The Theater and Cinema of

BUSTER KEAT

The Theater and Cinema of

BUSTER KEATON

Robert Knopf

PRINCETON UNIVERSITY PRESS • PRINCETON, NEW JERSEY

Copyright   1999 by Princeton University Press

Published by Princeton University Press, 41 William Street,

Princeton, New Jersey 08540

In the United Kingdom: Princeton University Press,

Chichester, West Sussex

Library of Congress Cataloging-in-Publication Data

Knopf, Robert, 1961–

The theater and cinema of Buster Keaton / Robert Knopf.

p.   cm.

Filmography: p.

Includes bibliographical references and index.

ISBN 0-691-00441-2 (cloth : alk. paper)

ISBN 0-691-00442-0 (pbk. : alk. paper)

1. Keaton, Buster, 1895–1966—Criticism and interpretation. I. Title.

PN2287.K4 K67 1999

791.43'028'092—dc21   98-51582

This book has been composed in Berkeley typeface

Designed by Frank Mahood

Composed by Robert E. Brown

The paper used in this publication meets the minimum requirements

of ANSI / NISO Z39.48-1992 (R 1997) (*Permanence of Paper*)

http://pup.princeton.edu

Printed in the United States of America

1   3   5   7   9   10   8   6   4   2

For my parents
WHO TAUGHT ME HOW TO LAUGH

and my wife and daughter
WHO SHARE MY LAUGHTER
EVERY DAY.

Contents

List of Illustrations

Acknowledgments

I WOULD LIKE to acknowledge the following people for their assistance with my work. Charles Silver (Museum of Modern Art) and Rosemary C. Hanes (Library of Congress) allowed me to screen many of Keaton's films during the early stages of my research, when many of the films were not easily obtainable. Eleanor Keaton and Ron Pesch were of invaluable aid in providing me with access to Myra Keaton's vaudeville scrapbook. Joan Franklin and the Columbia University Oral History Project gave me access to their transcript of a 1958 interview with Buster Keaton. Mary Corliss and Terry Geeskin (Museum of Modern Art), Kristine Krueger (Academy of Motion Picture Arts and Sciences), and Adele Blinston (British Film Institute) assisted me with my search for film stills to illustrate my work. The Rackham School of Graduate Studies at the University of Michigan supported my research and writing through a generous fellowship. My research assistants at Purdue University, Kristen Tripp Kelley, Mara Hesed, and Sarah Bay, helped me immensely during the revision process. Gerald Potterton graciously allowed me to interrogate him about his work with Buster on *The Railrodder* when we were both stranded in an airport following a film conference.

Special thanks to Bert Cardullo for his intellectual support and fervent editorial advice throughout this project. I would also like to thank Mike Gauger, Leigh Woods, Frank Beaver, and Enoch Brater for their comments on the early drafts of the manuscript. My editor Mary Murrell and readers Henry Jenkins and Charles Maland provided excellent suggestions for improving the manuscript in its final stages. James Lastra and Richard Abel guided me in my search for surrealist writings on Keaton. My wife, Liz, has been, and continues to be, unbelievably patient and insightful in talking with me about my work. Thanks for helping me make sense of it all.

The Theater and Cinema of

BUSTER KEATON

Introduction

DEPENDING UPON which criticism one reads, the films of Buster Keaton reveal either: a knockabout comedian from vaudeville who successfully adapted his act to silent films; an unintentional surrealist; or one of the earliest and finest directors of classical Hollywood cinema. Surrealist critics refuse to see Keaton as merely a vaudeville entertainer. Classical critics focus so completely on the structure of his plots and the geometric progression of his stories that they slight other attributes of his work. And those who view Keaton primarily as a vaudevillian tend to concentrate on recounting his most humorous gags and explaining how they work. For these critics, plot is a pretext for the ingenuity of Keaton's gags.

Of these three lines of criticism, the view of Keaton as an exemplar of classical Hollywood cinema is most widely accepted. Several film textbooks use *Our Hospitality* (1923) and *The General* (1927) to discuss causality and linear narrative in classical cinema.[1] In one of the most widely read books of criticism on Keaton, *Keaton: The Silent Features Close-Up*, Daniel Moews uses narrative structure as the central criterion for judging the relative quality of Keaton's films. By this standard, Moews rates *The General* as Keaton's strongest feature film and criticizes *College* (1927) as his weakest effort. Yet Luis Buñuel, widely regarded as the most successful surrealist filmmaker, praised *College* shortly after its release, singling out the film's simplicity ("beautiful as a bathroom, vital as a Hispano"), Keaton's work with objects, and his avoidance of sentimentality: "With Buster Keaton the expression is as modest as that of a bottle for example: although around the round, clear circuit of his pupils dances his aseptic soul. But the bottle and the face of Buster have their viewpoints in infinity."[2] Buñuel's evaluation of *College* testifies to his application of a vastly different set of aesthetic criteria, one which values attributes other than narrative structure.

Each line of criticism can be seen as a different "lens" through which the critic views Keaton's films. Like a camera lens, each of these critical lenses emphasizes different qualities, shaping the critic's perception of the films.

Each lens distorts the subject matter in different ways, magnifying some attributes and diminishing others. The disparities among the lines of criticism can be recognized, then, as different ways of seeing, rather than as simple differences of opinion.[3] Although the critics differ in their evaluations of Keaton's films, most consciously or unconsciously apply one of the three "lenses" as their dominant criterion for interpreting Keaton's work. Isolating the qualities of each lens allows us to examine Keaton's films with specificity; looking beyond the closely knit parameters of classical Hollywood cinema in particular encourages us to investigate the interaction among its elements and those of vaudeville in Keaton's films. By integrating these views of Keaton's films, I seek to arrive at a more complete understanding of his work, one that uncovers the interaction between the formative influences on his work (vaudeville and Hollywood), as well as the affinities he shared with his contemporaries from the 1920s, the surrealists.

The Lens of Classical Hollywood Cinema

In *The Classical Hollywood Cinema*, Bordwell, Staiger, and Thompson advance a dynamic theory of the emergence of classical Hollywood cinema from its origins in 1907 through its development to 1960. They endeavor to reveal the stylistic parameters within which classical Hollywood cinema has been, and to a great extent continues to be, produced. I will use their criteria to uncover the assumptions inherent in Keaton criticism from the classical point of view. Once I have laid out these assumptions, elements of classical Hollywood cinema in Keaton's films can be examined not merely for their function within the classical Hollywood style, but for their relationship to other elements—such as Keaton's visual gags and imagery—highlighted by the lenses of vaudeville and surrealism.

Classical Hollywood cinema is based first and foremost on the principle of narrative causality. Narrative causality is, to use formalist terminology, the dominant: "the focusing component . . . which guarantees the integrity of the structure."[4] Bordwell notes that classical Hollywood cinema carries over, with some changes, the formula of the well-made play from nineteenth-century theater: "The conventions of the well-made play—strong opening exposition, battles of wits, thrusts and counter-thrusts, extreme reversals of fortunes, and rapid denouement—all reappear in Hollywood dramaturgy, and all are defined in relation to cause and effect. The film progresses like a staircase: 'Each scene should make a definite impression,

accomplish one thing, and advance the narrative a step nearer the climax.'[5]
Action triggers reaction: each step has an effect which in turn becomes a
new cause.[6]"

Critics who analyze Keaton's films through the lens of classical Hollywood cinema stress narrative as the dominant feature in his work. Consequently, most of these critics neglect Keaton's short films in favor of his
feature films. In *Classical Hollywood Comedy*, a collection of essays on the
development of Hollywood's film comedy, Kristine Brunovska Karnick and
Henry Jenkins cogently argue that the assumptions of classical Hollywood
cinema color the scholarship of several prominent theorists of film comedy:
"The accounts of critics such as Donald McCaffrey and Gerald Mast presup-
pose the centrality of classical criteria of thematic significance, character
consistency, narrative unity, causal logic and psychological realism at all
stages of the genre's development."[7] Karnick and Jenkins challenge the classical standard as the sole criterion of value, building on Jenkins's earlier
book on the first sound film comedies, *What Made Pistachio Nuts?*[8] Yet the
classical line of criticism dominates the work on silent film comedy. By this
standard, Mack Sennett's Keystone comedies are frequently judged inferior
to the films of Keaton, Charlie Chaplin, Harold Lloyd, and Harry Langdon
on the basis of the former's lack of narrative thrust and coherence. McCaffrey, for example, perceives Keaton as part of a progression away from Sennett's "off-the-cuff, helter-skelter" style of slapstick toward a more story-
based form of comedy.[9]

When critics apply narrative causality as a standard of quality, they emphasize certain aspects of Keaton's films over others. Moews, for example,
declares *The General* Keaton's masterpiece on the basis of its symmetry and
the integration of gags into the narrative. Conversely, he criticizes *College*
for its lack of "dramatic tautness and rhythmic drive."[10] He recognizes the
superiority of the gags in *College* ("for the first time individual Keaton routines look rather better than the film in which they occur"[11]), yet fails to
appreciate the artistic integrity of his gags outside the realm of narrative. In
effect, Moews's narrative bias filters out other elements of the films—such
as gags and spectacle—making them appear subordinate to narrative. The
ingenuity of any individual gag or image appears to be less important than
the overall structure and shape of the films.

But to favor narrative over gag and image in viewing Keaton is to see his
films incompletely. For Keaton's spectacular settings and stunts command
attention in and of themselves even now; his images and gags are, to my
mind, the heart and soul of his work. Narrative might indeed contain Kea-

ton's artistically motivated gags and images, yet given the formulaic nature of the narrative—an aspect of Keaton's stories that even Moews concedes[12]—perhaps Keaton's narratives are best thought of as containers in a more literal sense. Keaton is able to fill his narrative containers with a special substance, an amalgam of vaudeville, melodrama, optical illusion, and his unique vision of the world. Although his films can serve to illustrate classical Hollywood cinema technique, they did not inspire generations of artists to copy his narrative techniques. For that there are models too numerous to mention. Keaton's influence, indeed his legacy, originates within and extends beyond his narratives. By examining Keaton's films solely as examples of classical Hollywood cinema—for their narrative structure and causality—we neglect the formidable artistry in his gag and stunt sequences and the complex ways in which these sequences interact with the narrative.

By focusing their attention on Keaton's narrative, classical critics limit the scope of their vision. Moews, for example, rejects the surrealist critics who see philosophical significance in Keaton's films, stating that the films evince "no serious interest in ideas."[13] Gerald Mast, however, infers substantial thematic intentions from Keaton's narratives. According to Mast, Keaton's plots reveal his predominant concern with morality.[14] Regardless of their differences, Moews and Mast focus on narrative as the sole source of potential meaning, missing ideas concealed from them in Keaton's imagery.

Through the lens of classical Hollywood cinema, all other major elements—time, space, and editing—are seen as serving the narrative chain. Classical Hollywood cinema generally portrays time chronologically. Chronology can be disrupted, but only as long as the filmmaker maintains the causal chain. The most common variation from the chronological presentation of time is the flashback. The classical Hollywood lens encourages the spectator to absorb or fuse the flashback into the causal chain of the narrative.[15] Surrealist critics and artists, however, might welcome the divergences from the causal chain that flashbacks provide, seizing these opportunities to wander into the past with little thought of the future. The single-minded focus of the classical lens on causality diverts attention from manipulations of time the surrealist critic considers essential.

In *Seven Chances* (1925), for example, Keaton uses temporal overlapping to create a surreal image that the classical lens might slight. Buster[16] drives to his girlfriend's house to propose to her. In the first shot, Buster gets into his car. But the film does not show Buster driving to her house; the house comes to Buster, the background of the shot dissolving from the outside of his house to the outside of his girlfriend's house, while Buster and his car stay in place. Keaton reproduced the exact placement of the car within the frame and cut the two shots together, so his car appears to be magically transported to his girlfriend's house.[17] Through the lens of classical Hollywood cinema, the narrative appears to absorb the gag, defusing it of its power as an image by viewing this artistic flourish as generically justified or motivated within slapstick comedy. The vaudeville critic would emphasize the origin of such sleight-of-hand in medicine shows and vaudeville magic acts, whereas a surrealist would stress the use of time in film to allow Keaton to change the laws of nature, transcending "what manifestly is" to reveal "what could be."[18]

Instead of searching for manipulations and distortions of time, the classical approach stresses unity of time. Thus, a classical critic such as Moews contends that time is a key element in achieving Keaton's classical style, noting that most of Keaton's films take place over a period of one or two days. Moews sees unity of time as central to Keaton's formula; in each film Keaton falls asleep only to successfully repeat the actions he failed to perform properly during the first twenty-four hours.[19] Moews emphasizes this use of time to the neglect of others. In *The Navigator* (1924), for example, he fails to observe that time has seemingly stopped for Buster and his girlfriend aboard the boat. Although surrealist critics favorably compare Keaton's use of time in these scenes to the sense of suspended time in the plays of Beckett, Moews finds these sequences lacking in narrative drive. Once again, classical assumptions divert Moews from the very attributes of this film that surrealists would most revere.

Similarly, the classical view of the use of space in film is inherently reductive. Classical Hollywood cinema favors many compositional techniques that it appropriates from ancient traditions in the visual arts: centered compositions, overall balance, and frontal views of the most important subjects.[20] These traditions also stem from practices originating with the Greek and Roman theater and further developed for the proscenium stage.[21] Keaton's use of space falls squarely within these traditions. His sense of space undoubtedly developed during his years as a vaudeville performer. Merely to pigeonhole Keaton's use of space as "classical," however, is to limit the scope of the investigation. Surrealist visual artists such as Dalí and Magritte also comply, on the surface, with the classical spatial conventions of centered compositions, balance, and frontality. Yet no one would classify these artists as "classical" without considering the content of their images. These artists achieve their surrealism precisely because of the contrast between classical form and surrealist content. The classical use of space encourages the viewer to situate their art close to realism, and the content of the image achieves surreality; not mere fantasy, but marvelous images contained in realistic forms.

Classical critics of Keaton prefer moments when his realistic use of space supports the logic of the story. David Robinson champions *The General* for the way Keaton grounds his comedy in realistic detail, seeing Keaton's films as most successful when he uses a realistic environment to support the film's "logic" or causality: "All the elements of the film—the dramatic integrity of the action, the conscientious period reconstructions, the use of locations of striking visual beauty and grandeur—contribute to the logic and realism that Keaton was by now seeking as a basis for his comedy. The gags are all the funnier because they are sprung out of a realistic situation and tried against the touchstone of reality."[22] By subordinating the use of space within a film to narrative causality, the classical lens ignores other functions of the seemingly classical portrayal of space in film. The classical lens perceives departures from compositionally motivated use of space as brief artistic flourishes, justified by the slapstick form. But these flourishes are precisely what most inspire the critics and artists who view Keaton through the lenses of vaudeville and surrealism. Therefore, classical critics do not merely disagree with the others; through the classical lens, they see a fundamentally different film.

The classical critic views space as subservient to the narrative, a narrative that is fueled by psychological causality.[23] Consequently, classical filmmakers endow objects and the environment with meanings that support the psychological development of the characters. Keaton, though, approaches objects and environment with the mind of a vaudevillian. He explores objects for their unforeseen functions, an obsession he shares with the surrealists. The environment, in Keaton's films, has a mind of its own and often appears to hold a hostile, or at least aggressively indifferent, position toward Buster. He learns to master the environment by applying his unique brand of illogic. In classical Hollywood cinema, space is "chiefly a container for character action; the story has appropriated it. . . . [A] locale is of little interest in its own right."[24] But in Keaton's silent features, space does not merely support the story; it creates the story.[25]

Moreover, Keaton distinguishes himself from the classical Hollywood tradition by his insistence on showing as much space as possible. The classical lens allows the viewer to make connections between shots to complete the space: "A convincing image need not show everything in the space as long as nothing we see actually contradicts what we expect."[26] Keaton, by contrast, goes out of his way to record as much of the environment as possible in long shots, particularly for his most expansive gags and stunts. Although Harold Lloyd constructs many of his stunts through editing and camera angles, Keaton studiously avoids substituting camera work for stunt work. Keaton's long shots and long takes confirm that his stunts are not the result of camera tricks and authenticate his virtuosity as a stuntman and acrobat.[27] By constructing his stunts within the mise-en-scène, rather than in the editing room, Keaton retains artistic control as a performer.

Conversely, classical Hollywood cinema favors the work of the director over the actor. The director constructs space in collaboration with the audience, which is trained by years of viewing to complete the space from clues provided by the director. As Bordwell states, the length of the shots, the number of sequences, and the duration of the sequences in classical Hollywood cinema dominate the creation of a film's rhythm.[28] In particular, classical Hollywood cinema favors short takes over long takes: "Using long takes was discouraged, since a paucity of shots took crucial decisions about timing and emphasis out of producers' and editors' hands."[29] Many critics have noted Keaton's use of long takes. Within Bordwell's definition of classical Hollywood cinema, long takes are perceived as a stylistic choice by the director. Yet from the vaudevillian perspective, longer takes focus attention on Keaton's virtuosity as a performer and enable him to be the center of attention. Moreover, by minimizing the influence of editing on the rhythm and tempo of the film, Keaton draws attention to the rhythm of his body.

The disparate views of Keaton's use of long takes indicate a fundamental disagreement as to how and why he exercised artistic control as a filmmaker. Classical critics assume that Keaton controlled the narrative structure of his films—during the process of developing the scenarios or while filming and editing—when most accounts of his filmmaking process indicate that this was a collaborative process involving Keaton, several gag writers, the cameramen, and sometimes a co-director.[30] Whereas Keaton's off-camera process for developing both gags and narrative was collaborative, once in front of the camera Keaton exerted near-complete artistic control over his gags, improvising and adapting the physical routines to the necessities and inspiration of the moment. I maintain, therefore, that Keaton exercised his strongest influence over the creation of gags, stunts, and images.[31] Not only can we trace his gags and visual images directly to the routines he performed and saw in his nineteen years as a vaudeville performer with The Three Keatons, but his gags evince an unmistakable style throughout his career, as I will examine in Chapter 2, "From Stage to Film: The Transformation of Keaton's Vaudeville."

How we define Keaton, as "an inventor of visual forms"[32] or as a storyteller, determines what we see as the most important structure in his films: the "horizontal" cause-and-effect chain of the narrative or the "vertical" chain of vaudeville based on the repetition of visual gags. Critics have disputed the conflicting claims of these two structures in film comedy.[33] As Karnick and Jenkins note, these critics present differing views of how narrative and gags interact:

> These various views on the relationship between gags and narrative can be seen as points along a continuum. Karnick and Palmer represent views in which jokes or gags are experienced within non-comic narratives. Crafton argues for the ultimate irreconcilability of gags and narrative. Du Pasquier, by contrast, argues that gags subvert narrative logic, which implies a close relationship between the two. Kramer, Neale and Krutnik find a closer connection between gag and narrative. Kramer, for example, argues that comic gags may disrupt the narrative, but that the gag also re-establishes the fiction. Finally, Bordwell and Thompson link these two elements in the most fundamental ways.[34]

All these critics, to some extent, examine the interaction between vaudeville and classical Hollywood cinema in film comedy. To the extent that they argue that narrative contains the disruptive effects of gags, they are using a classical lens, ultimately focusing on narrative as the dominant element. To the extent that they focus on the effect and techniques of gags, they view films through a vaudeville lens. This ongoing debate in film criticism will be taken up in Chapter 3, "Keaton Re-Viewed: Beyond Keaton's Classicism."

The Lens of Vaudeville

Regardless of the assumptions with which critics come to the study of Keaton's films, Keaton's background in vaudeville remains indisputable. It seems strange, therefore, that little attempt has been made to construct a theory or framework for understanding Keaton's transition from vaudeville to film. To me, this transformation reveals a wealth of information: how he adapted his performance skills to film; how he expanded and changed his artistic vision because of the attributes of film to which he was attracted; and how he blended the vaudeville tradition with conventions and structures from other traditions, such as stage melodrama, toward a new tradition of silent film comedy.[35]

Keaton's films, together with the silent comedy films of his contemporaries, survive as living artifacts from vaudeville. As such, these films can be explored as a way of tracing the "afterlife" of vaudeville. By gaining a better understanding of the techniques and aesthetics of vaudeville through Keaton's films, we might trace the influence of vaudeville on subsequent avant-garde drama and film through Keaton and his contemporaries. For when the body of vaudeville (the institution) died, its soul (its aesthetics and techniques) was absorbed into film comedy, avant-garde drama and film, and the circus. Thus, vaudeville experiences a rebirth, in altered form, in the drama of Beckett, Ionesco, and others, most recently in New Vaudeville and performance art.[36]

To begin, we must develop a method of reading Keaton's films for the vaudeville within them. Isolating the vaudeville allows us to compare his films to historical and biographical accounts of his vaudeville act with The Three Keatons. Such a comparison reveals the abundance of material Keaton drew from his vaudeville work and the ways in which he transformed the source material. In *What Made Pistachio Nuts?* Henry Jenkins identifies the key attributes of vaudeville to develop a framework for analyzing and appreciating the frequently maligned early sound comedies of the 1930s.[37] He argues that these films function in a fundamentally different way from classical Hollywood cinema. According to Jenkins, critics who value the classical norms of narrative integration and psychological causality overlook the vaudeville aesthetic at work in these films and thus underestimate the films' achievements.

Jenkins maintains that film producers embraced vaudeville at the start of the sound era by hiring a wave of stand-up comedians to respond to the new challenge of sound. He therefore re-evaluates the early sound films by the standards of the vaudeville aesthetic, which, he argues, is the most appropriate measure of the films' success. In an analysis of the vaudeville aesthetic in Keaton's films, the changes his vaudeville underwent in film become evident. Jenkins's framework of analysis can thus serve as a guide that enables us to read Keaton's vaudeville between the lines, as it were, of his classicism.[38]

Viewing Keaton's films from the perspective of vaudeville demands a different way of looking at the structure of his films. Although the classical lens foregrounds narrative structure, the vaudeville lens emphasizes the structural elements of vaudeville co-existing with the narrative in Keaton's films. The typical vaudeville bill consisted of eight to fourteen acts, each self-contained, running from eight to twenty minutes each. Each act was interchangeable; generally the most popular acts were put toward the end of the bill. Producers made no attempt to present a narrative for the entire performance. Spectators would have been unable to construct a comprehensive story, except perhaps within one of the brief acts. Instead, they viewed each act as a separate unit.

The lens of vaudeville calls for the spectator to watch films on this microcosmic level. As Jenkins justifies his appreciation of the lesser-known sound comedy *Stand Up and Cheer*: "To appreciate such a film, we need to think about comedy *atomistically*, as a loosely linked succession of comic 'bits.' That the parts are more satisfying than the whole may only be a criticism if we do not like the parts."[39] Looking at Keaton's films atomistically focuses attention on how he transferred his vaudeville to film and in the process transformed it; that the whole is also pleasing should not prevent us from perceiving, analyzing, and appreciating the parts.

A number of critics have implicitly approached Keaton's films from this point of view. J. P. Lebel, for example, recognizes Keaton's use of gags as the fundamental structural element in his films, devoting much of his analysis to Keaton's face, physical qualities, and exploits.[40] According to Lebel, to grasp the significance or meaning of Keaton's films, critics first must analyze Keaton's gags: "The gag is the form that Keaton's attitude takes in regard to the world; consequently, the study of Keaton's 'world action' can be nothing but the study of the structure of the gag in his films."[41] Similarly, in his seminal essay "Comedy's Greatest Era," James Agee emphasizes Keaton's face and mechanistic gags rather than the plots of his films, capturing the spirit of Keaton's world with a poeticism that has yet to be equaled: "In a way his pictures are like a transcendent juggling act in which it seems that the whole universe is in exquisite flying motion and the one point of repose is the juggler's effortless, uninterested face."[42]

Once we begin to look at Keaton's films atomistically—filtering through each for repeated gags and images—it becomes evident that the gag structure and narrative structure of the films operate on entirely different planes. Narrative structure develops horizontally, with one sequence building upon the next. Gags accumulate vertically—one on top of the other—each "step" in a gag repeating a step, culminating in a climactic gag that usually consists of a variation on its predecessors.[43] A gag rarely advances the story horizontally; the story seems to be treading water in one place as the gag transpires. It is almost as if all of the repetitions exist at the same time, like a triple image. Classical narrative structure reincorporates previous information to advance the story, but in gag structure repetition is significant in and of itself. It need not advance the story; it need only present a theme and variation.

Gags can be confined to a single sequence of a film or stretched out over the course of the film as a "running gag." Jenkins describes this quality as an "accordionlike structure," insightfully observing that gags potentially can be stretched and contracted temporally.[44] Within a narrative structure, the placement of each "step" or bit of narrative information will dramatically alter the shape of the narrative. Although it is possible to change the placement of different sequences in a narrative, classical narrative structure requires each sequence to build upon the previous one. Gag structure requires no such logical progression. A gag may be repeated at any time without risking damage to the overall progression. Therefore, when we view Keaton's films for their vaudeville—focusing on gag structure rather than narrative structure—the temporal and spatial qualities of the gags become more important than their narrative functions. Rather than examining Keaton's gags for their integration within the narrative, we focus on the structure of the gag: the set-up, repetition, and the spatial and temporal illogic of the gag.

Vaudeville's general neglect of narrative, with the exception of "playlets" that were frequently a part of the bill, stemmed from the form of the typical bill. The more descriptive name for vaudeville is "variety," a quality that vaudeville valued above all others. A typical bill might include jugglers, acrobats, knockabout comedians, stand-up comedians, animal acts, singers, dancers, magicians, novelty acts, and ventriloquists. Since each act was only eight to fifteen minutes long, and many of the performers came from traditions that did not value narrative, vaudeville constantly shifted acts to retain the audience's attention. If the audience disliked an act, it had only a brief wait for a new act. Acts changed weekly, so audience members could see new shows frequently.

Within the structure of each act, the only "rule" was that the act should have a "Wow Finish."[45] This rule illustrates that the structure of an act was designed to achieve a purely emotional climax.[46] The finish necessitated an emotional peak, a "topper" that surpassed the previous material within the act, be it comedy, acrobatics, or magic. In effect, the finish replaces narrative closure. For this reason, when we examine Keaton's films for their vaudeville, we focus on the escalation of gags and pure sensation within the structure of each gag sequence and over the course of each of his films.

In vaudeville, the members of each act controlled the structure of individual routines. Each team functioned as a self-contained economic and artistic unit, developing and polishing its routines, transporting its props, and financing all purchases of props and costumes. Theaters provided little for the performer beyond a performance space, stock backdrops and set pieces, and a repertory light plot. Producers limited their artistic control to the hiring and arrangement of acts within the bill; they rarely interfered with the acts unless presented with a pressing economic reason. Since the acts controlled artistic production, the chief selling point of a vaudeville act was the performer.

Having spent almost all of the first twenty-two years of his life in vaudeville, Keaton approached the new medium of film with a fundamental belief in his artistic control as a performer.[47] Because Keaton also became expert at the technical aspects of film directing, such as editing and composition, his work as a performer has rarely been considered in terms of artistic control. Many of his artistic choices—his preference, for example, for long shots and long takes—stem from his continuing belief in the performer as the locus of artistic control. As Lebel notes, action in Keaton's films develops from Keaton as a performer, rather than from dramatic action.[48] Consequently, the changes in his method that Irving Thalberg instituted when Keaton began working for MGM in 1928—from a flexible approach with considerable improvisation to MGM's carefully controlled, fully scripted style—contributed to Keaton's decline in the sound era. MGM's regimented production process and strict budget constraints stripped Keaton of the latitude for improvisation that he enjoyed in his pre-MGM films.[49] Even at the end of his career, one can still see Keaton exerting his artistic control as a performer. As an actor in *The Railrodder* (1965) and Samuel Beckett's *Film* (1966), Keaton insisted upon his right to improvise upon and shape the directors' and writers' ideas.[50]

Jenkins provides the foundation for understanding Keaton's adaptation of vaudeville to film, but his focus on early sound comedy limits the applicability of his work.[51] Because early sound film comedy culled performers from the ranks of vaudeville's stand-up comedians, Jenkins concentrates on "monologists, crossfire teams, and comic sketches" in developing his vaudeville aesthetic.[52] I examine a broader range of vaudeville artists who influenced Keaton: acrobats, magicians, physical comedians, and animal acts, to name just a few. In examining Keaton's use of his body, for example, I note the dependence of vaudeville performers, especially physical comedians, on props. Zooming in on props—and the performer's ability to transform the props through their use—will demonstrate other ways in which Keaton adapted his vaudeville skills to film. Keaton seized upon film's ability to display larger props and spaces more realistically than vaudeville.[53] As he set his films in more and more realistic environments, his visual gags with props can be seen as progressing from comic sketches on the vaudeville stage to vast canvases in the real world.

The Lens of Surrealism

In the Preface to *Surrealism and Film*, J. H. Matthews notes that "all surrealists claim certain rights and privileges" as filmmakers, screenwriters, critics, and spectators.[54] To understand the surrealists' approach to watching and making films, Matthews argues, we must apply the principles of surrealism to isolate "which features of filmmaking are accorded priority in surrealism . . . [and what] means surrealists consider relevant to granting these appropriate prominence, often to the detriment of other aspects of the filmmaker's art."[55] The aspects of filmmaking to which the surrealists grant prominence reveal the particular qualities of the surrealist lens: how it filters and distorts what the spectator views.

From this vantage point, surrealists reviled many of the most critically acclaimed films of the 1920s, and revered films that most critics widely regarded as inferior. Yet in the case of silent film comedy, surrealists championed the films of the most commercially successful comedians. Did surrealists suddenly accept the critical opinions of the mainstream? Or did they share certain aesthetic or thematic concerns with the silent film comedians? Matthews stresses that the surrealists' contribution to criticism of the silent comedians is not in the films that they championed, but in their way of looking at the films: "Their originality lies in a special angle of vision, shedding the light of surrealism upon the work of some of the most successful comedians in the movies."[56] Isolating the elements of the surrealists' "angle of vision" allows us to approach Keaton's films in a fundamentally different way from the examination of his films for elements of vaudeville or classical Hollywood cinema.

Surrealism was founded as a "movement" at the beginning of the 1920s, during the same period that James Agee acclaimed as "Comedy's Greatest Era." From the outset the surrealists were intrigued by film's ability to transcend the rigidity of everyday reality. Phillipe Soupault noted, "Already the richness of this new art appears to those who can see. Its strength is impressive since it reverses natural laws: it ignores space and time, upsets gravity, ballistics, biology, etc., . . . Its eye is more patient, sharper, more precise."[57]

Surrealists viewing films went out of their way to increase the disorienting effects of film. During World War I—a decade before founding surrealism—André Breton and Jacques Vaché would hop from cinema to cinema, watching a random segment of one film before switching to a new one:

> I never began by consulting the amusement pages to find out what film might chance to be the best, nor did I find out the time the film was to begin. I agreed wholeheartedly with Jacques Vaché in appreciating nothing so much as dropping into the cinema when whatever was playing was playing, at any point in the show, and leaving at the first hint of boredom . . . to rush off to another cinema where we behaved in the same way. . . . I have never known anything more *magnetizing*: it goes without saying that more often than not we left our seats without even knowing the title of the film which was of no importance to us anyway.[58]

In this journey, they allowed themselves to be guided by chance. They never bothered to find out what film was being exhibited. Instead, they viewed fragments from various films—absent a narrative context—and mentally assembled their own films consisting of short segments from a series of unrelated works.

Similarly, in Luis Buñuel's film programs at Cineclub Español during the 1920s and 1930s—which consisted of excerpts from various films, including those of the silent comedians, selected and arranged by Buñuel—he isolated particular film sequences and images that he valued.[59] Surrealists found surrealism in films by selective viewing, altering their perception of films by focusing on isolated imagery. To view Keaton's films through the lens of surrealism, we must therefore look at segments more closely, narrowing our temporal focus to examine sequences and moments rather than the entire film. Surrealist critics of Keaton's films rarely engage in lengthy plot synopsis; they analyze his films for the images and sequences that most appeal to their artistic sensibility. This is consistent with the surrealists' rejection of traditional narrative and places them squarely in opposition to classical critics who view the triumph and ultimate contribution of Keaton in terms of his ability to integrate gags into classically constructed narratives. Although the classical lens examines how sequences are integrated into the narrative whole, the surrealist lens isolates sequences for their own pleasureful sake, independent of, or in opposition to, the larger narrative.

In particular, surrealists valued films for their ability to disorient the spectator. J. H. Matthews defines disorientation (*dépaysement*) as "the power of the cinema to take man out of his natural surroundings, be these material, mental, or emotional."[60] Whereas classical critics view Keaton's films for the logic of their narrative structure, surrealist critics search for the ways in which Keaton questions the logic of the world. Keaton never intended to create surrealist films, yet the ways in which his films challenge logic, reason, and causality influenced the surrealists, who saw in his films and those of many of the silent film comedians an involuntary surrealism.[61] Surrealist criticism of Keaton results in a radical reinterpretation of his films, one that many scholars resist as inconsistent with Keaton's intentions. Yet by comparing the lenses of surrealism and vaudeville, similarities in their views of Keaton's films emerge, revealing latent links between popular entertainment and the avant-garde.

Many of the techniques the surrealists used in their artistic explorations overlap with those used in vaudeville comedy: the double meaning of objects and words, verbal and visual puns, the juxtaposition of two disparate images, the animation of inanimate objects, and the disruption of narrative continuity, time, and space. It remains for us to examine how Keaton transformed the techniques of vaudeville into silent film comedy that inspired the surrealists. Because film captures reality in a way that theater, and vaudeville in particular, only hint at, it provides the bridge from vaudeville to surrealism. When the reality of film supplanted the inherent theatricality of vaudeville, silent comedians were able to set marvelous gags in more and more realistic environments. More than any other silent film comedian, Keaton exploited film's ability to display the real world. By setting his films in meticulously real—and increasingly immense—American landscapes, Keaton accentuated the realism in his surrealism.

As Keaton progressed from two-reel shorts to full-length features, he avoided fantastic gags that were not believable within the context of his plots. Many critics argue that this change made Keaton's films more classical, yet I believe it also makes them more surreal. As he tailored his gags to feature-length films, his gags and images became increasingly surreal precisely because they were more believable. Keaton's classicism sustains the "reality" that his gags and stunts challenge and ultimately undermine. When vaudeville and classical Hollywood cinema meet in Keaton's films, the classical Hollywood style exposes the latent surrealism in vaudeville.

1

The Evolution of Keaton's Vaudeville

ACCORDING TO Keaton family legend, Buster Keaton spent only one day in school. Allegedly, the teacher expelled Keaton for answering her questions with punch lines he learned in vaudeville.[1] Regardless of the veracity of the story, for all practical purposes Keaton's "school" was the vaudeville stage; he learned his trade performing around the country for more than seventeen of the first twenty-two years of his life. Keaton first appeared in vaudeville when he was nine months old, and by the age of five he was a regular part of his parents' act, The Three Keatons. He quickly acclimated himself to the stage and almost immediately became The Three Keatons' star attraction. "Young Buster Keaton, who is only five years old, is a wonderful comedian," noted an early reviewer, "and he is ably assisted by his father and mother."[2] Subsequent reviewers recognized Buster[3] as the star of the act and frequently remarked that The Three Keatons received more laughter than any other act on the bill, often eclipsing the headline act.[4]

Joseph Frank "Buster" Keaton was born on October 4, 1895, in Piqua, Kansas. His parents, Joe and Myra, were performers; at the time of Buster's birth, they were touring with a medicine show, the lowest rung on the traveling entertainers' ladder. Joe met Myra when he began working for the Cutler-Bryant Medicine Show, a traveling tent show owned in part by Myra's father, F. L. Cutler. Joe first worked as the bouncer for the show but eventually developed skills as an acrobat, "eccentric" dancer, and "grotesque" comedian. Grotesque comedians portrayed stock characters based on exaggerated, stereotyped traits of a particular ethnic group. Joe Keaton played an Irishman, although the mainstay of his act was his acrobatics, a distinctive specialty best captured by the billing he gave himself in advertisements: "The Man with the Table." Joe performed his acrobatic act on, under, and around a table located center stage: "He would dive on it head-first, turn handsprings along its top, and then from apogee plunge head down almost to the floor before, with a catlike turn, he would land on his feet."[5] He was known for his ability to kick; his particular specialty was the "hitch kick," a high kick that he performed later in his career in Buster's films.[6] Myra sang and played the saxophone. In publicity releases and news clippings the Keatons claimed Myra was "America's first lady saxophonist."[7]

The Keatons worked their way up the vaudeville ladder slowly. Toward the turn of the century, they toured with Harry Houdini's family as part of another medicine show, Dr. Hill's California Concert Company.[8] As Buster's fame grew, the story of how he received his nickname "Buster" eventually incorporated the great Houdini, who by the early 1900s had already attained world recognition for his escape stunts. In later versions of the story, Houdini, seeing six-month-old Buster fall down an entire flight of stairs only to land unharmed, declared, "That's some Buster your baby took," using the vaudeville slang for a stage fall. According to Myra Keaton, "Joe looked down and said, 'Well, Buster, looks like Uncle Harry has named you.' He's been Buster ever since."[9]

Keaton biographers have always been quite generous in accepting this story as truth, as well as the rest of the Keaton family myths. Yet careful study of the newspaper clippings in Myra Keaton's scrapbook reveals that the story evolved over the years. In one version, Buster's nickname was coined by "George Pardey, an old-time legitimate comedian."[10] In another, Joe Keaton gave Buster his nickname because his son was always falling down. With the exception of Dardis, writers have been extremely reluctant to recognize these inconsistencies, perhaps because many have perceived the Keaton family stories as a source for Keaton's comedy.[11]

Recognizing these stories as fiction, or at the very least as embellishments of reality, does not discount their value for the study and understanding of Keaton's work. The stories reveal much about their author, Joe Keaton, who, in addition to his many physical skills, was an excellent public relations representative for The Three Keatons. His primary publicity tool was the newspaper "plant," a publicity stunt or story barely disguised as a news article.[12] Joe's creations included the staged kidnappings of both Buster and his younger brother Harry (nicknamed "Jingles"), as well as stories about the Keatons' chance encounters with train wrecks, hotel fires, and cyclones.[13] While some of these events might have some basis in fact, there is little doubt that Joe used them to garner as much publicity as he could for The Three Keatons. If Joe Keaton created these stories for publicity—or, for that matter, even if he merely elaborated on actual occurrences—he did so with an eye for the connection between the stories and The Three Keatons' act. The stronger the connection that Joe created between the publicity stories and The Three Keatons' act, the more successful the publicity was in generating audiences. Buster learned from his father how to transform the family's life story into publicity material at an early age. Many of the most striking elements of Keaton's films—natural disasters, last-minute rescues, and Buster's indestructibility—are contained in these early life stories.

Perhaps the most noted feature of The Three Keatons' act that influenced Keaton's films was the way in which he went about his vaudeville routines with a sense of serious purpose. As Keaton told the story later in life, his father taught him not to smile early on in their vaudeville career. If Buster smiled or laughed during their act, Joe would admonish him, "Face! Face!," which meant that he should freeze his serious facial expression.[14] But reviews from the 1900s are evenly split: reviewers just as frequently mention Buster smiling after his father tossed him across the stage as they note his seriousness. One reviewer notes of Buster, "His smile is happy,"[15] whereas another suggests, "The youngster should be encouraged to smile. As things are his intense gravity is too long maintained."[16]

Although the origins of Keaton's "Great Stone Face" have received the most critical attention, Keaton's vaudevillian influences extend far beyond his trademarked frozen face. One of the first skills Keaton acquired in vaudeville was mimicry. From the beginning of his performing career, he learned most of his physical skills by imitating other performers: first his father, and later the performers with whom the Keatons shared the bill. For Buster's first appearance on stage, Joe dressed him up in a grotesque Irishman's costume, a miniature version of his own outfit, and Buster imitated everything that his father did on stage. As one reviewer noted in 1903, "Keaton pere comes on the stage in the full glory of red galways, a comic makeup, consisting of face white-plastered to the cheek bones, where a rosy flush forms a sharp angle, coming to a point just beneath the eyes. He wears loose, baggy trousers, no coat, and white spats. Baby Buster is made up and dressed exactly like his father, but diminutive face and figure increase the ludicrous effect in his case."[17] As this review indicates, part of the appeal of their costumes lay in the replication of the same image: they appear to be the same person in different sizes. By mimicking Joe's every movement—"his great dark staring saucer eyes fixed on his father, his body and arms following every movement, his lips silently mouthing all the well-known lines"[18]— Buster further reinforced the audience's perception of him as a distorted double image of his father, almost like a funhouse mirror come to life.

Figure 1.1. A publicity shot of The Three Keatons. Joe Keaton was known as "The Man with the Table."

The image of Buster as a miniature of his father remained a central element of The Three Keatons' act throughout most of their vaudeville career (fig. 1.1). The Keatons' weekly advertisement in the *Dramatic Mirror* usually contained a photograph that captured Joe, Myra, and Buster in their trademark pose: all three of them in the identical posture arranged from tallest to shortest, with Joe and Buster in identical grotesque Irishmen's costumes. In the early days of their vaudeville act, Buster would remove Myra's costume with a burlesque "strip cord" to reveal Myra dressed in a third identical Irishman's costume, complete with red hair and bald cap.[19] Later, when Buster's brother Jingles and sister Louise joined the act for a short time, they were also outfitted in identical costumes. With five of them standing together in a line, as one reviewer chronicled, the Keatons looked "like the separated portions of a Chinese miracle box."[20]

Jingles and Louise remained in the act for a few years before they tired of performing, although they did little on stage beyond Jingle's occasional "flip-flap" (vaudeville slang for a somersault) and Louise's attempted headstands.[21] Joe and Myra recognized the value of the optical illusion created by five identical Keatons. Since Jingles and Louise entered at the end of the routine, their appearance seems to have been the act's topper: the final gag that served as a climax. In reviewers' descriptions of The Three Keatons' finale, there is a sense that the act achieved a sense of closure by taking the central image—Buster as a Lilliputian clone of Joe—and expanding it as far as possible. This type of image is evident in many of Keaton's most famous film sequences: the multiple Busters of *The Playhouse*, the hordes of policemen in *Cops*, and the hundreds of brides and boulders in *Seven Chances*. Not only did Buster learn to use multiple mirror images while he performed with his parents, but perhaps more fundamentally, he also discovered the power of the purely visual and physical climax.

When Jingles and Louise were not performing, The Three Keatons usually depended upon Buster to perform a spectacular fall as the climactic finish to their act; when Buster was younger, Joe threw him into the stock backdrop. Similarly, in most of the Keaton myths, Buster's ability to take a fall without injury is a central theme. His very name, "Buster," celebrates this ability and points to its origin in vaudeville. Although Keaton was frequently modest about his abilities as an acrobat, Keaton's falls were more spectacular than those of any other silent comedian. From the time Buster became a regular part of the Keatons' act, falling down was Buster's main occupation.

In vaudeville, Buster's falls were always precipitated by Joe's tossing or hitting him. This has led many critics, including Dardis, to hypothesize about the effects of this "violence" on Buster's early development. Combined with Joe's developing alcoholism, the case for Buster's abuse at the hands of his father is easy to make. Yet film critics are not alone in their concern for young Buster's welfare. From the start of Buster's vaudeville career, the Gerry Society—also known as the Society for the Prevention of Cruelty to Children—continually tried to bar Buster from appearing on stage. The Gerry Society dedicated its efforts to enforcing the child labor laws: "In theatre this meant that no child under seven might even walk on-stage; none under sixteen might juggle, do acrobatics or walk a wire, engage in bicycle riding, and on through a long list."[22] For a considerable time, Joe Keaton was able to defend Buster's right to perform. The Gerry Society wielded the most political clout in New York, but the Keatons' appearances remained mostly unchallenged while on tour. In New York Buster toned down his act, concentrating on his impressions of famous vaudeville performers and comic songs. Some theater managers claimed that Buster was a "midget comedian"[23] in their advertisements and at least a few reviewers seem to have accepted this story, perhaps because they had trouble believing that any child could do what Buster did. Although the Gerry Society rejected the claim that Buster was a midget—an assertion that became increasingly difficult to maintain as Buster grew taller and larger—Joe succeeded, with the help of an affidavit from producer Tony Pastor, in adding two years to Buster's officially recognized age,[24] enabling Buster to perform his entire act in New York by the age of fourteen.[25]

Moreover, the act appears to have resonated with audiences *because* of its suggestion of child abuse. Before tossing Buster across the stage, Joe would tell audiences, "He's got to learn to mind," or "Father hates to be rough," to which Buster, following each of his falls, replied, "I'm so sorry I fell down."[26] Reviewers frequently remarked that although male audience members laughed throughout the act, female audience members were often horrified. Almost all reviewers noted, however, that Buster was never injured—"The way the youngster is thrown about the stage without damage to else but his clothes is a thrilling sight," observed one[27]—and the violence in The Three Keatons' act rarely failed to induce laughter.

Based on the reports of reviewers, as well as the Keatons themselves, the laughter stemmed not from the violence itself, but from Buster's reaction to the violence: his ability to take a spectacular fall and land unhurt. It appears that the element of surprise led to a laughter of relief and awe when Buster escaped from his father's punishments unscathed. Moreover, Buster was not the only Keaton to absorb punishment in the act. Although the act was built around Joe's attempts to discipline his oldest son, Buster often retaliated in kind. Frequently Buster's own seemingly inadvertent attacks on his father led to his punishment in the first place.

The standard setup for their act involved Joe's entering the stage to perform a solo—usually a song, eccentric dance, or sketch—only to have Buster interrupt him unexpectedly. As Keaton describes the act in his autobiography,

> [Joe] had hardly started on "Maud Miller" or "Where Is My Wandering Boy Tonight?" when I'd come out and fastidiously select one of the thirteen or fourteen old brooms that were on the end of the battered kitchen table. . . . Ignoring him, I would carefully sweep off the table, then appear to see something that wasn't there. Picking up this imaginary object with my cupped hand, I examined it and then put it down on another part of the table. This distressed Pop. Stopping his singing or reciting, he moved the invisible thing back to the place where I'd picked it up. I'd move it to where I wanted it, he'd move it back.

That went on with our rage mounting until we were fighting wildly, blasting, kicking, punching, and throwing one another across the table and all over the stage.[28]

The act then evolved into a chaotic game of cat-and-mouse, as Buster continued to interrupt his father and Joe repeatedly tried to teach him to behave, usually by tossing Buster around the stage, into the wings, into the orchestra pit, or into the backdrop. Myra sewed a suitcase handle on to the back of Buster's costume to provide Joe with a firmer grip and improved leverage.[29] When reviewers proclaimed that Buster was the whole show, they rarely remarked on his ability to play the stock Irish character indicated by his costume, but instead complimented his ability to execute his physically astonishing falls. Buster's falls became the focus of the act and the main source of humor, disrupting and displacing the story or song with which Joe had opened the act.

The stories of the practical jokes of Buster's youth display a similar spirit of disruption. The Keatons spent their summers in Bluffton, Michigan, an actors' colony adjacent to Muskegon, where many vaudeville performers owned homes.[30] In Muskegon, Buster invented his first absurd machines, including the "Ed Gray Awakener," a device he built to help a fellow vaudeville performer wake up in the morning. If Gray failed to rise after his alarm clock went off, the clock set into motion a series of devices Buster designed to drive him out of bed: "A lever operated by the clock started weights and counterweights of the greatest complexity all going at once: the gas was turned on and lit under the coffeepot (by a match scratched on sandpaper); a mechanical arm snatched off the sheet and blanket, if any; and an electric motor, operating through eccentric cams, made the bed rock like a foundering ship. Another day had dawned for Ed Gray."[31] Keaton constructed machines like this one throughout his career. They appear, for example, in the automated gadgets of *The Electric House* (1922), the convertible room of *The Scarecrow* (1920), and the makeshift galley contraptions in *The Navigator*.

Although Keaton's machines eventually accomplish their intended objective, such as waking up Ed Gray, the objective merely provides a pretext for the disruptive gags that occur between the time the machine is put in motion and the time it completes its intended purpose. The achievement of the machine's initial aim provides a sense of closure, a *reincorporation* of its original objective.[32] But these machines inevitably focus our attention on the absurd logic of the connections linking all of the disruptions that occur between point A (the initiation of the action) and point B (the completion of the action). The progression of physical stunts in The Three Keatons' act evinces a similar logic: "He is hurled all over the stage, grabbed by the tails of his long Prince Albert, shot across a long table on a slide, turns a somer-sault and stands on his feet at the edge of the footlights with about the funniest grin on his face that a human being ever worked his countenance into. Then Joe Keaton grabs Buster by the nape of the neck, twists him around in several beautiful circles, lets go, and Buster slides about fifteen feet on his pedal extremities, and never loses his balance."[33] The significant element is not what happened but how it happened, and the "how" in this case consists of a series of interconnected gags.

Most of Keaton's films display a similar line of interconnected gags and stunts. One of the primary tools Keaton used to create these gags and con-nect them was improvisation. By improvising, he found new routes from point A to point B. As Keaton stated regarding the construction of his films, "At no time in the Keaton Studio did we ever have a script, for the features or the two-reelers. . . . When the three writers and I had decided on a plot, we could start. We always looked for the story first, and the minute some-body came up with a good start, we always jumped the middle. We never paid any attention to that. We jumped to the finish. . . . We always figured the middle would take care of itself."[34] Keaton learned that as long as he knew there was a point B, he could eventually reach it. The confines of the beginning and the ending, the very limitations they display, provided Kea-ton with the freedom to improvise.

Reviewers, as well as Buster himself, noted that The Three Keatons im-provised a great deal of their material. As early as 1904, a reviewer for the *Dramatic Mirror*, a theatrical newspaper, noted that Buster Keaton, al-though only eight years old at this time, "frequently surprises his father by springing new gags and bits of business on him without warning or re-hearsal."[35] Improvisation, according to Buster, kept their act fresh. Given that Buster's objective was to disrupt his father, the more he could surprise Joe with his actions, the more spontaneous the act seemed.

The Three Keatons did not confine their act to improvised knockabout comedy, however. Early in his career, as Buster started to become the focus of the act, audiences frequently called for him to perform encores. In 1902, a reviewer noted that Buster had "recently graduated into the line of talking comedy," citing one of his encores.[36] Reviewers often remarked that Buster performed songs, parodies, and impressions in response to these requests, indicating that the act could run up to thirty-two minutes—and on at least one occasion, when the next act was delayed, a full hour and a half—which was a great deal longer than the standard twenty minutes the act usually filled. Little is known about this material, although some of the reviews offer brief glimpses. Buster performed a song entitled "Waiting at the Church" costumed in a wedding dress, while standing "beside a church that was not half as big as himself."[37] Other song titles include "Somebody Lied to Me," "No, No, Emflatically, No [sic]," and "Fru-a-la-la."[38] He also regularly recited a poem, "The Village Blacksmith," by "Shortfellow."[39] More frequently, Keaton performed impressions of other performers. His repertoire included Dan Daly, Press Eldridge, Jimmie Russell, De Wolf Hopper, Sagar Midgely, Charley Case, former heavyweight champion John L. Sullivan, Charley Mitchell, and the Mooney Brothers.[40] Though The Three Keatons were known for their rough acrobatics, Buster received additional notice from reviewers for these impressions and his burlesques of other acts, usually developed while sharing the bill with them. Vaudeville acts toured widely enough for these impressions to be recognizable around the country. Buster continued this type of work in films such as *Frozen North* (1922), which burlesqued the Western films of William S. Hart, *The Playhouse* (1921), which mercilessly teased Thomas Ince for over-crediting himself in his films' credits, and *The Three Ages* (1923), which parodied D. W. Griffith's *Intolerance* (1916). As late as 1933, Keaton proposed a parody of *Grand Hotel* to Thalberg at MGM, to be released immediately after the original.[41]

Many of Keaton's films can be seen as parodies of melodrama, a form with which he was quite familiar from his vaudeville days. Not only did The Three Keatons frequently share the bill with a short melodrama, Buster even acted in melodramas during the season he and his father toured with the Fenberg Stock Company as a "special added attraction" performing between acts.[42] Wishing to increase Buster's range as a performer, Joe convinced Mr. Fenberg, the owner of the company, to cast Buster in straight acting roles in two melodramas; he played the title role in *Little Lord Fauntleroy* and "Little William" in *East Lynne*.

Several other acts that played on the same bill as the Keatons almost certainly provided the basis for material in Buster's films, although no evidence exists that he parodied them at the time. Buster's imitation of a performing monkey in a vaudeville act in *The Playhouse* (fig. 1.2) probably was inspired by Peter the Great, a monkey act with whom the Keatons performed in their short run in London.[43] The ventriloquist's dummy that scares Buster in a deserted vaudeville theater at the end of *Steamboat Bill, Jr.* appears to have been inspired by an incident that occurred in 1902 when Buster was seven years old. Trovollo, a ventriloquist, befriended Buster by

Figure 1.2. Buster imitates a performing monkey in *The Playhouse*.

conversing with him through his dummies. Buster, who had few friends his own age, decided to kidnap his favorite dummy, Redtop. Unbeknownst to him, Trovollo discovered his plan. When Buster reached for Redtop, Trovollo was already there and the dummy appeared to come to life, screaming, "Don't touch me, boy, or I'll tell your old man."[44] Buster also incorporated blackface, a type of performance he and Joe both parodied in vaudeville, into *The Playhouse* and *College*.

As he traveled with his family on the vaudeville circuits, playing with different acts wherever they went, Buster copied other acts he admired. "I was a natural mimic," wrote Keaton, "and could imitate everything from sword-swallowing to playing a musical saw."[45] Many of these acts would turn up later in slightly altered form in his films, from Annette Kellerman's "Original Aboriginal Splash" (a diving act) to the trick sharpshooting gunplay of the Great Bordeverry.[46] Often Buster would parody these acts as part of The Three Keatons' routine, as this review notes: "'Buster' Keaton introduced a burlesque on the shooting act of Colonel Gaston Bordeverry last week at Proctor's Twenty-third Street Theatre that was as funny as anything the little fellow has ever done. Colonel Bordeverry was so amused with the travesty that he loaned 'Buster' one of his small rifles for the entire week."[47]?

According to Keaton, many vaudeville performers befriended him as a boy and taught him their skills: "I also got instruction in soft-shoe dancing from George Primrose, the famous old minstrel man, and Bill (Bojangles) Robinson taught me soft-shoe and tap dancing, Herb Williams gave me piano lessons between shows, and Houdini showed me a few of his sleight-of-hand tricks."[48] Much of the diversity in Keaton's films stems from the fact that Keaton wholeheartedly embraced the variety in vaudeville and re-peatedly returned to the images and skills he learned in vaudeville when he turned to filmmaking. Yet it would not be until 1917 that Keaton seized an opportunity to begin learning about making films.

As early as 1913, William Randolph Hearst offered the Keatons the op-portunity to act in a film version of *Bringing Up Father*, a popular cartoon strip that ran in Hearst's newspapers, but Joe Keaton adamantly rejected this proposal because he believed film degraded actors' work.[49] At the same time, the Keatons faced two new pressures: the United Booking Office (UBO) conflict and Joe's drinking. The UBO was organized around 1906 by B. F. Keith and E. F. Albee, the most powerful producers in vaudeville, in a successful attempt to monopolize vaudeville acts and dictate terms of em-ployment and touring routes. F. F. Proctor, a rival producer, challenged the UBO monopoly openly by offering employment to those vaudeville acts who wished to work for him rather than Keith-Albee. Joe Keaton sided with Proctor in this feud. Without enough theaters to fight the UBO, though, Proctor eventually capitulated and became Keith's partner.[50]

In 1907, another competitor, the team of Klaw and Erlanger, attempted to fight the monopoly but Keith and Albee bought them out. Acts who had left Keith-Albee, including the Keatons, now found themselves "banished to vaudeville Siberia, the second-run, three-a-day Western Pantages Circuit. This spelled drastically lower salaries and . . . weeks lost in making the long Western jumps by rail."[51] After a year of this punishment, the UBO began to book the exiled acts in better vaudeville houses. Yet Joe retained a special resentment toward Martin Beck, the powerful theater manager who con-ducted the UBO's booking meetings; he blamed Beck for all his family's professional misfortunes. In 1916, Beck booked The Three Keatons at New York's Palace Theater as the opening act, an insult for an act of their stature. Following an argument between the two men in the middle of a perform-ance, Joe chased Beck out of the theater and, in retaliation, Beck sent The

Three Keatons back to the Western Orpheum Circuit. The arduous schedule of traveling long distances and giving an extra performance each day took its toll on the Keatons, especially Joe, whose drinking problem grew considerably more severe. In February 1917, Myra and Buster broke up the act and left Joe in Los Angeles. After leaving The Three Keatons, Buster traveled to New York and approached the family's manager, Max Hart, about finding work as a "single act," or solo vaudeville act. Hart quickly booked Buster as a single act in a Broadway revue produced by the Shuberts, *The Passing Show of 1917*. As he was in the process of developing a routine for the revue, Buster met Roscoe "Fatty" Arbuckle and began to act in his short films, which Arbuckle had started to direct for the Comique Film Corporation and his new producer, Joseph Schenck. As Keaton told the story to biographers and interviewers in the 1950s, the meeting was accidental: Arbuckle and he met on the street, introduced by Lou Anger, a "Dutch" comedian who had performed on the same bills with the Keatons in vaudeville. When Arbuckle invited him to visit his studio and try a small part, Keaton agreed. Once there, Keaton became enamored with filmmaking and he and Arbuckle became close friends and colleagues. He backed out of his contract with the Shuberts and began making films with Arbuckle full-time.

Keaton was immediately struck by the enormous differences between filmmaking and vaudeville and saw opportunities emerging from these differences. Before he left The Three Keatons, Keaton apparently shared his father's negative appraisal of film, considering it "derivative—a painting versus the real thing."[52] From the moment he entered Arbuckle's studio, though, Keaton began to see the opportunities that film offered him. First, film was a collaborative venture. Despite the fact that Keaton had performed solo in his vaudeville encores, he appears to have been reluctant, or at the very least cautious, about performing as a single act in *The Passing Show of 1917*. With Arbuckle and his company, Keaton could continue to work in the collaborative style he had enjoyed with his family. Second, he quickly seized upon film's potential for dissolving many of the limitations of the stage: "The greatest thing to me about picturemaking was the way it automatically did away with the physical limitations of the theater. On the stage, even one as immense as the New York Hippodrome stage, one could show only so much. The camera had no such limitations. The whole world was its stage."[53] From the moment he began making films with Arbuckle, Keaton relentlessly pushed the limits of what could be captured on film.

Keaton's timing was impeccable: Arbuckle had just started directing his own two-reel short films for Schenck. In March 1917, Arbuckle began shooting *The Butcher Boy* with Keaton playing a supporting role. Three short films and four months later, Arbuckle asked Keaton to work as his assistant director. After making six films in New York, the company moved to Hollywood, where Keaton made six more films with Arbuckle before he was drafted into the Army in June 1918.[54] After serving a short tour in World War I, in which his service was limited to entertaining the troops in France, Keaton returned to Hollywood to make three more short films with Arbuckle. Following this, Zukor offered Arbuckle a contract to make feature-length films, while Schenck offered Keaton the opportunity to make short films for him. Keaton accepted Schenck's offer and Schenck purchased Chaplin's Mutual studio for him—formerly the "Lone Star," where Chaplin filmed *Easy Street*, among others—which he renamed the "Keaton Studio."[55]

As part of a deal with Metro to release Keaton's short films, Schenck arranged for him to star in a feature film for Metro, *The Saphead*, based on *The Henrietta*, a popular Broadway play. In the four-week gap before he began to shoot *The Saphead*, Keaton starred in and directed his first short film, *The High Sign*, but he delayed its release for a year because he was dissatisfied with it.[56] Once Keaton settled into his new studio, Schenck gave him nearly unlimited artistic control over his films. Schenck was first and foremost a producer, a money man who knew about business and left the making of comedy to his talented stars. Keaton had total control over gags, stories, and the editing process; he cut his films himself. According to writer Clyde Bruckman, one of Keaton's closest collaborators for over thirty years, Keaton provided the overwhelming majority of the gags, stories, and direction in his films.[57]

Keaton made eighteen two-reel films before Schenck offered him the opportunity to progress to feature films. Since Keaton had already starred in the successful feature-length comedy *The Saphead*, Schenck had reason to believe that Keaton could make the transition to features. Moreover, the potential for greater financial rewards encouraged Schenck to move Keaton into feature films. Keaton began making features at a time when silent comedians had just started to expand their films to this length.[58] Although in 1914 Mack Sennett had produced the first feature-length comedy, *Tillie's Punctured Romance*, co-starring Charlie Chaplin, this early experiment remained an anomaly until 1921, when Chaplin directed and starred in *The Kid*. By the end of 1922, the overabundance of short silent comedies and the growing market for feature-length films by silent comedians convinced Schenck that the time was right for Keaton to make feature films. By switching to feature-length comedies, producers could charge exhibitors larger rental fees and obtain longer runs. The stage was set for Keaton's ascendance to features.

Keaton's first independent feature-length comedy was *The Three Ages*, a parody of D. W. Griffith's *Intolerance*. The film depicts Buster struggling to find love in three periods of history: the Stone Age, the Roman era, and modern times. The film's structure was a shrewd business move by Keaton and Schenck: if *The Three Ages* did not work as a feature film, Keaton could have easily divided it up into three short films, a possibility that Keaton himself realized.[59] Keaton also selected a form for his first feature film that eased his transition from short films to features by allowing him to link several short films through a common theme. In this way, Keaton produced his first full-length film without necessitating a major change in his thinking about narrative structure.

During the period from 1923 to 1928, Keaton produced two films a year: a spring and a fall release. In total, Keaton created eleven silent feature comedies in this period (as well as *The Saphead*, which he did not direct). Together with the nineteen short films he made between 1920 and 1923, Keaton's reputation as a filmmaker rests solely on these films. Although he frequently shared directing credit with other people, and occasionally gave away the credit outright, Keaton is widely regarded as the principal creator of these films. Regardless of who co-directed or collaborated on a particular film, the style of Keaton's independent short films and features is recognizably his own.

In 1927, Schenck ceased his operations as an independent producer amidst the transition to sound and the consolidation of Hollywood studios.[60] He joined United Artists and advised Keaton to make films for MGM, where Keaton could work for Joe Schenck's brother, Nicholas. Keaton made some attempts to find another studio that would allow him to continue making his films independently, contacting Adolf Zukor at Paramount, but found his options limited, in large part because his last few films for Schenck had made little or no money.[61] By 1927, when he made *College*, Schenck had already assigned two supervisors, Harry Brand and John Considine, to try to contain Keaton's production costs.[62] This trend accelerated rapidly when Keaton began working at MGM.

Keaton made his last two silent features with MGM, *The Cameraman* and *Spite Marriage*. With each film, he found his artistic freedom further curtailed. Keaton was MGM's first true comic star but the MGM system had not been designed to accommodate his working method.[63] At MGM, Keaton no longer worked with a small team of collaborators who knew his work and production methods. Instead, he was assigned teams of writers—as many as twenty-two—and a production staff, all of whom were accountable to the heads of their departments rather than to Keaton.[64] Although the studio promised Keaton he would work with his former production team as much as possible, following the success of *The Cameraman* Keaton usually found his favorite collaborators—such as writer Clyde Bruckman, cameraman Elgin Lessley, and technical director Fred Gabourie—working on other MGM films, effectively stripping him of his staff and friends.[65] Moreover, MGM selected most of Keaton's scripts for him. Under the supervision of Irving Thalberg and Lawrence Weingarten, Keaton's shooting schedule was strictly monitored, allowing him little room for improvisation. As an MGM star, he was limited in his range of expression by the studio's insistence that he no longer perform dangerous stunts.[66] MGM could not accept the risk of injury to Keaton, who was one of their most valuable properties at this time.

In 1929, the studio heads decided that Keaton should begin making sound films. Keaton welcomed this opportunity—indeed, he had lobbied for the opportunity to make sound films after shooting his first feature with MGM[67]—but he had particular ideas about how he should work in a sound film. He believed that the addition of sound did not necessitate constant speaking or singing. Instead, he wanted to continue making films that had little dialogue, but incorporated sound effects. In Keaton's words, "There's nothing wrong with sound that a little silence won't cure."[68] MGM, however, employed a large staff of writers who filled Keaton's sound films with dialogue. Spoken humor replaced physical comedy, a trend accentuated by the studio-enforced limits on Keaton's stunts. At this early stage in sound film, background noise and camera noise were still severe problems, causing most sound films to be shot in the studio, rather than on location, and consequently further limiting Keaton's artistic options.[69] Having sacrificed most of the freedom he had grown accustomed to in vaudeville and silent film, Keaton felt trapped in his new surroundings at MGM.

Dardis's biography documents Keaton's surprising financial success at MGM under these circumstances. But the studio, and Louis B. Mayer in particular, found it increasingly difficult to work with Keaton. Starting with *The Passionate Plumber* (1932), MGM paired Keaton with the overly verbal Jimmy Durante, a combination that still seems absurdly inappropriate more than sixty years later. Although the Keaton-Durante films continued to earn a profit, Keaton became expendable, especially as his alcohol problem grew and he began to miss shooting days. His personal problems were compounded when his first wife, Natalie, filed for divorce, gaining custody of Keaton's sons and leaving him with few assets other than his expensive "land yacht."[70] On February 2, 1933, when he failed to show up for a publicity appearance as ordered by Mayer, his contract was terminated.

Keaton never again enjoyed the artistic control or the popularity of his silent film days. He acted in low-budget two-reel sound shorts for Educational Pictures from 1934 to 1937 and later for Columbia Pictures from 1939 to 1941, working on production budgets under $5000 and shooting entire films in three to five days.[71] Even in this environment, his producers rarely allowed him to direct or write his own films. In *Grand Slam Opera* (1936), the only film he made for Educational Pictures in which he receives a writing credit, Keaton displays flashes of his former absurd imagination—including his appearance on a radio talent show as a *juggler*—indicating what he might have been capable of producing in the sound era had he been given the chance.

Keaton pieced together a decent living, supplementing his income from the short films by working as a gag consultant for MGM. He worked in this capacity on the films of the Marx Brothers, Red Skelton, Abbott and Costello, and later on the film version of his life story, *The Buster Keaton Story* (1957), starring Donald O'Connor. In the 1950s, he toured European circuses several times, performing vaudeville routines culled from his silent films. His third wife, Eleanor Norris Keaton, performed with him in these appearances. Chaplin invited him to play a small yet significant role as a former vaudeville performer serving as Chaplin's dresser in *Limelight* (1953), resulting in the only joint appearance of the two silent comedians. In 1949–50, Keaton created a short-lived television series, *The Buster Keaton Show*, but the show was broadcast only in the Los Angeles area. His second series, a syndicated weekly show, was cancelled after thirteen episodes in 1950–51.[72]

In the 1950s, two of his silent films, *The Navigator* and *The General*, began to be circulated and exhibited through film societies. This, together with Agee's homage to Keaton in *Life* magazine, brought renewed attention to his work. In the late 1950s and the first half of the 1960s, Keaton found himself offered more work than he could accept, including appearances on several television shows—including *The Ed Sullivan Show*, *Playhouse 90*, *Candid Camera*, and *The Twilight Zone*—and small roles in over a dozen films—including *It's a Mad Mad Mad Mad World* (1963), *The Railrodder* (1965), *A Funny Thing Happened on the Way to the Forum* (1966), and several of the Frankie Avalon and Annette Funicello beach movies.

In June 1964, Keaton starred in *Film*—Samuel Beckett's only movie script—directed by Beckett's long-time American theater director, Alan Schneider. Beckett had been a fan of Keaton's since the silent era and had offered Keaton the part of Lucky in the original American production of *Waiting for Godot*.[73] The two found little common ground for conversation, yet their work together is strangely powerful. In September 1965, *Film* was screened at the Venice Film Festival and Keaton, in attendance, was given a standing ovation by the audience. Five months later, on February 1, 1966, Buster Keaton died of lung cancer at the age of seventy.

From Stage to Film:
The Transformation of Keaton's Vaudeville

IN HIS STUDY of early sound comedy, Henry Jenkins suggests, "Perhaps, the habits of watching classical Hollywood texts had become so ingrained that spectators looked for causally integrated narratives even within films not primarily interested in telling stories."[1] If spectators watching early sound comedies, which frequently valued performers' virtuosity over narrative, found it difficult to break the habit of concentrating on narrative values, then spectators of Keaton's films, which hold narrative and gag values in a more precarious balance, may find it even more difficult to overcome the tendency to focus on narrative. Yet in order to see the vaudeville in Keaton's films, we must do precisely that: resist, albeit temporarily, the lure of the narrative. By doing so, I seek to answer the following questions about the influence of vaudeville on Keaton's films: 1) what elements of vaudeville influenced Keaton's filmmaking and remained in his films in some form?; 2) how did Keaton adapt his vaudevillian skills to film?; and 3) what attributes of film attracted Keaton and how did he use these attributes to expand and otherwise change his artistic vision?

One of the primary vaudevillian influences on Keaton's filmmaking may not be immediately apparent: his use of improvisation. For Keaton, as with many of the vaudeville performers who left the stage to make silent films, the practice of improvising was central to his working process. "Vaudeville acts were rarely scripted in advance or written down," notes David Robinson. "Generally they were developed in performance, and perfected against the reactions of an audience."[2] By polishing their acts during performances, vaudevillians exerted artistic control with unmatched immediacy. Although many of The Three Keatons' routines had a basic shape, Joe liked to change their act almost every night and encouraged Buster to improvise from an early age. Keaton observed, "We never bothered to do the same routines twice in a row. We found it much more fun to surprise one another by pulling any crazy, wild stunt that came into our heads."[3]

From the beginning of his filmmaking apprenticeship with Roscoe Arbuckle, Keaton learned to approach filmmaking with the same improvisatory skills upon which he depended in vaudeville. Like Keaton, Arbuckle started out as a vaudeville performer and, together with the less structured studio apparatus Joe Schenck had developed, this led Arbuckle to incorporate into his filmmaking the methods of improvisational comedy-making he learned during his stage work.[4] Arbuckle allowed Keaton to improvise extensively, so that when Schenck put Keaton in charge of his own studio in 1920 Keaton's use of improvisation was a firmly established part of his filmmaking approach.

During the years from 1917 (when he began making films with Arbuckle) to 1928 (when he moved from his own studio to MGM) Keaton, like most of his silent comedy colleagues, never used a written scenario—he worked from a rough, unwritten outline rather than a script.[5] As I noted in Chapter 1, to begin making a film, Keaton required only a beginning and an ending for the story. Frequently, a single idea or prop was enough to set a film in motion. In the case of *The Navigator* (1924), Keaton heard that the *S.S. Buford*, an oceanliner, was about to be demolished and was available for rent for $25,000.[6] Keaton, who had been fascinated by ships and trains since his youth, had his writers brainstorm the ideas for the film in order to make use of the ship; when Clyde Bruckman came up with the basic premise, Keaton rented the ship and began filming. Some of the most brilliant gags in the film were developed from the shape and configuration of the ship. Buster and Betsy, the woman he loves, find themselves stranded on a deserted oceanliner, yet they are unaware of each other's presence. In an elaborately choreographed chase sequence, Buster and Betsy continually fail to locate each other. As they rush up and down the decks and staircases of the ship, a long shot captures the action on three floors of the ship at once, their paths tracing interwoven patterns of simple geometric beauty suggested by the ship's architecture.

To permit himself the freedom to improvise in his filmmaking, Keaton developed particular stylistic preferences that had practical as well as visual aims. By using full or long shots, for example, Keaton allowed himself the opportunity to improvise at will during the production of his silent films, since these shots provided him with the physical space within the frame to improvise. The director and cameramen did not have to know what he would do next, so Keaton maintained the immediacy of his vaudeville act. Medium and close-up shots demanded that the cameramen know where Keaton would move next; long shots, by contrast, allowed him to move within a larger area and gave him the latitude to change his mind and follow his impulses. In addition, the full or long shot in film most closely replicates the vaudeville stage in terms of the performer's physical relationship to the frame.[7] Keaton's preference for long shots stems not only from the oft-quoted observation that tragedy is a close-up and comedy a long shot, but also from the complementary notion that long shots emphasize the body in space. By choosing the long shot for his most extraordinary physical gags and stunts, Keaton focuses the audience's attention insistently on his physical virtuosity as a performer.

To allow himself as much artistic freedom as possible in front of the camera, Keaton insisted that his cameramen continue to shoot film until he said to stop. As Bruckman told Blesh, "The cameramen . . . knew one thing: never stop cranking until Bus said, 'Cut!' Anything might happen. Once into action, it would unfold in his mind, developing as he went along, germinating from a gag to a scene, from a minor scene to a master scene."[8] By insisting upon this rule and retaining control over the editing process and final cut, Keaton retained artistic control even when he had a co-director: as long as the camera caught the action, it remained Keaton's choice whether to include the improvised footage later.

The nature of this artistic control arose from the unique aesthetics of vaudeville. Vaudeville bills were structured in a completely different fashion from theatrical bills; vaudeville producers valued different qualities in performers from those encouraged and emphasized on the "legitimate" stage. By the end of the nineteenth century, the emerging trend in legitimate theater favored ensemble acting as part of a desire for greater verisimilitude.[9] As Jenkins notes, "The focus shifted from the individual performer's ability to 'stop the show,' to 'command the stage,' toward a theater perceived as 'group art,' where each element had to assume its particular place within the overall work."[10] The rise of the director as the locus of artistic control subdued the virtuosic performances by lead actors that had dominated theater for much of the nineteenth century. As legitimate theater strove for greater realism, the interaction among actors took precedence over the power and artistic expression of any one actor. Theatrical conventions were modified to accommodate the change in aesthetic values: actors no longer addressed the audience directly, for example, imagining the presence of an invisible "fourth wall" separating the stage from the audience.

Vaudeville, however, maintained a set of conventions directly opposed to the trends of the legitimate stage. Vaudeville performers addressed the audience directly, soliciting immediate responses to their every joke, stunt, and move. The vaudeville aesthetic was based on "affective immediacy"[11]—performers looked for immediate response from the audience and altered their act from night to night, theater to theater, and town to town depending upon the audience's reactions.[12] This led to a necessarily flexible structure for each act. As one teacher of vaudeville writing suggested, routines could be written down, a joke at a time, on index cards and reshuffled on demand to fit the needs of particular audiences, bills, and venues:

> Have as many cards or slips of paper as you have points or gags. Write only one point of gag on one card or slip of paper. On the first card, write "Introduction" and always keep that card first in your hand. Then take up a card and read the point or gag on it as following the introduction, the second card as the second point or gag, and so on until you have arranged your monologue in an effective manner. . . . By shuffling the cards you may make as many arrangements as you wish and eventually arrive at the ideal routine.[13]

The order of the cards was manipulated for purely emotional effect. Vaudeville producers judged each act's worth by the audible and visible reactions of the audience.[14] Producers shared this information among themselves and with the booking agencies that dominated vaudeville from the turn of the century. This information played a major part in the establishment of the reputation of each act, so that the audience's reactions shaped not only the act's nightly performance, but also its future marketability, salary, and placement on the bill. Vaudeville acts, therefore, had to be structurally fluid to adapt to the differing tastes of individual audiences. The livelihood of the performers depended upon their ability to constantly shift the focus of their material for greater impact: more laughs, more gasps, more applause.

Although vaudeville performers retained artistic control over the content of their acts, the producer of each vaudeville theater selected and arranged the acts on the bill for any given week. An evening of vaudeville was never organized with a narrative throughline or any sort of thematic coherence; instead, the producer arranged the acts with an eye toward constant variety.[15] As Brooks McNamara notes, "The organization of acts on a bill was governed by practical considerations about balancing the elements of a show, by traditions about the location of certain kinds of material within the show's framework, and by the attempt to create a 'rising action' as the evening progressed, building toward a climactic act at or near the end of the show."[16] The shape not only of the vaudeville bill, but also of each of the acts contained within it, was developed along this rising curve. Each act tried to finish its routine with a topper: a final gag, joke, or stunt that capped their performance by evoking the largest audience response yet. Thus, an evening of vaudeville was designed to elicit a series of rising curves, each one the length of a vaudeville routine—fifteen to twenty minutes in duration. The overall pattern of the vaudeville bill replicated the shape of an act, building audience response toward the "headliner," the best-known and hopefully best-received act of the evening, which operated as a topper for the evening's entertainment. Usually the topper was followed by a closing act or two that settled down the audience. Needless to say, the spots following the headliner were not considered desirable by performers because they functioned as a sort of anticlimax.

Keaton's films reveal a variety of approaches to transferring this structure to film. Sometimes, as in *Our Hospitality* and *The General*, the vaudeville structure is blended with a strong narrative line, the positioning of the gags and stunts supporting rather than challenging the dominance of the more linear, causally linked narrative. Other films display a more complex and equivocal relationship between the two structures.[17] Yet another group of films, which includes many of Keaton's silent shorts and a few of his feature-length silent films, appears to depend upon vaudeville structure—the rise in pure emotional and comic effect—for cohesiveness, using narrative as a pretext for extended gag sequences. These are the films I will be examining below, because they provide the easiest *entrée* to Keaton's vaudeville.

One Week (1920), the first independent short film that Keaton released, exemplifies this group of films.[18] Inspired by *Home Made*, a Ford Motor Company promotional film on "do-it-yourself" prefabricated houses,[19] *One Week* wears its structure on its sleeve, so to speak: it is divided into the seven days of the week. Each day is indicated by a close-up shot of a daily calendar. At the beginning of each episode, the previous day is pulled off the calendar to reveal the day of the scene to follow. The plot serves little purpose other than as a pretext for gags: Buster marries a young woman, and his uncle gives the couple a lot on which to assemble a prefabricated house that he has delivered to them. Unbeknownst to them, a rival suitor for the woman's affections changes the numbers on the house kit, so that when they assemble the house all of the parts are completely out of order. After the house is nearly destroyed by a storm, Buster and his wife discover that they have built the house on the wrong lot. As they attempt to move the house, it gets stuck on a railroad track and is destroyed by a train.

The story, however, is not what attracts our interest; instead, Keaton displays his creativity through the ingenuity of his gags and the way in which he modulates them throughout the film. *One Week* displays many structural elements of vaudeville, and these elements can be read as a separate organizing principle of the film. In *One Week*, the house—and the machinations of Buster and his wife in first trying to build it and then trying to tame it— becomes the central focus of the film. Keaton directs each episode with an eye for variety, incorporating many of the skills he developed in vaudeville: acrobatics, transformation gags, and gags based upon incongruity and illogic. As in vaudeville, each episode functions as a discrete unit (with rising action and a "topper"), and Keaton modulates the rising action of the entire film along the same line.

The first episode, Monday the 9th, functions as an opening act and begins by warming up the audience with small gags before the action quickly escalates. One of the ways Keaton created rising action in his films was by enlarging the physical scale of his gags and the physical space that they occupy. In the first episode of *One Week*, the gags begin slowly with small sight gags. Buster and his new bride descend the church steps following their wedding ceremony. The guests throw rice at the happy couple, followed by old shoes.[20] Buster, who is wearing a pair of vaudeville flapshoes for his wedding day, sees the old shoes and reaches down to select a pair. The gag, although a minor one, works on two levels: Buster's behavior is inappropriate for the circumstances and at the same time it draws attention to his flapshoes, a "self-reference" to Keaton's extrafictional status as a film comedian.[21]

The next gag is based primarily on Buster's facial expressions and the movements of his head. "Handy Hank," a rival for the affections of Buster's wife, begins to chauffeur them to their new house, with the couple in the back seat. Buster turns to kiss his wife only to notice that Hank has turned to watch them. When Buster aborts the kiss Hank looks forward, yet each time Buster attempts to kiss his wife again Hank looks back at them, stopping them in mid-kiss. The gag depends upon Keaton's ability to perform a "take," freezing his movements for a brief moment before swiveling his head to stare down Hank. From this point the action escalates rapidly. The following sequence shifts the emphasis from Buster's comic takes to his acrobatic stunt work: in order to escape Hank's surveillance, Buster and his wife attempt to jump into a taxi traveling parallel to their car. Buster's wife succeeds in making the dangerous transfer, but Buster gets caught between the two cars in a spread-eagle position. When a motorcycle coming from the opposite direction drives between the two cars, Buster is swept off on its handlebars. The sequence is captured in a long shot with the cars facing full front; the camera tracks backwards at the same speed as the cars and captures Buster's entire body and both cars in the frame. By showing the stunt in one long take, Keaton draws attention to what Jenkins calls "performance virtuosity,"[22] preserving the integrity of the stunt in order to emphasize his performance skills as an acrobat. As Walter Kerr perceptively notes, "It was Keaton's notion that cutting, valuable as it was in a thousand ways, must not replace the recording function of the camera, must not *create* the happening. The happening must happen, be photographed intact, then be related by cutting to other happenings."[23] Keaton insisted upon capturing his stunts in their entirety—without the assistance of camera tricks or editing—throughout his career. This is not to say that he completely avoided using editing and camera tricks, but rather that he used them to increase the effects of his stunts rather than to substitute for the stunts themselves.

Buster pursues his wife and Hank on the motorcycle and, in the topper for the sequence, he passes them and rescues his wife by knocking out a traffic cop and using the policeman's hat and baton to stop Hank, who has commandeered the taxi. Buster and his wife then proceed to their new house, only to discover that it comes in a box: their uncle has given them a portable house that they must build themselves. The first two sight gags—the shoe gag followed by the aborted kisses—slowly build the opening of the sequence and prepare for the physical comedy and spectacle of the stunt work. The stunts—Buster and his wife jumping from car to car; Buster caught between the cars and nearly killed, but actually saved, by an onrushing motorcyle; Buster's rescue of his wife—intensify the impact of the episode on the audience.

Keaton relies on the variety of his gags and stunts, rather than the development of the characters and narrative, to sustain the audience's interest throughout the seven episodes. Just as vaudeville constantly changed gears by providing its audiences with a new act and a new type of entertainment every twenty minutes, Keaton shaped *One Week* by modulating his vast array of performance skills within each episode and between them. In the second episode, Tuesday the 10th, Keaton switches from the daredevil chase antics of the previous episode to an escalating series of gags involving his attempts to construct one wall of the house. First, while sawing a two-by-four on the second floor, Buster fails to notice that he is sitting on the section of the wooden beam that juts out over the edge of the outer wall of the house. His wife, who is cooking below, calls for him to join her for breakfast. Buster hollers back to her (communicated by an intertitle), "I'll be right down!" only to turn his statement into a self-fulfilled prophecy by sawing himself away from the house. His plunge from the second floor is captured in a long shot, providing him with the opportunity to display one of his most oft-noted vaudeville skills, the "buster," or acrobatic fall. Buster lands on his feet, but increases the perceived impact of the fall by immediately rolling into a back somersault, his legs stretched out and apart, so that he lands fully sprawled on his back.

Next, Buster is perched at the top of a second-story wall and his wife sits on the first floor window sill directly beneath him. When Buster hammers a board into place, the entire wall rotates 180 degrees from top to bottom, so that the first- and second-story windows trade places, with Buster ending up on the ground floor while his wife finds herself at the top of the second-story wall. Finding himself unexpectedly on the ground, Buster calls out for his wife. As he walks forward to search for her, the entire wall falls on Buster, but he escapes injury when the second-story window opening falls on him, allowing him to pass through it unharmed. This operates as the topper for the sequence and its impact is all the greater because it is unexpected. Keaton foreshadows the first gag with his intertitle, "I'll be right down." The second gag (the revolving wall) is executed on such a large scale that it appears to be the topper for the sequence. Consequently, the third gag comes as a complete surprise, heightening the humorous effect by unexpectedly topping the topper.

Arbuckle and Keaton also used a version of the falling-wall gag in *Back Stage* (1919). In this earlier version, Fatty is performing on stage and Buster accidentally trips the support post for a stage flat, causing it to fall on Fatty, with the window conveniently slipping over Fatty's body. It may be that this gag was originally Arbuckle's idea, yet in its initial form it has little of the power of Keaton's versions. The key difference is one of size and danger. By using a larger wall that appears to be real, Keaton expanded this simple vaudeville stunt into a visual metaphor for his relationship with the world. The world appears to be aggressively antagonistic, as if it has a mind of its own, yet Buster seems to know unconsciously where to stand in order to survive. Keaton used the same gag on an even larger scale in what remains perhaps his most famous stunt, the sequence at the end of *Steamboat Bill, Jr.* (1928) in which an entire three-story building façade falls down on him during a hurricane. The evolution of the gag from film to film demonstrates

Figure 2.1. *One Week*. The house that Buster built.

how Keaton constantly raised the stunt to a larger scale while continuing to preserve the integrity of his performance in a single long shot.[24]

In the next episode of *One Week*, Wednesday the 11th, Buster and his wife have completed the house and it looks completely ludicrous, as if it were deconstructed and reconstructed by a psychotic or a surrealist architect (fig. 2.1). Buster walks around the back of the house to finish installing the kitchen sink that is mounted on the outside of the house along with the cookware. Unfazed, he simply revolves the wall panel, simultaneously entering the house and putting the kitchen in its proper place. The repetition of a revolving wall provides a sense of visual continuity between this gag and the previous episode, which Keaton will continue to build on in the film.

The succeeding episodes continue the pattern of constantly shifting gag types, as well as the variation between small gags with props and larger ones involving the entire house. For Thursday's episode, Keaton intercut a gag in which he tacks down a carpet over his coat with a fairly routine sight gag of his wife splashing herself with milk while attempting to open the container. This episode introduces another form of spectacle derived from vaudeville:

the titillation of burlesque. As Buster executes a series of gags involving the installation of a chimney, his wife is revealed bathing, her breasts barely obscured by the edge of the bathtub from the view of the camera. She drops a bar of soap and starts to lean down to pick it up, but notices the camera. The cameraman then covers the lens with his hand so that her body remains hidden from us.[25] This sequence is intercut with Buster's chimney routine, so that when he falls through the chimney and into the bathroom (in Buster's oddly constructed house, the chimney is located directly above the bath), we expect him to fall on his wife. His wife, however, is now in the shower and orders Buster to leave the bathroom. Temporarily flustered, Buster rushes out of the bathroom door only to discover that it leads directly from the second story to the outdoors and he performs a flip as he tumbles to the ground.

Much of the rest of this episode depends upon Buster's use of transformation gags,[26] in which an object, body, animal, or setting is used as if it were something else. When Buster and his wife attempt to haul a piano into the house by attaching a rope to the first-floor chandelier, the first-floor ceiling stretches down, as if it were made of rubber. When Buster releases the rope, the ceiling snaps back into place, catapulting Hank, the repairman working on the second floor, through the roof, as if he were on a trampoline. In order to rescue Hank, whose head is stuck in the roof, Buster detaches the porch railing and uses it as a ladder. There is a search for constant variety in this sequence, as Keaton looks for a new gag every time he comes into contact with a prop. Having used the railing as a ladder, he must use it differently as he descends. As he comes down the ladder, he reaches out as he talks to his wife below, tipping the ladder out from the wall. After balancing it away from the wall for a moment, Buster climbs to the inside of the ladder and travels the rest of the way down on the wall side of the ladder.

The episode for Friday the 13th gradually increases the physical scale of Keaton's gags beyond that of any of the preceding scenes. Before doing so, however, Keaton reincorporates the second-story exit gag at the end of a fight with Hank during a house-warming party the couple hosts for friends and family. In the midst of the fight, Buster dashes upstairs with Hank in pursuit. Buster reaches the bathroom a few feet in front of Hank and quickly opens the second-floor exit so that Hank sprints directly out of the house, falling from the second story and crashing into the backyard fence. By using this gag on two different "days" within *One Week*, Keaton demonstrates how gags can be temporally extended—exhibiting what Jenkins calls an "accordionlike structure"[27]—by spacing the variations on a single gag over several episodes. These repetitions provide the film with a certain structural stability; each repetition reminds us of the previous gags of this type and thus serves to unify the film. In this way, gag structure takes the place of narrative structure. Although Hank reemerges as a character in this scene, we never hear from him again and his reappearance serves little purpose in this episode other than to provide an opportunity to extend the running gag. Rather than pushing the narrative further, the repetition of the gag suggests that the film has circled back to the previous episode, creating stasis rather than progress.

Instead, Keaton achieves a sense of progression by escalating the size and visceral impact of the stunts that follow. As in *Steamboat Bill, Jr.*, Keaton uses a cyclone as the agent for the chaos that ensues. As the storm builds, the house begins to rotate on its central axis, an effect Keaton achieved by putting the entire building on a revolving platform.[28] He alternates long shots of the house spinning with interior shots of the guests and Buster tumbling around inside it. In both cases the shots emphasize the acrobatic maneuvers of the actors, rather than the damage that the storm inflicts on the house. As the gags unfold, Keaton goes out of his way to isolate his own acrobatics. Having unsuccessfully tried to stop the house from spinning by holding it in place from the outside, Buster jumps inside the house and performs his stunts in the living room. Yet there is a noticeable inconsistency here: the guests, who have just been seen spinning around the kitchen, are not visible in the shots of Buster. Rather than attempting to upstage his fellow actors in a group scene, Keaton simply cleared the room for his shots in this sequence, isolating himself to emphasize his acrobatic performance.

Within the overall pattern of the film, Keaton balances the apocalyptic proportions of the spinning house with contrastingly small gags in the following episode. On Saturday the 14th, upon awaking "after the storm" as the intertitle indicates, Buster and his wife turn to survey the damage to their house. Devastated by the sight of the ravaged house, which looks all the worse for the combination of its absurd construction and the damage that the storm has caused, Buster and his wife stand side-by-side and collapse toward each other, forming an inverted "v" with their bodies; the only thing that prevents them from falling to the ground is the inward pressure of their bodies. Keaton uses a long shot that shows the entire house in order to emphasize the parallels between the couple and the structure of the house, both of which stand on their "last legs." A neighbor points out that they have built the house on the wrong lot and must move it. The episode then ends with two transformation gags: Buster's wife uses a car jack to elevate the house, while Buster puts barrels under the house so that they can roll it to its new location.

The final episode, by vaudeville's aesthetic standards, must have a topper or "wow finish" and, following the spinning-house episode, this is no easy task. One way that Keaton attempts to top the spinning-house episode is by opening up the physical scale of the film even further. Buster and his wife attempt to tow the house to the proper lot, but they find themselves unable to haul it over the railroad tracks. Here, Keaton appropriated one of the oldest stock finishes from melodrama—the damsel in distress on the train tracks—but substituted a house for the damsel, parodying the conventional melodramatic ending. After several attempts to move the house, they hear a train whistle and rush from the house. The train appears ready to destroy the house, but at the last minute it actually passes by when it is revealed to be on a parallel set of tracks. Just as Buster and his wife think they have survived this ordeal, another train plows through the middle of the house from the opposite direction. The actual destruction of the house is preceded by a false alarm, allowing the second train to catch the audience by surprise. This "one-two punch," a rapid repetition of the same gag, provides the topper and saves the ending from reverting to pure melodrama for its conclusion. At the end of the film, Buster places a "For Sale" sign and the assembly instructions in front of the house, then walks away from it with his bride. This closing, and minor, anticlimactic gag serves as a counterweight to the enormous scale of the destruction of the house. It also reincorporates the gag from the first episode when the couple first realized that their house came in a box with instructions. By depositing the instructions with the demolished house, the couple has come full circle and the audience, too, has returned to the first gag involving the house. Stripped of the minimal plot, the film retains its interest through the purely visual pleasures of the spinning walls of the house, its eccentric construction, the unexpected transformations of floors into catapults and the entire house into a merry-go-round. On the visual level, the film takes joy in disorienting the spectator with its playful revision of reality, shifting the focus from the story to the shapes, turns, and twists of Buster and the house.

One Week quickly established Keaton's reputation as a filmmaker and slapstick comedian independent of his work with Arbuckle. Although it was his first release as an independent filmmaker, *One Week* was not the first film Keaton made. In the four weeks preceding his work as an actor in the feature film *The Saphead*, Keaton wrote, directed, and starred in *The High*

Sign (1921).[29] Yet he withheld release of this film for nearly a year and then only released it at the request of his producer, Joe Schenck. A comparison of the two films reveals structural differences that may partially explain why Keaton was disappointed with *The High Sign*.

The High Sign contains many ingenious gags, but Keaton's over-attentiveness to narrative development and details hinders the film's drive. Out of work and destitute, Buster gets a job at a shooting gallery, where he is employed as a trick-shot artist, a task he executes by rigging the targets so that they ring whenever he depresses a foot pedal. This allows him to put on an impressive display of sharpshooting wizardry, no doubt incorporating material from his vaudeville parody of the Great Bordeverry.[30] His employer is a member of the "Blinking Buzzards," a small-time crime organization. The Buzzards have unsuccessfully attempted to extort money from August Nickelnurser, the town miser. Consequently, they hire Buster, whom they believe to be a sharpshooter, to shoot Nickelnurser. Nickelnurser's daughter sees Buster performing his (faked) trick shots at the arcade and hires him to protect her father from the Buzzards. Thus, Buster is the hitman and bodyguard for the same man. Nickelnurser has furnished his house with a series of trapdoors, false walls, and hidden escapes for his protection. Buster, whose sympathies lie with Nickelnurser (in part because he has fallen for Nickelnurser's daughter), pretends to kill Nickelnurser in front of the Buzzards, but the Buzzards discover the fraud. The last five minutes of the film involve a complex chase throughout the house. Eventually, Buster captures the leader of the Buzzards by triggering a trapdoor to the cellar, saves Nickelnurser, and is united with the daughter. In comparison to the pared-down narrative of *One Week*, the story of *The High Sign* seems bulky, and the narrative exposition contributes little to the humor, serving only to slow down the pace of the film.

A comparison of the chase within the house in *The High Sign* with the storm sequence in *One Week* illustrates the development of Keaton's thinking as a filmmaker, particularly in his use of space. The chase in *The High Sign* primarily consists of shots of individual rooms, in which Buster and the criminals move from room to room by virtue of revolving walls, trapdoors, and hidden escape routes, such as the body of a grandfather clock that Buster jumps through. In one long shot, he shows a cut-away of the entire building, so that the camera follows the chase from one room to another without a cut. Here Keaton tries to preserve the integrity of his acrobatic performance, tumbling and leaping from room to room, as well as his skill in conceiving and building the set for this sequence. Yet the mise-en-scène remains essentially theatrical in these shots; Keaton could have performed the scene on a stage. He fails to take advantage of the flexibility of his medium, opting to keep the action on a single plane and the camera in a relatively static alternation between the long shot of the entire house in cut-away and the full shots of the action in the rooms.

In *One Week*, however, Keaton begins to make fuller use of space and exploits film's ability to expand space beyond the three walls of a stage set. The entire house moves, both revolving during the storm sequence and being pulled by a car in the final sequence. The revolving house, of course, utilizes technology that had been a part of theatrical practice since the 1890s: the turntable. But the towing of the house could not have been done convincingly on stage, and the topper for the film—the destruction of the house by a speeding locomotive—shows Keaton beginning to reach for a level of spectacle toward which melodrama and spectacular theater had been striving in the latter part of the nineteenth century, but which they could never attain.[31]

These differences, though representative of the development of Keaton's use of space, could scarcely have been the reason he withheld the film from circulation for so long, however.[32] Ultimately, it is by the vaudevillian standard of affective response that *The High Sign* falls short of Keaton's other two-reel films. The gags are inventive and abundant, but the film fails to build momentum because of the overemphasis on plot development: in a reversal of current theories about the relationship between gags and narrative, the narrative disrupts the gags.[33] Although two-reel slapstick comedies as a genre tend to favor gags over plot, the progression from *The High Sign* to *One Week* reveals that Keaton first attempted a more plot-based short film and then retreated from it. Few of his subsequent shorts were dominated by plot development. While *The High Sign* depends upon plot for coherence, in *One Week* Keaton retains one prop, the house, as a central image and finds as much variety as possible through his interactions with it, sacrificing narrative development for the escalation of gags. The conclusion of *One Week* brings the couple back to where they started—the house is in pieces and they have only each other—whereas the conclusion of *The High Sign* relies on the progression of the narrative: Buster has foiled the Buzzards and won at love.

In exploring the relationship between narrative and gags in his early feature films, Keaton initially retained a more gag-based structure in *The Three Ages* (1923), before experimenting with more narrative-based forms in some of his subsequent films. At this early stage in his directing career,

Keaton had already grasped film's ability to jump back and forth through time and the usefulness of parallel plots. The film presents a scene in one age and then reworks it in two others, ending in three parallel conclusions that mirror each other. This structure allowed Keaton to make his first feature film with relatively little economic pressure, as Schenck could have released the film as three separate short films with little difficulty.[34] By choosing to appropriate the basic structure of Griffith's film, Keaton was able to ease his transition to feature length by staying close to the format of his earlier two-reel films.

In each of the film's five major sections, we see essentially the same plot played out in all three eras. Since the story and outcome remain essentially the same in each era, the focus shifts from *what* will happen to *how* it will happen, emphasizing the variety of ways Keaton performs similar gags from era to era. In the first section, for example, Keaton repeats two central gags in each era: one on modes of transportation and the other showing how the parents of Margaret Leahy (Buster's love interest) decide who is the most appropriate suitor for her. In the Stone Age, Wallace Beery (Buster's antagonist) rides a mastodon, while Buster rides a dinosaur; in the Roman Age, Beery has a chariot, while Buster's chariot is pulled by donkeys;[35] in the Present Age sequence, as Buster and Beery drive their cars side-by-side, Buster's ramshackle car collapses when they drive over a ditch. In the Stone Age, Margaret's father decides who is the appropriate suitor by hitting Buster and his rival on top of the head with a club; the Roman Age father decides the matter by military rank; while the Present Age father defers to his wife, who selects Beery because he has the larger bank account. By extending the gag variations over the three eras, Keaton demonstrates how gags can be expanded temporally over the course of a film. While a narrative-based reading of this structure might be that love never changes, a vaudeville reading suggests that humor never changes. At the same time, the outcome of the plots also remains consistent, indicating that Keaton was more interested in generating funny gags than propelling the plot forward in time. Instead, each variation of a gag reminds the audience of the previous gag upon which it was based, leading the audience around in circles through the ages.

In his later films, Keaton did not completely abandon the structure he began to work with in *The Three Ages*. *Sherlock Jr.* can be seen as two nearly autonomous films, each approximately the length of a two-reel short. Indeed, this notion of the film is latent in much of the criticism of *Sherlock Jr.*: scholars frequently refer to the "inner film" and the "outer film" when dis-

cussing the narrative.[36] Both the inner and outer films concern love trian-
gles (Buster, the Sheik, and the woman) and the search for stolen property
(a watch in the outer film; pearls in the inner film). Yet by focusing on the
similarities between the inner and outer films, scholars have neglected to
notice just how apt the descriptive terminology is. The inner and outer films
are each twenty-two minutes long, approximately the length of a two-reel
short and, not coincidentally, also the length of a vaudeville act; moreover,
as in *The Three Ages*, Keaton unifies the two films by repeating the same gags
with variations in both. Yet the inner and outer films of *Sherlock Jr.* differ
greatly in structure and dominant gag types.[37] The outer film depends upon
narrative and one very good gag for closure, while the inner film depends
much more upon pure sensation and spectacle.

In the outer film Buster, the would-be detective, searches his girlfriend's
family and the Sheik in a failed attempt to discover who stole the father's
watch. In the inner film Buster, as "Sherlock Jr.," searches the family of the
inner film by merely staring intently at each person. By reincorporating this
gag, Keaton stretches it temporally across the film, as he had done in *The
Three Ages*. Yet it is more successful in *Sherlock Jr.* because it is less predictable and more subtle: the repetition of each gag is no longer emphasized by
the strict tripartite structure of *The Three Ages*.[38] Keaton achieves a similar
effect when he "tails" the Sheik. In the outer film, Buster follows the Sheik,
mirroring his every move, including tripping, catching the Sheik's discarded
cigarette in mid-air, and sidestepping an oncoming automobile with identical footwork to the Sheik. When the Sheik discovers Buster, he traps him in
a railroad car. Buster escapes through the roof hatch and runs from car to
car as the train rushes forward. When there are no cars left, he grabs onto a
water spout that hangs above the train and, as his weight pulls him slowly
towards the ground, the water explodes from the spout, knocking him to
the ground and drenching him to the bone. In the inner film, the Sheik
tricks Buster into climbing onto a roof and locks him up there. As the Sheik
heads off in his car, Buster jumps from the rooftop to a railroad-crossing bar
and, recapitulating the movement of the water spout in the inner film, he
sails toward the ground, this time landing safely unseen in the backseat of
the Sheik's car.

In this way, Keaton continued to experiment with the structure of his
films in two-reel, twenty-minute units. From his experience as a vaudeville
performer, Keaton was already used to thinking in such units. In *Sherlock
Jr.*, the outer film can be seen to rely on simple slapstick humor—the stuck-
paper gag, the lost-dollar gag, the banana-peel gag[39]—while the inner film

places greater reliance on more physically elaborate magic tricks and optical illusions, such as the scene in which Buster appears to jump through his assistant's stomach and the sequence in which he appears to walk through a mirror.[40] It is as if we see two vaudeville acts—a slapstick routine and a magic act—except that Keaton has melded them together in one film. By carrying over key gags from the outer film to the inner film, Keaton provides a sense of continuity between the two and thus compensates for the inner film's divergence from the narrative line of the outer film.

The expanded accordion structure, previously seen in *One Week*, is present to some extent in almost all of Keaton's films, but is perhaps most evident in *College* (1927). *College*, I must reiterate, was a favorite film of Luis Buñuel, and his comments on the film bear repeating here at greater length:

> Asepsia. Disinfection. Liberated from tradition, our outlook is rejuvenated in the youthful and temperate world of Buster, the great specialist against all sentimental infection. . . . There are those who have sought to believe Buster the 'anti-virtuoso', inferior to Chaplin, to reckon it some sort of disadvantage, a kind of stigmata in him, what the rest of us reckon a virtue, that Keaton arrives at comedy through direct harmony with objects, situations and other means of his work. Keaton is full of humanity: but of actual and not synthetic humanity. . . . Superfilms serve to give lessons to technicians; those of Keaton give lessons to reality itself, with or without the technique of reality.[41]

What makes *College* unsentimental in Buñuel's eyes is Keaton's constant focus on physical gags—in Buñuel's words, "through direct harmony with objects"—precisely the quality of this film that Moews most maligns.[42] In *College*, Keaton focuses his attention almost exclusively on his physical work as a performer. Perhaps this is one reason why he grew despondent when he was forced to hire Olympic pole-vaulter Lee Barnes to perform a crucial stunt, which he himself was unable to learn, for the end of the film.[43] Nonetheless, Keaton's own physical gags and his overriding emphasis on his body provide the film's primary attractions.

The majority of the film's gags concern Buster's attempts to become a successful athlete in order to win back his girlfriend, Mary. But the causal line from athletics to romance is attenuated and put, quite literally, in the background. At each sporting event in which Buster participates, Mary dutifully appears to watch Buster and her new boyfriend, Jeff, the star athlete of the college. Yet her reactions to Buster's failure at baseball and track are essentially inconsequential; the gags gain little from her presence and Buster gains little from his athletic performance. His later success—in typical Keaton form he helps the college crew team win by attaching the rudder to his posterior and steering with his hips—is not even witnessed by Mary.

Keaton manages to pull all of these gags together in the final gag sequence, which fuses them in a flurry of gag and spectacle. The narrative sets the sequence in motion, yet narrative concerns are clearly overshadowed by Keaton's physical work as a performer. Jeff has locked Mary in her dormitory room in a desperate attempt to force her to marry him. She calls Buster and, as he speeds to her rescue, Buster performs every physical task that he had failed to perform earlier. The rows of hedges he encounters in his rush to Mary's dormitory provide him with the opportunity to remedy his earlier failure at the high hurdles; the pools of water in his path allow him to master the long jump. When he reaches the dormitory, he pole-vaults into Mary's second-story room, rectifying his earlier failure on the track when he broke the pole. The reincorporations of previous gag material come so quickly in this sequence that it is almost like a flashback montage of the best gags and stunts in the film. Keaton reprises the rest of his track-and-field gags, including his work with the shot-put, the javelin, the discus, and the hammer. He suddenly possesses the baseball skills that he lacked earlier, catching, throwing, and batting objects at Jeff in order to chase him from Mary's room. As he does so, he seems to spin back through the film, correcting all of his previous failures. The entire film serves as one giant, expanding, accordion-like gag, with the earlier gags establishing a foundation for their eventual reincorporation in the final rescue scene.

Critics have argued that Keaton's final sequences, which often involve Buster succeeding at tasks that had been impossible for him to perform earlier in the films, can be difficult to believe; after all, how could his character have developed these skills so quickly? Rather than a weakness in Keaton's films, I see Buster's instantaneous acquisition of these skills as a confirmation of the relative unimportance of narrative consistency to Keaton's success as a filmmaker. Keaton's acknowledged status as the master of these stunts is a vital element in his filmmaking. As audiences came to expect spectacular acrobatics from Keaton, the endings of the films became almost a convention—extended sequences that draw attention to Keaton's extrafictional reputation as a physical comedian. All of Keaton's feature films depend upon his performance of extraordinarily demanding physical tasks for closure: an urban escape across rooftops (*The Three Ages*), a waterfall rescue (*Our Hospitality*), a battle with cannibals (*The Navigator*), ocean and river rescues (*The Cameraman, Steamboat Bill, Jr.*), elaborate chases (*Sherlock Jr.*,

Figure 2.2. The Keatons' vaudeville act frequently ended with the
revelation of multiple, miniature versions of Joe Keaton, as
in this publicity shot of The Four Keatons.

The General, Seven Chances, Go West), boxing (*Battling Butler*), and acrobatic balancing acts (*Spite Marriage*). Although Keaton depended upon stories to entice audiences to root for his character through the final reel, the

films' climactic sequences are ultimately about Keaton's physical performance at least as much, if not more so, than his performance of his character.

Keaton's use of the spectacular final sequence may be traced to The Three
Keatons' vaudeville act. As I described in Chapter 1, the final gag of The
Three Keatons' act normally involved a revelation of multiple Keatons in
identical costumes. Buster was dressed as a miniature duplicate of his father,
Joe; his mother, Myra, was frequently revealed to be wearing a costume
identical to Joe's and Buster's underneath her original outfit; and the act's
topper, in later years, involved Jingles and Louise entering the stage in
matching costumes, further extending the miniaturization of Joe's stage
image (fig. 2.2). The Five Keatons would stand in a line, organized from
tallest (Joe) to smallest (Louise). The resulting image created an optical
illusion, as if through some bit of stage magic Joe had successfully cloned or
replicated himself. The image was all the more astounding, however, because it was *not* an illusion. Keaton learned two lessons from this image: 1)
that extending a gag image to absurd dimensions was both humorous and
startling; and 2) that gags work best when they appear to be possible.

The latter lesson has been misunderstood in Keaton criticism to date. In
his autobiography, Keaton stated that he "discontinued using what we call
impossible or cartoon gags"[44] when he made the transition from two-reel
films to feature films. In interpreting this statement, scholars have emphasized Keaton's rejection of impossible gags. There is a fine distinction I
would like to make here, one that will become more important in Chapter
4 when I look at Keaton's films for their affinities with surrealism: while
Keaton may have rejected impossible gags, he regularly used and in fact
depended upon *improbable* gags. As an example of an impossible gag, Keaton cited the sequence in *Hard Luck* when Buster dives from a balcony into
an empty swimming pool, creating a large crater, only to emerge "years
later" with a Chinese wife and children. Yet Keaton did not consider the
cyclone sequence in *Steamboat Bill, Jr.* to be an impossible gag. It seems safe
to say, therefore, that Keaton had an extremely broad conception of what
was possible.

In skirting the line between the improbable and the impossible, Keaton
draws from the spirit, if not the literal tradition, of farce. The combination
of fact and fantasy is one of the distinguishing marks of farce. As Eric
Bentley aptly notes, "Farce brings together the direct and wild fantasies and
the everyday and drab realities. The interplay between the two is the very
essence of this art—the farcical dialectic."[45] While comedy always remains
connected to reality on some level, farce tests and frequently breaks this
bond. Although Keaton did not consider his films to be farces, Albert

Figure 2.3. *The Boat*. Buster and sons.

Bermel suggests that Keaton's judgment most likely stemmed from a narrow definition of farce: "Evidently he, like so many others, thought of farce restrictedly as being that specialized, nineteenth-century type of boulevard play known as bedroom farce. He believed himself to be a realist, while "farce" was synthetic, phony. In some respects his pictures support that belief. Keaton insisted that his backgrounds look geographically and historically authentic."[46] Bermel observes that Keaton's landscapes and his preference for beautifully composed long shots drive his films from farce into other genres. "How can such a figure on such landscapes be farcical?" asks Bermel. "The answer is that he is not. Keaton is giving us flashes of lyrical respite while the farce cuts in and out."[47] Yet Keaton's farce often invades his lyrical landscapes and his landscapes, in turn, provide the sense of the everyday that his farce assaults. By setting his farcical actions in a vividly created world, Keaton brings the maniacal power of farce to bear on the real world, suggesting what Peter F. Parshall describes as "a world moved by darker forces than our comfortable rationality would admit."[48]

When Keaton did go "over the line" into farce and fantasy, he usually provided a justification for the excursion—in *Sherlock Jr.*, for example, he bracketed the use of impossible gags within the inner film's "dream." By doing so, Keaton was able to treat the inner film as a completely different piece from the outer film, with a distinct aesthetic and special rules for acceptable gags. The distinction between the impossible and the improbable is particularly important when we look at Keaton's use of multiple images.[49] Five identical Keatons were not impossible, just biologically improbable. The greater the ranks of the multiples, the more improbable and hence the more startling the image. Keaton would take these multiples to unprecedented and unequaled dimensions in his short and feature-length silent films; they are noticeably absent from his sound films for MGM and his subsequent short films for Educational Pictures and Columbia Pictures, most likely because of the strict artistic and economic constraints under which these films were made.

Keaton's independent short films exhibit numerous uses of multiple images. In *The Boat* (1921), Buster's family is comprised of his wife and two children; both children sport porkpie hats identical to his (fig. 2.3). This type of multiple-image gag directly appropriates the basic gag of The Three Keatons: an entire family in matching costumes. The only differences are that Buster has taken over the role of father and the gag is entrenched in the entire film. Rather than using the revelation of multiple, miniaturized Busters as a topper as The Three Keatons did, Keaton merely incorporated his sons' matching outfits without comment. This choice does, to some extent, dampen the theatricality of Buster's multiples; he draws less attention to the gag than The Three Keatons did on the vaudeville stage. Yet the use of Buster's porkpie hat as the main prop in establishing his sons' "multiplicity" is ultimately extrafictional and self-referential, highlighting Buster's identity as an already established star performer.

In his study of "comedian comedy"—film comedy featuring comedians with reputations previously established in other media—Steve Seidman defines extrafictional as "anything that interrupts the smooth exposition of a fictional universe, or anything that intrudes upon the depiction of a 'real' fictional universe to give the sense that 'it's only a movie.'"[50] Keaton frequently incorporated into his films vaudeville performance conventions and aspects of his vaudevillian persona, breaking the reality of the scene by re-

Figure 2.4. "Buster de Milo." A publicity shot of Keaton.

minding the audience of his existence as a performer within a larger body of work. Whenever Buster the character performed an acrobatic stunt, spectacular fall, or eccentric dance, the audience recognized the vaudeville skills of Keaton the performer. Initially, Keaton may have self-consciously displayed his vaudeville skills out of habit, but these extrafictional moments also satisfied the audience's desire for virtuoso performances.

Yet Keaton straddled the line between the extrafictional—as indicated by his acrobatics, stunts, and porkpie hat—and the fictional by normalizing the appearance of his character while still incorporating his vaudeville skills into his performance. In their vaudeville act, the Keatons wore character make-up that almost completely obscured their facial features: the false beards, hats, and bald caps of the standard, stereotyped vaudeville costume for an Irishman. In his films, however, Keaton emphasized his natural facial features; his screen image required only his porkpie hat, although his tie, collar, and flapshoes remained optional accessories. With this subtle change, Keaton moved away from the stereotypes of the vaudeville stage toward a more realistic and human characterization. In his films Keaton appears to be a normal human being, certainly when compared to the more clown-like image of the cross-eyed comic Ben Turpin or the more obviously dysfunctional characterization of Harry Langdon. In contrast to his appearance, Keaton's extrafictional stunts and gags seem all the more remarkable.

Seidman argues that extrafictional moments "point to an attitude of *self-reference* as part of the films."[51] The most common moments of self-reference in Keaton's films involve his alleged "stone face," his ability to take a fall, and, perhaps most notably, his porkpie hat. Over the course of his films with Arbuckle, Keaton's porkpie hat became a standard signifier for Keaton the performer, in the same way that Harold Lloyd was identified by his horn-rimmed glasses.[52] Several publicity photographs from Keaton's silent-film period rely upon his porkpie hat for their humor. In a frequently reproduced photograph, Keaton poses as a Greek sculpture—his arms are lopped off, his body is wrapped in a sheet, his face is angled serenely upward, yet his porkpie hat remains firmly atop his head (fig. 2.4). In another photograph, Keaton is seen reading a newspaper, the paper held up so that it covers all of his face except for his eyes and his porkpie hat. The back of the newspaper, which faces the camera, contains an advertisement that proclaims, "Hats Tell Tales."

In several of his films, Keaton builds gags around his porkpie hat. At the beginning of *Our Hospitality* (1923), Buster wears a top hat. During his trip south in an old-fashioned train coach, he attempts to put on the top hat, only to find that he does not have enough head room in the coach to manage the task. He slumps down in his seat in order to put on the top hat, but when the train hits a bump, Buster bounces in his seat and the hat is forced down over his eyes. After removing the top hat, he replaces it with his familiar (and conveniently *flat*) porkpie hat. The fact that the film is set in the

Figure 2.5. Keaton and his writing staff (left to right: Keaton,
Clyde Bruckman, Joseph Mitchell, Jean Havez, and Eddie Cline).

1830s—an inappropriate time period for a porkpie hat—further emphasizes
the self-reference in the gag. In *Steamboat Bill, Jr.*, Buster's father, annoyed
by the foppish beret that Buster wears upon returning home from school,
takes him to a clothing store to buy him a new hat. The salesperson repeatedly places hats on Buster's head only to have his father quickly remove
them. As the tempo of the scene increases, the three men become a veritable
hat assembly line. When his father looks away for a brief moment, the salesman offers Buster a porkpie hat. For one brief moment of stillness, Buster
looks at himself in the mirror wearing the hat. He appears to recognize the
porkpie hat, but with a glance towards his father, he immediately returns it
to the salesman. As in the hat scene from *Our Hospitality*, Buster faces the
camera full front, tacitly acknowledging his screen persona to the audience.[53]

In several other photographs from this period, the porkpie hat becomes
instrumental in creating multiple images. In a photograph of Keaton with his

Figure 2.6. "Hear no evil, see no evil, speak no evil."

writing staff, all four of Keaton's writers wear matching porkpie hats and stone-faced expressions (fig. 2.5). Keaton was frequently photographed with his female co-stars in matching hats and even at times in complete matching outfits.[54] Another shot captures three identical Busters, each with a porkpie hat, posing with their hands over their ears, eyes, and mouths, respectively (fig. 2.6). In a series of photographs with one of his girlfriends, Keaton and Viola Dana perform acrobatic stunts together with both in full Buster regalia, from identical porkpie hats down to matching flapshoes (fig. 2.7).

Keaton quickly found other ways of adapting multiple images to his films. In the short film *The Playhouse* (1921), Keaton used trick photography to produce an astounding number and variety of multiple Busters.[55] The film divides neatly into two sections, each one reel long. In the first reel, Keaton uses trick photography to produce an entire vaudeville cast and audience populated by multiple Busters—he plays, quite literally, every

Figure 2.7. Keaton with Viola Dana.

role. Buster is the conductor of a six-piece orchestra in which he plays all of the instruments (bass, cello, violin, clarinet, trombone, and drums); each half of the orchestra is shown in a separate three-shot. Keaton devised a system of shutters for the camera lens, so that he could expose the film in sections, one-third of the frame at a time, and he used this technology, in

Figure 2.8. *The Playhouse*. Three of the eight identical minstrels.

different fractions, throughout the film.[56] The first act in the show is a minstrel act (fig. 2.8). In one shot, Keaton expands the effect to include nine nearly identical minstrels all played by Buster. Meanwhile, in three balconies, double Busters interact with each other: an elderly couple, a young socialite couple, and a mother and son. Keaton timed each couple's interactions so closely that they genuinely appear to be conversing with each other. Moreover, he edited interactions between the balconies to achieve an elaborate extension of the successive revelation of multiple Keatons. The most immaculately timed sequence is a two-man eccentric dance by identical Busters. The timing is so precise that it appears as if the two men are duplicate images. Yet Keaton produced the effect on stage, rather than in a film lab. By using a two-section shuttered lens, he filmed each dancing Buster separately and synchronized his steps to live music.[57]

In the second half of *The Playhouse*, the action in the first reel is revealed to have been Buster's dream: he is actually a vaudeville stagehand who dreamed of playing every role. Although the second half of the film does not extend any narrative impulse from the first half, Keaton achieves unity within the film by continuing his obsessive exploration of multiples. In contrast to the multiples in the first half of the film, which were created with

Figure 2.9. *Cops.*

trick photography, the multiples in the second half of the film are real.
Buster falls in love with a woman who has an identical twin and spends
most of the remainder of the film trying to distinguish between the two
women. Keaton creates additional multiples with mirrors—when the twins
stand in front of their dressing mirrors, Buster sees identical quintuplets.
After he retreats to a back room to swear off drinking, he glances into a
three-part mirror only to see three Busters staring back at him. In the end,
the only way he knows which woman to marry is by painting an "x" on her
back.

Although Keaton had already worked with multiple images of others in
Arbuckle's *Moonshine* (1918),[58] *Cops* (1922) represents Keaton's first attempt to weave increasing multiple images into the climactic sequence of a
film. In the final chase sequence of *Cops*, which runs six minutes out of
eighteen minutes total running time, hundreds of policeman chase Buster
through a maze of city streets. The shots of Buster dashing toward the cam-

Figure 2.10. *The Three Ages.* Stone Age Buster and family.

era capture the action in a long shot from an elevated camera position in order to reveal the swelling ranks of policemen behind him, thus showing as fully as possible the multitude of identical cops. Keaton employs many times the number of policemen in any Keystone film, taking the cop chase to unprecedented dimensions and heightening the absurdity of these images (fig. 2.9). As opposed to Mack Sennett's Keystone Cops, whose identities were somewhat distinguishable because of the variety of their shapes and sizes, Buster's cops move as one gigantic machine, chasing him *en masse.*

Keaton's cops operate as a machine in a variety of ways and formations. Buster continually evades them by setting them against each other and causing their machinery to self-destruct. The cops appear to cancel each other out, as in the shots where Buster stands between two of them so that they hit each other when he ducks. In one of the most startling visual images in the film, Buster climbs a ladder that is leaning against a fence. When a cop starts to follow him, the ladder tips so that Buster and the cop are balanced precariously on the edge of the fence, rocking back and forth on each end of the ladder as if they were on a see-saw. As several cops grasp each end of the ladder, Buster scampers to the center, poised at the vertex as the cops rock the ladder back and forth. By taking advantage of the physics of the cops' own movements, Buster turns their efforts against them.

In the first feature film he directed, *The Three Ages*, Keaton also used multiples for the film's final topper. As I have noted above, *The Three Ages* is comprised of three two-reelers, following Buster's romantic pursuits in the Stone Age, the Roman Age, and the Modern Age. The final sequence in the film compares Buster's final situation in each era. In the Stone Age, Buster comes out of his cave followed by his wife and a horde of children, the smallest one straggling behind, in matching caveman costumes (fig. 2.10), a reprise of The Three Keatons' standard topper. In the Roman Age, Buster exits his house followed by his wife and four children in matching togas, the smallest one once again lagging behind. The final image from the Modern Age shows Buster and his wife leaving their house followed only by a small dog. Keaton thus reverses his usual progression of multiples, going from large to smaller numbers of children and culminating in the tiny, solitary dog.

Yet only when he expands the quantity of multiples to unprecedented numbers traveling across vast geographic spaces does Keaton truly seize upon film's potential to open up this gag and simultaneously extend the bounds of improbability. In *Go West* (1925), he had tremendous difficulty working with the hundreds of bulls that he leads through the Los Angeles city streets to the stockyard, while perched atop his beloved cow, Brown Eyes. Although Keaton had no trouble training Brown Eyes to follow him around, he encountered great difficulties with the final chase scene: "We didn't dare speed them up . . . or we would have had a real stampede."[59] Yet despite Keaton's disappointment with the speed of the chase, the image of Buster with hundreds of bulls in such an alien environment retains a certain power purely through the bovine numbers (fig. 2.11). Furthermore, Keaton doubles the effect by incorporating a corresponding number of policemen into the chase, emphasizing the animalistic nature of the police by having them all grasp coattails in a long line, as the bulls chase the "bulls."[60] Keaton raises a cow to the level of a human by casting Brown Eyes as his love interest, yet simultaneously lowers the police to the level of animals, a strategy that allows the audience to laugh more freely at their depersonalized antics. The greater the number of policemen, the more they appear to take on the quality of a machine, and the greater emotional distance we feel from

Figure 2.11. *Go West.*

the mechanistic operation of the police allows Keaton to unleash the violent energy of farce upon them in the climactic chase.

Keaton had made more successful use of the image of double sets of multiples in his preceding film, *Seven Chances* (1925). He devotes the entire second half of the film—twenty-two of fifty-six minutes total running time—to the permutations and pratfalls of hundreds of brides and boulders pursuing Buster. In order to assure his inheritance of seven million dollars, Buster must marry by 7 p.m. His friend places an advertisement in the paper telling of his predicament and requesting prospective brides to come to the church at 7 p.m. if one would like to marry a millionaire. Seven hundred brides (in keeping with the reiteration of sevens?) appear at the church (fig. 2.12). When Buster flees, the brides chase him through the city streets and into the hills. Keaton makes extensive use of long shots to fully create and display the spectacle of several hundred nearly identical brides dressed in matching bridal gowns.

Figure 2.12. *Seven Chances*. Buster and his hopeful brides-to-be.

Yet despite the visual pleasure of this sequence, Keaton was not satisfied with the film when he exhibited it for preview audiences. At the time of the preview, he had no conclusion for the film; he simply faded out on the brides chasing Buster. Just before the fade-out, Keaton and his staff noticed that something got a huge laugh, but they did not immediately realize what had caused it and projected the film again to examine the sequence more carefully. "There it was," said Keaton to his biographer, Rudi Blesh. "I had accidentally dislodged a rock. It started to roll after me. On its way, it knocked a couple more loose and there were three little rocks chasing me."[61] From the audience's response to this accidental gag, Keaton created the boulder sequence that serves as the film's topper. The brides have chased Buster to the top of a hill and decide to go around to the other side to intercept him ("I know a short cut—we'll head him off," says the intertitle), in a parody of Western films. In running down the hill, Buster accidentally dislodges a few small stones, causing an avalanche of boulders to cascade down the hill with and over him. The boulders get progressively bigger in size, with the largest ones exceeding eight feet in diameter. As he darts and ducks the mighty boulders falling from the top of the hill, the brides appear at the bottom of the hill, only to be confronted by the even greater force of the boulders. Keaton pits the two against each other—brides and boulders—with Buster trapped between two irresistible forces of nature.

In his films, Keaton consistently strove for larger numbers of multiple images in more vast spaces, taking full advantage of the cinema's potential to capture action in realistic detail. He expanded his family's simple vaudeville gag—Three Keatons, Four Keatons, Five Keatons—to unprecedented magnitude in space and number—two sons, multiple Busters, dozens of children, dozens of cops, hundreds of bulls, seven hundred brides and boulders[62]—always capturing the action in long shot in order to display its actual occurrence. He varied the figures and objects that are multiplied (son, cop, Buster, bull, bride, boulder) as well as the ways in which he created and deployed the multiples (camera tricks, increasing and decreasing numbers, double sets of multiples). Moreover, Keaton put his multiples in action, creating vast chase scenes virtually unparalleled in film history. As the multiples expand and interweave in the chase scenes, Keaton's cinematic world appears to consist of carbon-copied people, animals, and objects, all of which are reduced to cogs in an absurd machine.

Tom Gunning notes that the absurd machines of silent film comedy reflect America's obsession at this time with what he calls the "operational aesthetic": "Silent American comedy developed a form which drew its inspiration from gags rather than plotting. . . . But their explosive counterlogic also found embodiment in devices of balance and trajectory, antimachines which harness the laws of physics to overturn the rules of behavior. Simultaneously revolt and engineering, these devices mine the fascination that spectators of the industrial age had with the way things work, the operational aesthetic."[63] Gunning correctly notes that Keaton was one of the acknowledged masters of this type of gag, observing that the illogic of Rube Goldberg–type machines is central to the artistry and interest of Keaton's films. "A Keaton film is . . . a maze of such devices, gags that often serve little narrative purpose, but which provide the essential fascination of the films."[64] If Gunning is right in noting that these gags serve little narrative purpose—and I believe his observation is correct—then what function do they serve in Keaton's films? In particular, how are we to understand the function of these gags in those films in which Rube Goldberg–type devices play an integral part in the film's climactic sequence?

The important elements of this type of gag are the illogical connections between elements of a makeshift machine and a blatant display of the way the machine works. One of the most visually explicit examples of this type of machine occurs in the first reel of *The Scarecrow* (1920). Buster and his friend (actor Joe Roberts) live in a house that is filled with makeshift time-saving gadgets. The house is small, only one room, so the devices serve not only to expedite the two men's morning routine, but also to convert the room from bedroom to kitchen to living room. The breakfast table is rigged to allow all of the utensils and condiments to be shared by the two men without moving. The two men share the sugar by means of a pulley system that shuttles the sugar back and forth across the breakfast table. Salt, pepper, and other spices are mounted from strings suspended from the ceiling; Buster and Joe swing them effortlessly back and forth above the table. Buster receives a bottle of milk from the refrigerator by means of a lever and swings it back across the room effortlessly on yet another string tied to the ceiling. When they finish breakfast, the two men hoist the entire table top onto the wall with another set of ropes and pulleys and wash their plates clean with a hose. Nothing is wasted: as the bath flips over to become a sofa, the bath water is jettisoned outside for the farm animals.[65]

Other silent film comedians also worked with this sort of gag: Snub Pollard and Harold Lloyd come to mind immediately. Yet Keaton's work with Rube Goldberg contraptions differs in two vital respects. First, he almost always goes out of his way to display the entire mechanism. For Keaton, the way in which such machines functioned was essential to their appeal, and he almost always captured the entire machine in a single long shot so that the viewer could see that it worked and, as with his physical stunt work, that the machine was real. In contrast, Lloyd and Pollard frequently assembled their machines in the editing room. In *It's a Gift* (1923), for example, Pollard used ropes to connect various devices for waking up in the morning, but the actual connections between the parts that make up the devices are never shown in one shot. Similarly, in *The Chef* (1919), Lloyd cuts as the action shifts between rooms, so that he never reveals the action of more than half of a machine in one shot. Second, while Lloyd, Pollard, and Arbuckle frequently employed Rube Goldberg devices as time-saving gadgets developed by an eccentric inventor, in Keaton's films the whole world frequently seems to operate as a gigantic Rube Goldberg device. Keaton thus shifts the illogic of these devices from the area of invention to that of existence.

When his Rube Goldberg devices come to encompass the entire world of his films, Keaton comes closest to capturing the spirit and vision of farce, albeit in a more realistic form. This vision, "a world all its own," as Bentley observes, borders on the delusional: "There is something frightening about such worlds because there is something maniacal about them. Danger is

omnipresent. One touch, we feel, and we shall be sent spinning in space."[66]
At the end of his films, Buster frequently stabilizes this world by mastering
its most disruptive elements: the objects that gave him so much trouble
earlier in each film. Yet the danger remains present, for Buster's resolutions
accept the maniacal illogic of farce. Though the objects rarely defeat him,
his solutions fail to defuse their disruptive power. Instead, Buster survives
by blending into the world of objects.

There is the sense that the world of Keaton's films is governed by what
Walter Kerr describes as the "Keaton curve,"[67] a circular path that brings
Buster right back to where he started. In the climactic sequence in the Present Age in *The Three Ages*, for example, Buster flees over the rooftops to
escape from a police station. When he reaches a gap between two buildings,
he swings out a wooden platform that extends slightly over the edge of the
roof and jumps from it as if it were a diving board. He barely misses the edge
of the next building, sliding down through three awnings until he latches
onto a drainpipe. Unfortunately, the drainpipe disconnects from the wall of
the building due to Buster's weight and flips one hundred and eighty degrees, catapulting Buster down through a window below that happens to
belong to a fire station. Propelled along the floor of the fire station, he slides
into a hole in the floor and down the fire station pole, landing on the back
bumper of a fire truck. As an alarm has apparently just sounded, Buster is
carried along with the truck to a fire that happens to be in progress at . . . the
police station.

Although Buster's circular path in this scene from *The Three Ages* does
not, strictly speaking, advance the narrative, it expresses a large thematic
point on a purely visual level: the absurdity of a world controlled by coincidence. As Bentley observes, "In farce chance ceases to seem chance, and
mischief has method in its madness. . . . [M]ischief, fun, misrule seem an
equivalent of fate, a force not ourselves making, neither for righteousness
nor for catastrophe, but for aggression without risk."[68] By expanding the
level of coincidence to absurd dimensions, Keaton makes fate, in the form
of the irrational, visually and physically concrete.[69]

Keaton frequently makes irrational visual images the touchstones of his
films' climactic sequences. In the cyclone sequence at the end of *Steamboat
Bill, Jr.*, for example, he performs a series of gags involving his improbable
passage through a seemingly endless succession of windows and doors. It
appears as if the cyclone is pushing Buster through a world that has become
one gigantic Rube Goldberg device, blowing him from a hospital to a stable
to a theater until finally he is almost magically transported to the river

where needs to be. In this sequence, Buster's repeated passage through windows and doors lends structure to his seemingly endless series of escapes, giving concrete form to the illogic of his *Weltanschauung*.

The inner film of *Sherlock Jr.* begins with Keaton's most cinematic Rube Goldberg device: the "graphic-match montage" in which Buster, having jumped onto the screen at the theater where he is a projectionist, is buffeted across time and space from one locale to another along with the film he has entered.[70] The montage vastly exceeds the requirements of the narrative; all that is required to advance the plot is for Buster to jump into the inner film.[71] The two-minute sequence is magical, a virtuosic piece of filmmaking that had cameramen of the day watching the film numerous times to try to figure out how Keaton and his staff had achieved the effect.[72] Yet it is the quintessential Keaton sequence in many ways: it depends on Keaton's acrobatics for continuity; it has a circular shape, in that Buster ends up right where he started; and it features the basic conflict between Buster and an unaccommodating world, one that propels him from one place to another as if he were part of some unseen and unintelligible plan.

At the end of the inner film, Buster is propelled through a series of stunts that once again suggest a world operating like a Rube Goldberg invention. As Buster rides on the handlebars of his assistant Gillette's motorcycle, Gillette is thrown from the motorcycle when it hits a bump. Buster remains blissfully ignorant of this development, never losing his balance as the motorcycle careens through a world fraught with hazards. Yet the world appears to take care of Buster; through a series of coincidences, objects appear precisely when needed to save him, as if Buster had set into motion a machine-like world that functions for his benefit.[73] As the motorcycle heads toward a twelve-foot gap in a bridge that is under construction, two trucks, each the same height as the bridge, drive through the gap at precisely the moment Buster arrives on his motorcycle and he drives right over their rooftops. As he approaches the end of the bridge with no landing space in sight, it collapses forward and Buster rides it safely to the ground, as if it were an off-ramp on a highway.

Next, a large log that blocks the road is detonated by a road construction crew just in time for Buster to drive through the gap unharmed. A large tractor approaches, seen from the side, which appears headed for a collision with him. As the tractor turns left so that it is rushing directly toward Buster and the camera, it is revealed to be hollow in the center, permitting Buster to pass underneath it. After a near miss with a train, Buster's motorcycle crashes into the shack in which the Sheik's accomplice, the butler, is holding the heroine, propelling Buster through a window and feet-first into the chest of the servant. As the rest of the Sheik's criminal accomplices pull up in a car and storm into the shack through the door, Buster and the heroine escape through a window on the other side and flee in the criminals' car. As the criminals pursue them, Buster reaches into his pocket, extracts an exploding billiard ball from an earlier scene, and uses it as a grenade to derail the criminals. Just as Buster prevails, his car approaches a lake. He slams on the brakes and the chassis stops, but the body of the car slides onto the lake with Buster and the heroine aboard. Buster remains calm, lifts the convertible top upright, and, using it as a sail, steers a course as he embraces the heroine. It is as if the world is a huge, irrational machine, and only Buster is capable of understanding it and using its illogic to his own ends.

Keaton links these stunts in a single trajectory across varied spaces: from the billiards room of a mansion, down roads, through buildings, and across a lake. This trajectory has often been identified as "narrative"—the chase being a primitive narrative-ordering device—yet the mere linking of the illusions through the continuity provided by Buster does not place these sequences firmly within the confines of the narrative.[74] It is the excess in these sequences, created primarily by Keaton's use of long shots to capture the actuality of the stunts, that lifts them from the confines of the narrative and draws attention to Keaton's physical work, illusions, and camera techniques.[75]

The chase sequence in *The Navigator*, in which Buster and his girlfriend discover each other on board the ship, is one of the most precise, physically realized Rube Goldberg devices that Keaton created. As Buster and his girlfriend search the ship for each other, we see them as they continually just miss each other. Long shots down the length of the ship's decks capture Buster running the length of the ship; then just as he turns the corner, his girlfriend appears at the other end of the deck. The shot is repeated several times as they run faster and faster in an attempt to catch each other, like mice on a treadmill.[76] In the most visually spectacular shot in the sequence, we see the entire stern of the ship in one long shot, enabling us to see the patterns created by the two characters as they chase after each other across three levels and from aft to port. A close analysis of the shot reveals that the two characters follow the same path; their movements are synchronized so that they each cross the decks in opposite directions and ascend or descend the staircases at the same time.

Moreover, the sequence is framed by another of Keaton's self-referential hat gags. Just before the chase, Buster steps outside his stateroom and a gust

Figure 2.13. *The Navigator.*

of wind blows his hat overboard. He quickly steps back in to get another
one, holding it carefully in place with the handle of his walking cane. When
he returns to his stateroom a moment later, another gust of wind blows the
second hat overboard and this time Buster retrieves a top hat from his stateroom. At the end of the chase sequence, Buster and his girlfriend sit on
different decks, having given up the chase: his girlfriend sits in the galley,

while unbeknownst to her Buster is directly overhead, leaning against a large tube that leads down to the galley. A gust of wind blows Buster's hat down the tube; as he reaches for it, he tumbles down the tube and lands beside his girlfriend, crushing his top hat in the process (fig. 2.13). When we next see Buster, he is wearing a *porkpie* hat. Keaton extends the hat gag temporally, using it as a warm-up gag at the beginning of the chase sequence and reincorporating it as part of the topper at the end of the sequence. As Buster and his girlfriend chase each other round and round the ship, it is the hat that eventually unites them.

If the hat brings an end to the circular chase, the ship exists to keep the two of them apart, at least as long as they are actively seeking each other. As Gilberto Perez astutely observes, "The arrangements of the inanimate world exert everywhere in Keaton a governing influence on the dramatic development. All his films may be said to enact a dramaturgy of mechanics."[77] Perez's interpretation successfully accounts for the differing narrative and visual shapes of Keaton's films. The linearity of *The General* arises from the single line of railroad tracks, "the course of the action thus exactly coinciding with that railway line, as if foreordained by it."[78] The stasis and circularity of *The Navigator*, on the other hand, stem from the self-enclosed floating island of the ship, with its labyrinth of hallways and staircases, while the fluidity of the world of cinema is reflected in the amorphous shape of the inner film in *Sherlock Jr.*

By building gags from the environments in which he shot his films— ships, trains, buildings, cars, theaters—Buster Keaton remained true to the working methods he developed in vaudeville. His pride in his own physical performance may have led him to use long shots and to capture his stunts and gags without cuts, but it also created something new: a vast vision of a world controlled by unseen, interconnected forces that Buster must learn to accept in order to harness them to his advantage. Keaton's use of long shots accentuates the spectacular, irrational functioning of his mechanistic world, while his insistence on maintaining the "integrity of his performance" keeps his spectacle grounded in reality. For despite the scholars' claims for Keaton's classicism, the climactic sequences of his films overreach classicism, resulting in spectacular displays that can only be called "excess."[79] It is precisely these moments of excess that frequently become the centerpiece of documentaries on Keaton, for they create what comedian Richard Lewis refers to as the "visual intoxication" of Keaton's films.[80]

Keaton Re-Viewed:
Beyond Keaton's
Classicism

BUSTER KEATON began making films with Roscoe Arbuckle in 1917, as the American film industry was in the midst of a massive stylistic and economic transformation—from a "cinema of attractions"[1] to classical Hollywood cinema; from a loose association of independent producers into what was becoming the Hollywood industry. Bordwell, Staiger, and Thompson's seminal work, *The Classical Hollywood Cinema*, marks 1917 as the beginning of the classical Hollywood era, when the classical Hollywood style and industry came of age. As Thompson suggests, "The formulation of the classical mode began quite early, in the period around 1909–11, and . . . by 1917, the system was complete in its basic narrative and stylistic premises. During the early and mid-teens, older devices lingered, but classical norms began to coalesce."[2] Keaton's introduction to filmmaking comes at this crucial juncture in the history of American filmmaking, just as his loss of independence as a filmmaker when he signed with MGM in 1928 coincides with the next major phase in the development of classical Hollywood cinema—the introduction of sound films. Although Keaton's sound films at MGM were financially successful, he was never again given the opportunity to direct his own work. His reputation as a film director is therefore based on the silent films he made during the 1920s, the so-called "classic era" of slapstick film comedy.

Neale and Krutnik observe, however, that the classic era of slapstick comedy is not nearly as stylistically monolithic as scholars have traditionally portrayed it. Instead they argue that "these films are a specific and unstable combination of slapstick and narrative elements rather than the final flowering of an authentic slapstick tradition, which is how they have generally tended to be seen."[3] Perhaps because the first sound comedies in the late 1920s and early 1930s exhibit a more disruptive relationship between gag and narrative, the silent comedies of the 1920s appear in contrast to be more firmly classical than they actually are. It may be more accurate, therefore, to view the silent comedies of the 1920s as part of an ongoing negotiation between gags and narrative, one that shifts its favor toward gags with the onslaught of stand-up comedians from vaudeville into film at the beginning of the sound era.

Although Keaton developed stronger narratives after he made the transition to feature-length films, his vaudeville training—his knowledge and love of gags, gag structure, acrobatics, and improvisation—remained a dominant part of his film practice, as I have demonstrated in Chapter 2. In this chapter I will investigate the range of relationships between gags and narrative with which Keaton experimented in his feature films. I will examine four films that encompass the scope of Keaton's experimentation with the gag-narrative dynamic: *The General* (1927), *Seven Chances* (1925), *Steamboat Bill, Jr.* (1928), and *Sherlock Jr.* (1924).[4] To understand the shifting relationship between gags and narrative in Keaton's films, we must first locate his work within the historical evolution of Hollywood cinema as an industry and a form.

The films produced from the advent of cinema in 1894 through approximately 1908 have been labeled "primitive" by many film historians. In recent years, scholars have challenged the suitability of this term.[5] Tom Gunning cogently argues that film historians view these films as primitive only in retrospect.[6] Once film historians have assumed that the tight linear causality of later cinema is the inevitable form of filmmaking, they then find early cinema lacking in this regard. Gunning emphasizes the roots of early cinema in vaudeville and popular entertainment and advances the theory that early cinema, rather than being a nascent form of narrative-based film, comes from an entirely different tradition, one that valued variety over unity. During this transition, "The US cinema moved from a narrative model derived largely from vaudeville into a filmmaking formula drawing upon aspects of the novel, the popular legitimate theater, and the visual arts, and combined with specifically cinematic devices."[7]

Because of early cinema's dependence on the vaudeville theater as an exhibition site, vaudeville exerted a strong influence on the forms of early cinema: "Exhibition circumstances, short length, and small-scale production facilities dictated the creation of films which modeled themselves largely on types of stage acts: the variety act, the fictional narrative, the scenic (views of interesting locales), the topical (presentations of current events), and the trick film."[8] From 1903 to 1908, films began to exhibit one of the fundamental features of narrative—linear causality—with the chase film emerging as one of the first genres to temporally extend a single action across an entire short film. As Thompson observes, "Rather than confining itself to a simple, brief slapstick fight, the film might prolong its action by having one combatant flee, with the other chasing and passersby joining in."[9] Two vaudeville forms—the vaudeville skit and the playlet—exerted a powerful influence on the forms of early cinema. A vaudeville skit "usually involved a couple of comics performing verbal and sight gags in a relatively static situation."[10] Vaudeville playlets told a story in extremely compressed form—a "highly episodic series of highlights from existing works."[11] Neither skits nor playlets encouraged the tight and prolonged line of cause-and-effect seen in classical Hollywood cinema, however; skits were too brief, while playlets were too episodic and depended too much on coincidence to prolong the action.[12]

As the film industry expanded, several factors encouraged producers to switch from vaudeville structure to a more classical structure inspired by fiction and drama. First, producers increased the length of their films in order to meet audience demand for more of their product. As Thompson observes, the film industry rapidly discovered that narrative films were the most cost-effective and reliable form to expand to greater length: "Because of film's success, more footage was needed, and it proved more predictable to manufacture staged films than documentaries. In addition, all other things being equal, a longer narrative film was proportionately cheaper than a short one, since the same sets and personnel could be used to create a greater amount of footage."[13] Second, classical narrative films were much easier to mass produce than documentaries because of the classical narrative's reliance on formulaic plot constructions.

Full-length dramatic films became the norm after 1915, while comedy was mostly confined to shorter films of one- and two-reel length: "Relatively few feature-length comedies were produced before 1920, and even in 1925, the year of *The Gold Rush*, *The Freshman*, and *Seven Chances*, almost one thousand reels of short comedies were released."[14] As early as 1914, Mack Sennett produced the feature-length comedy *Tillie's Punctured Romance*, starring Mabel Normand and Charlie Chaplin, but this one-time experiment was not repeated for several years. The few feature-length comedies produced in the late 1910s, such as those of Douglas Fairbanks, tended to be more realistic and character-based comedies, as compared to the gag-based shorts popularized by Chaplin, Lloyd, and Arbuckle in the mid- to late 1910s. Richard Koszarski notes that high and low comedy were polarized in the film industry during this time: "Audiences now began to see two distinct types of comedy. The more 'high-class' comedy descended from Broadway adaptations and portrayed recognizable characters in believable situations. It was generally to be seen only in features. Short films were the province of 'low comedy,' a continuation of the slapstick tradition of nickelodeon days."[15]

With the popular success of *The Kid* (1921), Chaplin proved that a slapstick comedian could produce a commercially viable full-length comedy. Although Chaplin did not release another feature-length comedy until 1925, Lloyd began releasing one or two features per year in 1921 and Keaton proceeded at the same pace beginning in 1923 with *The Three Ages*.[16] In order to overcome the industry-wide reluctance to produce feature-length films by slapstick comedians, the comedians (and their producers) incorporated stronger narrative elements into their feature films. Yet even as he introduced more developed narratives into his feature films, Keaton retained much of the spirit of his vaudeville routines in his gag sequences, which were sometimes quite extensive. For this reason, his films exhibit a wide range of relationships between gag and narrative, as he experimented with different ways of balancing the demands of vaudeville and Hollywood.

Keaton in Context: Keaton, Chaplin, and Lloyd

We have seen in Chapter 2 how Keaton enlarged the scope of his vaudeville gags, particularly in his feature films. Yet Keaton was only one of the many vaudeville comedians who tried their hands at blending slapstick comedy with traditional narrative in the 1920s. By the time Keaton began making features, classical Hollywood cinema had become entrenched as an industry and a style, both in dramatic features and in the genteel comedies of actors such as Sidney Drew. It was left for comedians such as Keaton, Chaplin, and Lloyd to find the means to blend slapstick into traditional narratives, though each of them did so in a somewhat different way.[17]

Because Lloyd's films were heavily influenced by the classical style of director and producer Hal Roach, his films consistently subordinate gags to narrative. As Frank Krutnik cogently argues, in Lloyd's films "gags tend to *arise from* the narrative rather than competing with it. Both the status of

Lloyd-as-comedian and the gags themselves are 'naturalized' within a narrative process."[18] His gags therefore lose much of their power to disrupt. Conversely, Chaplin—primarily because of the great freedom he enjoyed as an
independent director—was less concerned with the unity and driving force
of the narratives in his feature-length films than he was with the dynamism
of individual scenes and his own performance. Chaplin constructed his
films by a method of accretion rather than depending upon the strict causality of classical narrative structure.[19] Keaton was more concerned with narrative structure than Chaplin, yet he was less classical than Lloyd in his subordination of gags to narrative. As he displayed in *The General* (1927), Keaton
was capable of constructing classical narratives, yet he enjoyed enough freedom under producer Joe Schenck to diverge into extended gag and stunt
sequences. He was therefore able to combine the most fantastic gags and
stunts with traditional narratives.

For the most part, Keaton's vaudeville—the gags, acrobatics, and optical
illusions Keaton learned in vaudeville with The Three Keatons—provided
the inspiration for his disruptive flights of fantasy, while his realism came
from film, or more accurately from the attributes of film to which Keaton
was attracted: long shots, long takes, and the composition of shots within
the mise-en-scène. By its nature, vaudeville (particularly The Three Keatons' style of knockabout comedy) was disruptive and chaotic. In contrast,
while film is not inherently orderly, Keaton created his short and feature
films in Hollywood, where the commercial film industry was rapidly turning its filmmaking process into inarguably the most systematic or standard-
ized style of storytelling in movie history—classical Hollywood cinema. As
a result, Keaton's films evince a fundamental conflict between vaudeville
and Hollywood, gags and narrative, fantasy and realism. In using the word
"conflict," I do not mean to depict this relationship in Keaton's films as
counterproductive. On the contrary, I believe that Keaton's unique combination of theatrical slapstick and visual realism goes to the heart of his
achievement as a film artist.

Like Keaton, Chaplin groomed his skills on the stage—specifically, in the
British music-hall—before he started making films. Chaplin, however, remained much more closely wed to his popular entertainment roots than
Keaton. In Chaplin's films we see music-hall gags transferred to the screen
fairly intact; his routines retain much of their original scale and style. He
rarely uses film to enlarge the physical scale of his gags. On the contrary, he
brings in the camera in order to focus more closely on smaller-scale gags.
While Keaton's camera captures his body in relationship to a very real and

potent world, Chaplin's camera tends to isolate him from the world so that we can revel in the charm and physical grace of his performance. We need only think of each comedian's most famous gag to understand this basic distinction: the "Oceana Roll" from Chaplin's *The Gold Rush* (1925) and the falling-wall sequence from Keaton's *Steamboat Bill, Jr.* (1928). In the former, Chaplin executes a classic transformation gag, spearing two dinner rolls with the ends of two forks and moving the forks and rolls as if they were a pair of dancing legs. The scene is captured in a medium shot (almost a close-up) of Charlie at a dinner table. The closeness of the camera to him allows Chaplin to emphasize the delicate motions of the dancing rolls. This scene is emblematic of Chaplin's approach to transferring his vaudeville to film: he uses film to bring the audience closer to the action. He also achieves greater intimacy through his use of medium and close-up shots, a preference that supports his somewhat sentimental narratives as well as his fine, detailed gag work.

Conversely, Keaton's trademark gag, the falling wall, evinces a different aesthetic. Rather than moving the camera closer for greater detail and intimacy, Keaton pulls it back in order to capture Buster's relationship to his environment. While Chaplin uses medium and close-up shots to create audience empathy for the plight of his character, Keaton prefers to use the long shot to create a larger image, one that visually exceeds the boundaries of his body. Particularly in his climactic sequences, Keaton's use of extreme long shots provides the audience with greater emotional distance from his character, a quality that is amplified by his understated acting style. Buñuel commends this aspect of Keaton's work when he designates him "the great specialist against all sentimental infection."[20] While Chaplin usually concludes his feature films with an emotional catharsis naturally deriving from the story (as in the close-up shot at the end of *City Lights*), Keaton frequently fails to provide the emotional release of the sentimental ending. Instead, he resolves his films in physical chases executed on the largest possible scale, depending on his acrobatic grace for closure rather than the audience's emotional identification with his character.

The larger physical scale of Keaton's gags and stunts contributes to their status as attractions. On the basis of sheer size alone, Keaton's gags tend to break free of the confines of his narratives. From the rotating house in *One Week* (1920) to the multiple Busters of *The Playhouse* (1921) to the cyclone in *Steamboat Bill, Jr.*, Keaton's films demonstrate his decided preference for sequences that are more concerned with showing than telling. In comparison, although Chaplin's gags may also be disruptive of the narrative, he is still bound to the aesthetic of the music-hall. Chaplin makes little attempt to transform his vaudeville aesthetic visually; he is more concerned with developing the emotional and social aspects of the story than with exploring film's ability to enlarge the visual realism or physical scale of his comedy. In *The Gold Rush*, for example, Chaplin juxtaposes the realistic opening sequence of the westward migration for gold with artificial-looking studio shots of the interior of the cabin as well as exterior shots in which he makes no attempt whatsoever to disguise his use of a rather flimsy-looking model of the cabin. When Chaplin does move to the larger scale, therefore, his films rarely inspire in us a sense of wonder as to how he created the world of his films. Instead Chaplin astonishes audiences with his individual work as a performer, creating in the words of Dan Kamin a "one-man show."[21] In Keaton's films, the world itself is an integral part of the show, and consequently the world embraces the illogic of his vaudeville comedy rather than serving merely as a background for it.

Although Keaton and Chaplin shared a background on the popular stage, their differences were already evident in their vaudeville and music-hall stage acts. We must resist the temptation to lump all comic performers from the variety stage into the single category of "comedian." The variety stage (I include both vaudeville and music-hall in the larger category of "variety") encompassed diverse types of performers within every category of performance. Not only was variety comprised of musicians, comedians, magicians, dancers, and specialty acts, but each category contained subcategories. Just as the larger category of dancing acts include everything from tap dancing to chorus lines, so did "comedians" include double-talk teams, stand-up comedians, and mimes.

Despite the range of work that The Three Keatons performed, Keaton was primarily a knockabout comedian—a comic acrobat. Because of the spatial requirements of his family's acrobatics, Keaton learned to work in a deep stage space early in his career. Whereas Keaton rarely performed without his family, Chaplin frequently worked as a solo act on stage and was always the center of theatrical attention. He was first and foremost a mime.[22] From his early days as the star of Fred Karno's comedy troupe "Karno's Komics," he grew accustomed to being the driving force of the comic action, while Keaton learned to collaborate, building comic action in reaction to a larger power (his father). In silent film comedy, Keaton displaced the driving force of his father into the world around him, while Chaplin remained the disruptive center of attention in a smaller world that revolved around him.

Like Keaton, Harold Lloyd sought to expand the physical scale of his comedy, particularly in his feature films. Yet Lloyd's approach differed from Keaton's in several key respects. First, as I pointed out in Chapter 2, Lloyd did not use long shots and long takes for stunts as frequently as Keaton did. Lloyd simply was not as skilled an acrobat as Keaton, and therefore he was forced to construct many of his most daring sequences in the editing room. When the three-story wall falls on Buster in *Steamboat Bill, Jr.*, there is no doubt that Keaton actually performed the stunt. When Lloyd clings to the hands of the tower clock in *Safety Last*, the action is shown predominantly in deceptive full shots. The director used progressively higher camera angles to suggest a height that is illusory—Lloyd later admitted that he was only two stories off the ground with a padded platform beneath him—and chose a building that was located at the top of a hill, so that the buildings below the hill contributed to the visual deception.[23] Whereas Lloyd's use of the full shot draws attention away from the larger world and toward his own character, Keaton's use of the long shot emphasizes the patterns his stunts create. His stunts become inseparable from his environment, drawing our focus to the mechanisms of the world he inhabits. By projecting his comic vision onto the world rather than keeping it contained within his character, as do Chaplin and Lloyd, Keaton suggests that the world itself may function according to the irrational and ephemeral dictates of vaudeville.

The Gag-Narrative Relationship in Keaton's Films

As propounded by Bordwell, classical Hollywood cinema follows a linear series of cause-and-effect actions that advance the central character toward a goal or goals. There are normally at least two lines of action: one, the pursuit of a love interest; the other, an activity such as business or sports. According to Bordwell, "The tight binding of the second line of action to the love interest is one of the most unusual qualities of the classical cinema, giving the film a variety of actions and a sense of comprehensive social 'realism' that earlier drama achieved through the use of parallel, loosely related subplots."[24] The central character unifies the two lines of action, which are further linked by a tight cause-and-effect chain of events.

Keaton's films generally follow the classical Hollywood model in fusing romantic action with the pursuit of another goal. In *Steamboat Bill, Jr.*, Buster must learn to navigate a steamboat and save several people in order to marry his girlfriend. In *The General*, he must rescue a train and become a soldier in order to regain his girlfriend's love and respect. The formula is reversed in *Seven Chances*, in which Buster must marry in order to receive an inheritance of seven million dollars. Yet despite his superficial adherence to these classical Hollywood norms, Keaton reveals a much more ambivalent relationship to classical Hollywood style in his handling of gags within the narrative.

Although Bordwell notes that comedies and musicals depart from strict narrative causality for artistic flourishes more frequently than other genres, he is, I believe, too quick to dismiss such departures as generically motivated.[25] In this way, Bordwell broadens his definition of classical Hollywood cinema to include virtually any stylistic variation that can be accounted for by the appropriation of conventions from other media. Yet it is clear that the gag and stunt sequences in Keaton's films often exert a disruptive force on the narrative's causal line. To return to the example of the deck chase in *The Navigator* (1924),[26] by choosing to show the multi-deck chase in a single long shot, Keaton emphasizes visual forms and the actors' physical performance over the narrative. Without a linear space such as the railroad tracks of *The General* to guide the chase forward, *The Navigator* focuses more on gags and circularity, reflecting the aimlessness of the ship that is, after all, the title character.

The night scenes in *The Navigator* exhibit a similar aimlessness, as Buster and his girlfriend attempt to survive their second night together on the ship. Daniel Moews criticizes these scenes as structural flaws, failing to appreciate their disruptive value: "There is no larger formula to organize the individual comic actions and to create a narrative thrust that drives inexorably onward to a fated and satisfying conclusion."[27] Moews clearly declares his preference for narrative over gag when he argues, "Where Keaton is at his best in the film, there is such an irresistible narrative, most typically created through simplifying and orderly symmetries, a classical order that effectively carries the hero and the audience into the future."[28] His interpretation of these symmetries is problematic because they may serve comedic as well as narrative purposes, for vaudeville and narrative both utilize the reincorporation of previous material. By assuming that most if not all reincorporations possess narrative significance, scholars with a classical bias ignore the disruptively comic force of Keaton's gags.

For example, in arguing for the subordination of gags to narrative in *Our Hospitality* (1923), Bordwell and Thompson analyze what they term the "fish-on-the-line" motif in the film: "Soon after [Buster] arrives in town, he is angling and hauls up a minuscule fish. Shortly afterward, a huge fish yanks him into the water. Later in the film, through a series of mishaps,

Willie becomes tied by a rope to one of the Canfield sons. Many gags arise from this umbilical cord linkage, especially one that results in Canfield's being pulled into the water as Willie was earlier."[29] Bordwell and Thompson argue that Keaton's repetition of the fish-on-the-line motif furthers the narrative, but it is difficult to see the contribution of the first sequence to this progression. We can just as easily attribute Keaton's use of the motif to vaudeville structure: it is simply a running gag. By seeking to absorb the first "fish-on-the-line" sequence into the path of the narrative, Bordwell and Thompson engage in precisely the same over-inclusiveness that they exhibit in *The Classical Hollywood Cinema*. Such analysis does not correspond with the actual experience of viewing the film. When we see the first fish-on-a-line sequence in *Our Hospitality*, we are unaware that it will be subsequently reincorporated; no future repetition of the gag can erase the disruptiveness of the first sequence.

Bordwell underestimates the power of such disruptive passages when he argues for the neutralizing force of the conventional narrative that envelops them: "Genuine breakdowns in classical narration are abrupt and fleeting, surrounded by conventional passages. In Hollywood cinema, there are no subversive films, only subversive moments. For social and economic reasons, no Hollywood film can provide a distinct and coherent alternative to the classical model."[30] Bordwell thus envisions the classical narration of Hollywood cinema as all-powerful; within its grip, all momentary stylistic departures are almost immediately squelched. Yet stylistic departures from Hollywood norms are most readily discerned in comparison to those norms. While non-Hollywood cinema may completely reject classical norms, Hollywood films are capable of simultaneously accepting and critiquing them. Momentary departures from classical narrative may indeed be most powerful within Hollywood films, since the norms of classical Hollywood cinema serve as a "straw man" for powerful, albeit "fleeting," reversals and disruptions.

One line of recent scholarship on silent film comedy does analyze the relationship between gags and narrative for its potential disruption of classical Hollywood norms. Donald Crafton argues that gags—which he implicitly defines in a broader sense to include all comedic moments and sequences—always oppose the progress of the narrative.[31] Crafton observes that many film scholars value narrative over gags, a bias he rejects: "I contend that it was never the aim of comic filmmakers to 'integrate' the gag elements of their movies. I also doubt that viewers subordinated gags to narrative."[32] In his critique of the prevalent view of the history of film comedy, Crafton convincingly argues that the preference for narrative over gags blinds scholars to the pleasures and functions of gags. In the eyes of these scholars, "Slapstick is the bad element, an excessive tendency that narrative must contain. Accordingly the history of the genre is usually teleological, written as though the eventual replacement of the gag by narrativized comedy was natural, ameliorative or even predestined."[33] Crafton argues that gags are like a pie in the face—momentary bursts of nonlinear excess—while narrative is like a chase: a linear, causal trajectory that fuels the progress of the film. It should be noted, however, that Crafton uses these terms metaphorically; actual film chases may function as "pies" within Crafton's theory if they are sufficiently disruptive.

In contrast to Crafton, who perceives the gags and narrative of slapstick film comedy as separated by "an unbridgeable gap,"[34] Tom Gunning contends that narrative "absorbs" gags in its wake. By functioning as obstacles *within* the narrative, gags contribute to the overall development and construction of the narrative.[35] Gunning recognizes the potential "show-stopping character" of gags, noting the origin of this quality in the theatrical forms from which they grew: "The Commedia dell'Arte *lazzi* (which provided schemata for many gags which survive into film comedy) were devised precisely as autonomous routines which could be inserted willy-nilly into almost any comic plot."[36] Yet Gunning argues that in this battle between the driving narrative and the disruptive gag, the narrative is victorious: "Narrative acts as a system of regulation which ultimately absorbs non-narrative elements into its pendulum sways."[37]

While Gunning contends that gags serve a similar function as obstacles within more traditional narratives, we can still distinguish diverse uses of gags on the basis of their relationship to the narrative. Neale and Krutnik's distinction between "comic events" and "gags" aptly captures the difference between gags that serve the narrative and those that disrupt the narrative. According to Neale and Krutnik, "comic events" are comedic moments or sequences that are inseparable from the narrative, while "gags" disrupt the narrative.[38] Perhaps the distinction may be better thought of as a continuum in which moments of comedy may contribute to—or detract from—the narrative to varying degrees.[39]

Gags that disrupt the narrative may be considered excessive by the standards of classical Hollywood cinema. Thompson defines "excess" as "an inevitable gap in the motivation for the physical presence of a device; the physical presence retains a perceptual interest beyond its function in the work."[40] In this way, gags that exceed the requirements of the narrative will be perceived as more disruptive than gags that are closely tailored to narrative requirements. Consequently, such gags draw the viewer's attention from the narrative to the performers and their performance.

Despite his belief in the dominance of narrative over gag, Gunning recognizes that gags retain this disruptive quality even when contained in more classical narratives: "In the later period of film comedy, when comedians were saddled with plots and characterization, gags appear in their films as *attractions*, momentary and hilarious distractions from the narrative aims of the plot."[41] Gunning first uses the term "attractions" in his 1986 article "The Cinema of Attraction: Early Film, Its Spectator and the Avant-Garde," in which he argues that prior to 1906–7, when filmmaking began to be dominated by narrative films, the dominant cinematic form—uniting the work of both Méliès and Lumière—was the cinema of attractions, "an exhibitionist cinema" that celebrated film's "ability to *show* something."[42] Gunning appropriated the term "attractions" from the Russian film director and theoriest Sergei Eisenstein, who coined the term while working as a stage director under the tutelage of Vsevold Meyerhold.[43] As Gunning explains, "I pick up this term partly to underscore the relationship to the spectator that this later avant-garde practice shares with early cinema: that of exhibitionist confrontation rather than diegetic absorption."[44] Regardless of whether Keaton's attractions are ultimately absorbed by the narrative or not, they possess the potential to be a disruptive force, at least momentarily. The four films I will examine in this chapter—*The General* (1927), *Seven Chances* (1925), *Steamboat Bill, Jr.* (1928), and *Sherlock Jr.* (1924)—display Keaton's mastery of a wide range of uses of the gag-narrative relationship. From the classicism of *The General* to the more gag- and stunt-driven structure of *Sherlock Jr.*, Keaton was constantly experimenting with comedic film form.

One reason that *The General* exhibits such a dominant narrative line may be that Keaton felt stronger about the story of *The General* than he did about the stories of his other films. Clyde Bruckman brought the book *The Great Locomotive Chase* to Keaton days after they had completed *Battling Butler*.[45] Originally written in 1863 by William Pittenger, *The Great Locomotive Chase* is a factual account by one of the participants in a cross-country train chase during the American Civil War. A band of Northern soldiers, led by a professional spy, James J. Andrews, masqueraded as Southern civilians and commandeered a Southern train, destroying telegraph wires key to the Southern war effort as they headed north aboard the train. William A. Fuller, the conductor of the stolen train, pursued them—initially on foot,

then in a handcar, and finally with a locomotive he discovered along the
way. Assisted by men he recruited during the chase, Fuller reclaimed the
train after the Northerners abandoned it.[46] Keaton added two central features to this story: 1) a second train chase, in which the Northern soldiers
chase Buster south after he recovers the stolen locomotive; and 2) a romantic plot that parallels the train chase, as Buster's love interest, Annabelle, is
abducted and later rescued along with the train. Both elements contribute to
scholars' claims for *The General*'s classicism.

Several scholars argue that *The General*'s symmetrical structure is the
hallmark of Keaton's classicism.[47] For example, Giannetti observes, "The
plot moves forward with such smoothness and poise that we're hardly aware
of its dazzling symmetry until the second chase."[48] He further argues that
the "combination of realistic execution with a formally patterned narrative
is typical of classical cinema."[49] What has received less attention, however,
is the function that vaudeville structure plays in the film's symmetry. Not
only does the film involve a symmetrical chase—first from south to north,
then from north to south—but it also contains numerous gags—such as
those involving a water spout, a runaway train, and a detached railway car—
that are established in one part of the film and repeated with variations later
on. The symmetry of *The General* may be seen on two levels, then: the
reincorporation of gags reflects the influence of vaudeville structure, while
the symmetry of the chase itself, first going north and then south along the
same tracks, dictates the film's narrative shape.

Because the gags are almost always contained by the narrative represented
by the linear tracks, their disruptive potential is limited. In the first chase,
for example, the Northern soldiers open up a water spout in order to hinder
the progress of Buster, who is following the stolen train, the *General*, aboard
a second train, the *Texas*. Buster is so intent on chasing the *General* that he
fails to see the water spout; as he sticks his head out the side window of the
locomotive in order to see better, he is blasted by a cascade of water from the
spout. Because of his inattentiveness—or more accurately, because his attention is so single-mindedly focused on chasing the *General*[50]—he does
not even realize the source of the water and looks up to the sky, holding out
his hand out to see if it is raining. During the second chase, Buster and his
pursuers revisit the water spout. This time Buster, in his attempt to refill the
engine's radiator, unintentionally separates the spout from the connected
water tower, which results in the drenching of Annabelle by a flood of water.
As the Northern soldiers follow in pursuit, they too are inundated by the
torrential downpour from the water spout. In terms of the narrative, these

gags function as obstacles to the forward movement of the chase. Although they temporarily impede the progression of the narrative, they simultaneously contribute to it. The water may momentarily hinder the passage of the Northern soldiers, but this serves a particular narrative purpose by advancing Buster's goal of trying to stay ahead of them. These gags are thus examples of Neale and Krutnik's "comic events," since they are directly related to the causal chain of the narrative. To use the railroad as a metaphor, comic events may reverse the direction of the train (the narrative), but gags derail it.

Perhaps the most thematically significant gag repetition in *The General* involves the coupling arm of the locomotive. In the first part of the film, Annabelle rejects Buster because she believes he is a coward; unbeknownst to her, the army would not allow Buster to enlist because he is more valuable to the war effort as an engineer. After Annabelle turns away from Buster, the camera captures him facing full front in a long shot as he sits down dejectedly on the coupling arm of his beloved train, the *General*. When another engineer starts up the train, the movement of the coupling arm lifts and drops Buster in time to the motion of the engine. As he moves with the train, Buster stares forward forlornly, blinded to the train's movement by his sadness. Just before the train transports him out of the view of the camera, he awakens to his dilemma with a start and does a double-take as he discovers himself unexpectedly moving.

This shot ends the introductory section of the film (the next scene occurs one year later and leads into the train chase), and a variation on this gag becomes the final image of the entire film. Buster has won the battle and been made an officer. Moreover, he has regained his two great loves: Annabelle and his train, the *General*. He and Annabelle sit on the coupling rod (now aptly named) and attempt to celebrate with a kiss, but they are continually interrupted by passing soldiers; now that Buster is an officer, all the soldiers salute him and he must salute back. He switches positions with Annabelle so that he can kiss her while he simultaneously salutes passing soldiers with his right hand. Thus, the film ends with the image of Buster repeatedly extending his arm—a veritable saluting machine—while he kisses one love, Annabelle, perched atop the coupling arm of his other love, the train.

These two gags are exemplary models for the blending of gag and narrative. On the level of vaudeville structure, we see the reincorporation of the original gag with a variation. By stretching out the gag repetition over the course of the film, Keaton takes advantage of the accordion-like structure of repeated gags. Nevertheless the final gag gains immeasurably from its narrative context, as Moews aptly notes, "The scene provides his last demonstration of ingenious efficiency, of how to do two things at once. . . . Appropriately, too, in the final shot Johnnie, Annabelle, and The General are together again. . . . Posed together now—boy, girl, locomotive—they form a romantic and dynamic trio, whose shared adventures have happily united them at the end."[51] Each gag evinces a reciprocal relationship between its humor and its narrative content. The humor of the first gag is increased because Buster is unaware of what is happening to him due to his depression over having lost Annabelle's love. Unlike the "fish-on-a-line" sequences in *Our Hospitality*, the first coupling-arm gag serves an explicit narrative purpose: it caps this part of the story by communicating that Buster will remain wed to his train rather than Annabelle. The humor of the second gag is augmented by our knowledge of how hard Buster has fought to win both Annabelle and the train. At the same time, the second gag concludes the narrative by displaying the compromise Buster must make to keep both of his loves. Almost all of the gags in *The General* serve similar double duty as gag and narrative element.

A second factor that helps the gags in *The General* achieve a close fit with the narrative is their role in propelling the narrative forward. One of the reasons *The General* makes such an excellent textbook example of the classical style is that a majority of the film consists of a chase along a railroad track. As I note above, the tracks serve as the perfect visual metaphor for the linearity of classical narrative. Moews observes, "The two chase sequences . . . are among Keaton's most remarkable achievements. In them the narrative line of the film is also the spatial line of the film, the distance traveled; and both are none other than the actual railroad line itself."[52] As the narrative follows the line of the tracks, almost every gag consists of Buster and the Northern soldiers placing and overcoming obstacles to each other's progress. Thus in a concrete way all of the gags contribute to the forward movement of the narrative.

Then what of the vaudeville structure that had such a strong influence on Keaton's early development as a filmmaker? Why does vaudeville structure appear less dominant in this film as compared to others by Keaton? First, I should like to emphasize that the symmetry and classicism of *The General* are most prominent in the two chase sequences that comprise the center of the film, a total of half the running time of the entire film. The symmetry is noticeably absent, for example, in the battle scenes that follow the railroad chase. In these scenes, Keaton returns to the more gag-based format he derived from vaudeville.

If we limit ourselves for the moment to an examination of the chase sequences, the reasons for their classicism become evident. Unlike the chases
in *Seven Chances* or *Cops*, where the geography of the terrain takes Buster
and his pursuers on a convoluted course, the railway chases provide only
two possible courses—forward and back, or in this case, north and south.
Yet the scale of the chase is nearly limitless, extending as far north and south
as the tracks will permit Buster to travel. At the same time, the scale of
Keaton's gags in *The General* tends to be small, limited to the confines of one
railway car or, at the most, the distance between the *General* and the *Texas*.
Even the larger-scale gags, as when Buster attempts to fire the cannon, are
always contained by the width of the two tracks on which the trains travel.
The gags in the chase sequences rarely reach the level of Gunning's "attractions"; they never overpower the cause-and-effect chain of the chase
through visual spectacle. In this way the narrative, described by the width
and length of the railroad tracks, literally as well as figuratively *contains* the
gags.

By comparison, the gags in *The Navigator* exist within a more amorphous
space—a ship adrift in an infinite sea, floating aimlessly without any dis-
cernible navigator. Just as the narrative of *The General* holds closely to the
line of the railroad tracks, the narrative of *The Navigator* takes its shape from
the geometric form of the decks of the ship, as I noted in Chapter 2. Both
films illustrate Keaton's interest in circularity: *The General* through the elaborate counterpoint of gags during the round-trip chase, *The Navigator* on
the microcosmic level of individual gags. The different physical and visual
strategies of the films are evident, however, in the sequence in which Buster
and Betsy first discover each other on board the ship. In the climactic shot
of this sequence, Keaton captures the entire stern of the ship in a long shot,
placing a strong visual emphasis on the patterns created by Buster and
Betsy as they continually miss each other. This shot pulls the viewer away
from the narrative by virtue of its visual excess, an exemplary instance of an
attraction.

In *Seven Chances*, Keaton also uses large-scale attractions to expand the
scope of the narrative; the climactic chase sequence in this film threatens to
overwhelm the narrative altogether. Because Keaton did not approve of the
play upon which the film was based, he approached it with less deference
than he did the source of *The General*, which was a story that he chose for
adaptation. Schenck purchased the rights to *Seven Chances* for $25,000
without Keaton's approval or knowledge and presented the script to Keaton
as a *fait accompli*.[53] Although Schenck granted Keaton greater control over
production than most Hollywood producers, he still exerted control over

Keaton's artistic and economic decisions when he deemed it necessary; Keaton did not have complete artistic control over his films, nor even over their subject matter. Keaton felt that *Seven Chances* (the play) was unsuitable material for him—"The type of unbelievable farce I don't like."[54] For this reason, he approached *Seven Chances* from a somewhat antagonistic point of view, which manifests itself in the film's adversarial gag-narrative relationship.

To begin, Keaton condensed most of the action of the play into the first half of the film, which runs approximately twenty-seven minutes. He presents the exposition of the first act of the play—the information that Jimmie Shannon must marry in order to receive his inheritance—in the first ten minutes of the film. While Act 1 of the play fleshes out the exposition with verbal jokes about Jimmie's fear of marriage and the pros and cons of marriage as an institution,[55] Keaton achieves the same effect through physical comedy. In the film, Buster (who plays Shannon) and his business partner Meekin are on the brink of financial disaster. When a lawyer arrives to tell them of Buster's inheritance, they mistakenly believe that the lawyer has come to serve them a summons and consequently evade him by slipping out the back of their office to their country club. The majority of this "opening act" of the film thus revolves around a small-scale slapstick chase in which the lawyer tries to catch Buster and Meekin.

Keaton further alters the characterization of the central character to fit his screen persona. In the play, Jimmie Shannon is a confirmed bachelor. Although at the beginning of the play he may be secretly in love with one woman, Anne, he does not realize this until the final, climactic scene and exhibits fearful, if not hostile, feelings toward women and marriage throughout most of the drama. His pursuit of a wife appears to be solely motivated by his desire for his grandfather's inheritance. In the film, however, Buster is obviously in love with one woman, Mary, from the beginning of the story. In the opening sequence, Buster and Mary talk in front of her house during each of the four seasons, yet Buster repeatedly fails to profess his love. In this way Keaton adapts the character to his screen persona: Buster may be afraid to tell Mary he loves her, but this fear stems from an initial social awkwardness that he must overcome, not from ambivalent feelings about women, as it does in the play.

In the film, Buster's reaction to the news of his inheritance is to propose to Mary immediately. The potential inheritance merely triggers an action (his proposal to Mary) that Buster has been dreaming of for at least a year.[56] Unfortunately, Buster is unable to make his intentions clear and Mary mistakenly assumes that he wishes to marry her only for the money. When Mary's mother intercedes, suggesting that Mary give Buster a chance to explain himself, Mary sends a servant to Buster with a note implying that she will marry him.[57] In the meantime, however, Buster has headed to the country club with Meekin, who urges him to marry the first woman he can in order to save them from financial ruin.

The country-club sequence is the equivalent to the second act of the play, in which Jimmie proposes to seven women (the "seven chances" of the title) and is in turn rejected by all of them. Keaton condenses the action of Act 2 into ten minutes of visual gags. While the play concentrates on the different ways in which Jimmie tries to propose and the many reasons why the women turn him down, the film finds variety in the visual manifestations of Buster's rejection. After the first two rejections, Buster makes his third proposal by tossing a note to a woman from the landing one flight below her. Her answer is evident from the fluttering of little bits of paper from above, which rain down on Buster in a veritable blizzard of rejection. Buster is rejected by another woman as they ascend a grand, curving staircase, and a moment later by yet another as he descends with her. After seven rejections, Buster is accepted, only to discover that the girl is underage, a sequence Keaton lifted directly from the play.[58] Buster and Meekin then agree to meet at a church at 5 p.m.; each will try to find a bride for Buster before then. Thus concludes the first half of the film—the action Keaton adapted from the play—which has established the central goal for the second half of the film.

The action of the entire second half of the film was created by Keaton and his writers, and it is for this material that the film is justifiably praised. Keaton immediately accelerates the pace of the proposals. While it takes Buster ten minutes to deliver his first eight proposals, he proposes to the next seven women—including a woman in blackface, a mannequin, and a female impersonator—in approximately two minutes of running time. Intercut with Buster's proposals, we see Meekin and the lawyer place an advertisement in the newspaper telling of Buster's dilemma. In response to the advertisement, hundreds of women flock to the church, where Buster, exhausted from the futility of his proposals, lies sleeping in the front pew. When the minister disperses the would-be brides by telling them that the advertisement must be a fraud, they chase Buster from the church. As Buster flees, Mary's servant finally intercepts him with her note, which establishes Buster's goal for the remainder of the film: in order to reach Mary's home by 7 p.m. and claim his inheritance, he must elude the hundreds of brides dogging his every step.

Figure 3.1. *Seven Chances*. Buster pursued by hundreds of brides.

It is this part of the film that comprises—at twenty-seven minutes of
fifty-five minutes' running time—a full half of the film and represents Keaton's expansion of the play. A careful analysis of the relationship between
gags and narrative in the second half of the film reveals much about Keaton's approach to the adaptation of the play. The majority of the remainder
of the film is made up of a chase so vast—on such a large physical and
spatial scale and so greatly exceeding the narrative requirements—that it
nearly consumes the narrative altogether. By judicious use of cross-cutting,
however, Keaton manages to preserve the integrity of the narrative while
pushing the chase to unparalleled dimensions. He intercuts brief shots of
the clock at the top of the town hall's tower and shots of Mary, her mother,
Meekin, and the lawyer waiting for Buster to arrive, regularly reminding the
audience of Buster's deadline (seven o'clock) and his goal (to marry Mary).
In this way, Keaton supports his gag structure with a key element of classical Hollywood cinema: the deadline. As Bordwell suggests, "The deadline
proper is the strongest way in which story duration cooperates with narrative causality. In effect, the characters set a limit to the timespan necessary
to the chain of cause and effect."[59] The deadline establishes a finite limit to
the film—it will end shortly after 7 p.m.—yet it also frees Keaton to expand

the boundaries of the narrative. The very limit of the deadline provides him with the freedom to indulge in expansive attractions.

Although Keaton uses periodic reminders of the deadline to lend minimal narrative structure to the second half of the film, he depends primarily on vaudeville structure for cohesiveness. The final chase sequences are built upon the vaudeville principle of the topper, as well as one of Keaton's favorite comic devices, the use of multiples, which he adapted from his family's vaudeville act, as I discussed in Chapter 2.[60] Despite Keaton's objections to the source material, the play already provided the opportunity for Keaton to use multiples by virtue of its central premise and title. Keaton expands upon this premise in many ways. First, he changes all the numbers in the film to sevens: Buster's inheritance becomes *seven* million dollars; he must marry by the age of twenty-*seven*; and one can even argue that he is chased by *seven* hundred brides and boulders, though an exact count would be inadvisable, to say the least (fig. 3.1). To the seven rejected proposals at the country club, Keaton adds another seven as he heads toward the church. Once he escapes from the church, he loses his watch and attempts to find out the time; coming to a watch store, he finds multiple clocks in the window, all with different times. As the brides pursue Buster, he tries to hide in a formation of multiple cops; later, they chase him through a multitude of swarming bees emerging from multiple beehives. Finally, as the brides try to "head him off at the pass," Buster sets in motion an avalanche of boulders.

The escalation of multiples—from clocks to brides to boulders—is what drives the latter half of this film, and the boulders serve as the final topper for these gag sequences. They are the final gag sequence in the series, the unpredictable natural and comedic element that finally defeats the brides in their rush to marry Buster. Quite appropriately, the boulders were improvised by Keaton after he and his writers screened the film for a preview audience. As Keaton told Blesh,

> Our fade-out was on me, running down the side of a hill, all those [brides] after me. . . . Then suddenly, just before the fade, a real belly laugh. I whispered to Bruckman, "Now what the hell caused that?" He didn't know, so we ran the ending slow at the studio. There it was. I had accidentally dislodged a rock. It started to roll after me. On its way, it knocked a couple more loose and there were three little rocks chasing me. . . . So we went back and milked that gag.[61]

Thus Keaton's impulse to improvise lured him away from the strict causality of classical Hollywood cinema in this sequence.

In this respect, the chase that ends *Seven Chances* is more representative of Keaton's work than the one in *The General*.[62] For in *Seven Chances*, despite the reminders of Buster's deadline and his goal, the chase is shot on such a large scale—captured predominantly in extreme long shot to emphasize that scale—that its visual imagery overwhelms the narrative. Although Crafton uses "the chase" as a metaphor to describe the linearity of narrative, the brides and boulders of *Seven Chances* ultimately function as "the pie." Keaton's acrobatics in response to these brides and boulders reach the level of attractions, crossing the line from gag to spectacle by their sheer visual impact and consequently diverting the viewer's attention from Buster's story to Keaton's performance. In sequences like this one, which often occur at the end of Keaton's feature films, he takes delight in the act of "showing" and goes out of his way to show as much as he can, to convince us that what we see actually occurred. These stunts and gags reveal a second structure operating within Keaton's films: in addition to the horizontal progression of the narrative, there is a vertical accumulation of gags and stunts.[63]

The next two films I will examine, *Steamboat Bill, Jr.* and *Sherlock Jr.*, display an increased tension between narrative and attractions. Of the two films, *Steamboat Bill, Jr.* holds more closely to a strongly causal narrative throughline, yet the excesses of its final "cyclone sequence" disrupt this line. During the first three-quarters of *Steamboat Bill, Jr.*, Keaton's gags serve to advance the narrative, as he moderates the gags' potential for disruption by integrating them with the narrative and characterization, and by keeping them on a physically and spatially small scale. The opening of the film introduces Steamboat Bill, Sr., and Mr. King, the richest man in town. The two men are engaged in a bitter rivalry over the steamboat business. Mr. King has just christened his luxurious new steamboat, which he believes will put Bill out of business. In the midst of their confrontation, Bill receives a telegram from his son, Bill, Jr. (Buster), whom he has not seen since Buster was a little boy. The telegram says that Buster is coming to visit and will wear a carnation so that Bill will be able to recognize him.

Until now, there has been little indication that the film is a comedy. The shots of the river and the steamboats establish an overall scenic realism that Keaton will fully exploit to a comic end in the cyclone sequence. Once Buster enters the film, he embarks on the first of a series of extended gags. At the train station where Buster is scheduled to arrive, Bill discovers that almost every young man there is wearing a carnation, yet none of them appears to be his son. Meanwhile Buster has gotten off the train quite literally on the "wrong side of the tracks," an appropriate image for Buster's first appearance in the film, as the plot capitalizes on the class differences between Bill and Buster, as well as between Bill and Mr. King. As Bill wanders off in search of Buster, the latter repeatedly shows his carnation to well-dressed strangers in the hope that one may be his father. This series of gags revolves around the different expectations that Bill and Buster have of each other; Bill expects a tall, muscular son and Buster expects a more refined father. Thus, the gags serve to advance the story by emphasizing the mutual disappointment of, and conflict between, father and son. Although the gags exhibit their own structure based upon repetition and reversal, the comedy still serves the story. The gags thus qualify as comic events according to Neale and Krutnik's definition.

The second extended gag sequence occurs in a hat store. Bill is unhappy with the way Buster dresses; in particular, he does not approve of Buster's beret and pencil mustache. In attempting to find a new hat for Buster, father and son discover that their tastes in hats distinctly differ. Buster finds a plaid cap that he likes, but Bill makes it clear by his reaction that he does not approve of Buster's choice. Each time Bill takes the cap off Buster's head, Buster puts it back on. Next, Buster tries on a series of hats offered to him by Bill and a salesman. The humor derives from a combination of the mechanical way in which Buster tries on the hats and the inherent conflict between Buster's self-image and the image of him held by his father.[64] In the two parts of this gag sequence, the comedy concerns Buster's refusal to conform to his father's wishes and thus builds on one of the primary conflicts in the story. Similarly, the succeeding gag sequences on the steamboat display Buster's inability to adjust to Bill's life and routine and thus are subsumed by the narrative. By this time, Buster has discovered that Mary, a woman from college in whom he is romantically interested, is also in town visiting her father. Unfortunately, her father is Bill's rival, Mr. King, and Buster and Mary become caught in the crossfire of a family feud.

These gag sequences fit neatly within the confines of classical Hollywood cinema because they serve a narrative as well as comic function. If we extract these gags from their narrative context, they are still funny, yet they gain humor from their relationship to the story. They are narrowly tailored to the demands of the story, neither exceeding the narrative requirements nor disrupting narrative continuity. Rather, by contributing to our understanding of the class conflict between father and son—between Buster's collegiate life in Boston and Bill's life as a riverboat captain—the gags are absorbed into the narrative.

In the final reel of the film, a cyclone hits the town and Buster must save all of the main characters—Mary, Bill, and Mr. King—in order to prove himself to his father, end the feud, and wed Mary. Yet in his rush to escape from the cyclone, Buster appears to have entirely forgotten about his father and girlfriend. The stunts and gags in this sequence no longer advance the story as the earlier ones did. Instead, it is as if Keaton has built up enough narrative momentum to justify an extraordinary explosion of attractions.

If we examine the cyclone sequence for its narrative purpose, it divides quite neatly into two sections. In the first section, the storm rolls into town and blows Buster from one end of town to the other. In the second section, after the storm magically transports Buster to the river, Buster rescues Mary, Bill, and Mr. King. In part, the inclusion of the cyclone sequence was accidental. Keaton had originally intended to end the film with an extended flood scene on the river. When his supervisor, Harry Brand, objected to this idea, Keaton substituted the cyclone sequence. Yet the second part of the cyclone sequence takes place entirely on the river, leading me to conclude that this section of the film remained essentially true to Keaton's original ideas for a flood scene. In fact, it looks like a flood scene; apparently the suggestion of a cyclone in the first section of the sequence was sufficient to gain Brand's approval for the river rescue. It is the first part of the cyclone sequence I will now examine more closely, because it depends on vaudeville structure more than narrative for unity.

The cyclone is established by two intertitles: first, by a clipping from a newspaper weather report that warns, "Storm clouds in the offing"; and second, by an intertitle, "The pier is not strong enough to hold the boat against the wind." Keaton used powerful wind machines to produce the near gale-force winds that rack the town and blow newspapers, boxes, and people around the streets. In one long shot, he captures the main street in the town from classical perspective. The shot draws the viewer's eyes deep into the frame by focusing attention on the narrowing road that recedes into the frame, lined by buildings on the left half and telephone poles on the right. An automobile stands just right of center at the bottom of the frame. As dozens of people race down the street, one man attempts to start the car. The wind raises the car's convertible top; the top acts as a sail, catching the wind and dragging the man, who was attempting to crank the car's engine manually, down the street into the distance. In this way, Keaton transforms the car into a sailboat, a trick he also used at the end of the inner film in *Sherlock Jr.* Although this shot helps establish the storm, it also provides the first transformation gag of the sequence, one that will be repeated several times with variations.

Shortly thereafter, the film returns to the actions of Buster. Dozens of patients run from the town's hospital, where Buster has been taken. Buster is revealed when the cyclone blows off three walls and the roof of the hospital. He is the only patient who has remained in bed, an ice-bag perched atop his head. As Buster attempts to flee toward the building behind the hospital, it collapses entirely. He retreats to his hospital bed and hides under the covers, but the cyclone now blows the bed down the street and into a stable. Buster raises his head, notes his new location and bed partners (several horses), and does a double-take. This scene establishes several actions and images that Keaton repeats throughout the sequence.

First, the sequence establishes the recurring image of Buster passing through doors and windows. In this way, Keaton relies on a vaudevillian structure of repetition for cohesiveness. The cyclone blows him, still lying on his bed, into the stable through one door and, after Buster's double-take on the horses, the doors open again and Buster is blown out through a door on the far side of the barn. In both shots, Buster fits perfectly through the door, as if he were meant to be there, or as if the cyclone somehow had something in mind for him. The shots of Buster entering and exiting the barn on his bed place a heavy visual emphasis on the silhouette of the barn door opening. He rolls into the dark rectangular opening of the barn and out through the light rectangular opening of the back door. Moreover, the wind has transformed the bed into a mobile vehicle, as if it were now a car, echoing the previous transformation of a car into a sailboat.

The scene draws additional humor from the incongruity of a bed in a stable. His double-take when he sees the horses, his trademark stone face registering his surprise in spite of himself, punctuates the gag. There is a strange other-worldliness to this section of the cyclone sequence, as if time and the rational laws of the universe have been suspended. In his rush to escape from the cyclone, Buster appears to have forgotten about the narrative of the film, almost as if he were trying to escape from the film itself. The spectacle of Keaton performing these dangerous stunts and magical transformations overshadows any concern we might have for the story.

From the barn, Buster, still lying on his bed, is blown in front of a three-story building. He tumbles from the bed as it stops in front of the building and seeks refuge under the bed, not a particularly safe place to wait out the storm. A man jumps from the third-story window onto the bed, drawing attention to the window while simultaneously disorienting Buster with the force of his jump. As Buster stands before the teetering wall rubbing his neck, the wall falls, yet he miraculously escapes injury: the window opening falls around him. The central shot in the sequence captures the entire action

Figure 3.2. *Steamboat Bill, Jr.* The falling wall.

of the falling wall without a cut. Buster faces the camera full front; he is seen in a long shot standing about eighteen feet in front of the three-story building. The third story is an attic with a rectangular window opening. The camera captures all but the very top of the third story, so that the slanted angles of the roof point to the third-story window. The shot balances Buster and the window on the central vertical axis of the frame: Buster at the bottom of the frame and the window at the top of the frame. Buster shakes his head, trying to regain his equilibrium following the preceding action. Unaware that the wall is about to fall, he stands still, oblivious to the tilting wall as the winds of the cyclone appear to pull it away from the rest of the structure. The entire front wall falls toward the camera and directly on top of Buster, yet he escapes unharmed because he is standing exactly under the descending window frame (fig. 3.2).

In this shot, Keaton far exceeds any reasonable demands for realism that the norms of classical Hollywood cinema would require. He easily could have constructed the same scene through editing. A long shot of the wall starting to fall would establish the situation; from there he could have cut to a medium shot showing the wall falling on top of him. With this closer second shot, a small piece of the wall would have sufficed to create the cinematic illusion. If he wanted to, he could even cut back to a long shot of the entire wall on the ground, with him standing in the middle of the window. Yet Keaton risked his life to produce this effect, which by classical standards was clearly excessive. Why?

By showing the wall fall in one shot, Keaton emphasized his own performance: his ability to calculate and execute this stunt as well as his bravery (some would say his foolishness) in performing it himself. The result is, quite literally, breath-taking. It completely transforms this simple vaudeville gag into an image that has become forever identified with Keaton: Buster as a round peg in a square hole, or, in this case, an almost square window frame. The falling-wall sequence repeats the image of Keaton passing through a window or door unharmed for the third time. This image is the central focus of the cyclone sequence, providing a sense of cohesiveness to Buster's seemingly endless series of narrow escapes.

Throughout the cyclone sequence, Keaton creates increasingly complex variations on the central image of Buster passing through windows and doors. As Buster attempts to escape from the cyclone, he seeks refuge in a theater. Finding himself backstage, he notices a painted backdrop of an ocean scene upstage and runs toward it, attempting to leap into the ocean. Here Keaton transforms one of the set routines from his vaudeville act with his father—in which his father would throw him into the stage backdrop—into a surreal manifestation of his hyper-literal imagination. The thinking behind this gag—Keaton's acceptance of a stage convention for reality—shares a common artistic and philosophical outlook with René Magritte's *The Wind and the Song* (1928–29), in which Magritte juxtaposes a painting of a pipe with the subtitle "This is not a pipe." The painting is not a pipe, but a representation of a pipe, just as Keaton mistakes a painting of the ocean for an actual ocean. Buster seems unable to distinguish between reality and representations of reality, between theater and life, and once again he gravitates toward a window, in this case a rectangular backdrop, in a frantic attempt to escape.

In the final gag in the theater scene, Buster steps into a magician's mechanism for a disappearing act. He climbs on top of a platform and suddenly a curtain draws around him. When the curtain rises, Buster seems to have disappeared. In this sequence, however, Buster is privy to information that the camera does not pick up. Buster knows where he is, but the audience does not until he pops his head up from under a trap door in the platform (yet another door!). After examining the trap door and the curtain, he realizes how the curtain serves to hide the action of the trap door. For the first time in the film, Buster comprehends how a mechanism works. This brief epiphany, which occurs appropriately enough in a vaudeville theater, serves to reconnect Buster's chaotic trajectory with the narrative line. Armed with this knowledge, he heads back out into the world—and back into the narrative of the film.

While in *Steamboat Bill, Jr.*, Buster returns to the storyline having unexpectedly gained knowledge from the narrative disruption, in *Sherlock Jr.*, the film's structure—a film-within-a-film—allows Keaton to completely disrupt the narrative of the outer film with the vaudeville-inspired magic of the inner film. Keaton's account of his process in developing *Sherlock Jr.* demonstrates his predilection for gags and stunts in the film. For a considerable time, Keaton had wanted to make a film incorporating all of the best illusions he had learned in vaudeville. He approached his cameraman, Elgin Lessley, with this idea and Lessley created the concept of an outer film to accommodate the magic tricks of the inner film. As Keaton recounted in an interview,

> I laid out some of these gags, and showed the technical man how to get the sets built for the things I had to do. When I got that batch of stuff together, [Elgin Lessley] said, "You can't do it and tell a legitimate story, because there are illusions, and some of them are clown gags, some Houdini, some Ching Ling Foo. It's got to come in a dream. To get what we're after, you've got to be a projectionist in a projecting room in a little local small-town picture theatre, and go to sleep, after you've got the picture started. Once you fall asleep, you visualize yourself as one of the important characters in the picture you're showing. You go down out of the projection room, walk up there on the screen and become part of it. Now you tell your whole story."[65]

Keaton's account of the creation of *Sherlock Jr.* reveals that the gags and magic tricks led to the story rather than growing out its given circumstances. Keaton's main concession to classical Hollywood style was suggested by Lessley—the use of a dream as the justification for the magical illusions in the inner film.[66]

Nonetheless the first plot device Keaton decided on—Buster's falling asleep and dreaming that he enters a film—is the single most disruptive moment in the film, the moment when the film veers most strongly away from the narrative line.[67] While working as the projectionist at the local movie theater, Buster falls asleep and his dream "alter ego" slips out of his body, a shot Keaton captures with a double exposure. The "dream Buster" sees the characters in the inner film transform themselves into the "people" from the outer film. The villain and heroine in the inner film become trans-

Figure 3.3. *Sherlock Jr.* Buster prepares to jump into the inner film.

formed into Buster's girlfriend and rival suitor from the outer film. When he observes his girlfriend being seduced by his rival suitor in the inner film, Buster becomes incensed. He walks directly to the screen and into the inner film (fig. 3.3).

Although the plot merely requires that Buster enter the inner film, Keaton created one of the most startling special-effects sequences in the history of film to bridge the gap between the outer and inner films. As Buster attempts to enter the inner film he is rebuffed; once he succeeds in staying in the inner film, Buster finds himself unable to keep his bearings. The film makes a series of cuts, going from a park to a lake to a desert, and each time Buster struggles to make the transition with the film. As he starts to adjust to one environment it becomes something else. When he leans against a door frame, the scene cuts and he nearly falls over a cliff. The sequence calls attention to the fragmentary nature of film in comparison to the continuity of life. As Garrett Stewart observes, "Real men are mobile in real spaces;

stage men know limited mobility within abstract or symbolic spaces; screen men must face the sometimes paralyzing paradox of space that is itself mobile."[68] Buster, the "reality" from outside the inner film, remains consistent while the film shifts beneath him; at the same time, his ability to move from place to place with each cut is a bit of film magic in and of itself.

Keaton achieved Buster's jump into the screen through the use of lighting. As he told Kevin Brownlow, "We built a stage with a big black cut-out screen. Then we built the front-row seats and orchestra pit. . . . We lit the stage so it looked like a motion picture being projected on to a screen."[69] To create the graphic-match montage, Keaton measure the distance from the camera to his position in front of the camera at the end of each shot. "As we did one shot, we'd throw it in the darkroom and develop it right there and then—and bring it back to the cameraman. He cut out a few frames and put them in the camera gate. When I come [sic] to change scenes, he could put me right square where I was."[70]

The graphic-match montage is a remarkable effect, not only for its time, but even today for contemporary audiences who have been spoiled by extravagant special effects. But the sequence is all the more remarkable for its disruption of the narrative. In *The Purple Rose of Cairo* (1985), Woody Allen reverses Keaton's idea by having a fictional character walk off the screen into the outer film. While Allen subordinates the technique to the plot of *The Purple Rose of Cairo*, Keaton uses the idea to diverge into a hilarious parody of film technique, completely foregoing the demands of the narrative for the more ephemeral pleasure of the gag.

We can trace the origin of this sequence back to The Three Keatons. Instead of Joe Keaton's tossing young Buster around a vaudeville stage, now the medium itself, the film-editing process, transports Buster from place to place, abusing him with the violence of a vaudeville knockabout act. In The Three Keatons' vaudeville act and the graphic-match montage of *Sherlock Jr.*, the humor is based on the same concept—unflappable Buster upended by a larger force, forever struggling to regain his equilibrium—yet Keaton exploits film's ability to replicate reality in order to carry this image into a new realm, where the pure theatricality of vaudeville meets the concrete (if two-dimensional) reality of the oceans, mountains, and trains of the real world.

Having succeeded in "breaking into pictures," Buster next appears in the inner film as "The crime-crushing criminologist—SHERLOCK JR." The Sheik has stolen a pearl necklace and the father in the inner film (played by Joe Keaton) calls on Buster to solve the crime. From this point on, the gags and stunts steadily escalate in scope, rapidly eclipsing the narrative as the locus of the audience's interest. Contrary to Mast's assertion, the inner film of *Sherlock Jr.* gains momentum from its attractions, not its narrative line.[71] Through Keaton's repetition of imagery, these attractions form a visual pattern throughout the film, one in which Buster continually flirts with disaster only to narrowly escape.

Keaton first establishes this pattern with several small gags. The Sheik plots to kill Buster with the aid of his co-conspirator, the butler. He invites Buster to the billiard room, where the butler has set several traps: an ax rigged to fall on whoever sits in a chair directly below it; a poisonous drink; and an exploding billiard ball. Buster avoids all these traps through a combination of ingenuity and coincidence. When he realizes that it is his turn to shoot in the pool game, he stops himself just before sitting on the chair; the butler, in turn, almost triggers the ax to fall on himself when Buster jams him with his pool cue in the midst of a shot. When the butler offers him the poison drink, Buster hands it to the Sheik in a gesture of proper etiquette. With these smaller gags, Keaton begins to establish a pattern that he repeats throughout the inner film.

Yet it is the pool game itself that displays the first spectacular example of Keaton's realization of the visual pattern. Buster begins to sink the pool balls, putting together a run of fourteen balls before missing. With each shot he succeeds in pocketing at least one ball, simultaneously missing the explosive thirteen ball by only a hair. All of Buster's pool shots are captured in full shot from one end of the table, so that the pool table and Buster's body are completely visible. In this way, Keaton insures that the audience knows he actually executed all of the pool shots in the sequence. The visual pattern created by his shots' criss-crossing the table and repeatedly missing the exploding ball so greatly exceeds the narrative demands of this scene that the narrative fades into the background—quite literally so, as the only thing left to remind us of the inner film's narrative is the reaction to Buster's shots by the Sheik and the butler, who are hiding in the next room. The only narrative detail necessary to appreciate this sequence is the knowledge that the ball Buster repeatedly misses may explode. The sequence thus functions more like a gag than a comic event, as these terms are defined by Neale and Krutnik.

Several optical illusions—magic tricks that Keaton appropriated from vaudeville—subsequently disrupt the narrative of the inner film through a combination of their excess and their independence from the narrative. In the next sequence, Buster appears to be dressing himself in a mirror in his

Figure 3.4. *Sherlock Jr.* The mirror sequence.

home. In a full shot, we see him in profile facing a mirror to his left (fig.
3.4). As he finishes checking his appearance, he walks through what we had
perceived as a mirror (fig. 3.5). The shot reveals that the mirror image was
an illusion; all the objects in Buster's living room are duplicated in the corresponding place in the "mirror room." Buster then walks over to a large wall
safe, works the combination, and opens it, revealing that it is actually his
front door. He strolls outside into the criss-crossing traffic. These gags serve
little narrative purpose; at most they advance the story by telling us that
Buster is getting ready to leave his house. Yet such minor information is
communicated in grand style; the optical illusions are so visually stunning
that they easily outshine their narrative implications. At the same time, another visual motif is established, indeed the same visual motif that serves to
unify the cyclone sequence in *Steamboat Bill, Jr.*—the image of Buster unexpectedly passing through windows and doors. Recurrent visual images such
as these compensate for the diminishing narrative line in the inner film.

By reincorporating visual images from the outer film in the inner film,
Keaton achieves the illusion of a greater connection between the two narra-
tives than actually exists. In both the inner and outer films, for example,
Buster tails the Sheik. In the outer film, the Sheik tricks Buster into walking

Figure 3.5. *Sherlock Jr.* The mirror sequence.

into a railroad car and then locks the door behind him. The scene is repeated in the inner film when the Sheik traps Buster on the roof of a building with a similar ploy. In the outer film, Buster escapes from the railroad
car and grasps a water spout, which unleashes a torrent of water on top of
him as it bends toward the ground. In the inner film, the movement of the
water spout is duplicated by the movement of a railroad crossing arm,
which Buster holds onto as it gently transports him to the back seat of the
Sheik's departing car. Scholars point to this type of gag as evidence of Keaton's use of narrative symmetry, yet in *Sherlock Jr.* the narrative contribution of the repetition is negligible compared to the "visual intoxication" it
provides.[72] By duplicating images from the outer film in the inner film,
Keaton is arguably playing with the way in which events in people's real
lives reappear in their dreams.[73] Yet I would note that the net effect of such
duplication on the narrative line of the film is zero. The inner "dream" film,
which comprises half the total running time of the film, cannot possibly
affect the outcome of the film because that outcome is already achieved
before the inner film starts: Buster's girlfriend has already solved the crime
and discredited the Sheik.

The following sequences repeat the "Buster through a window" image

Figure 3.6. *Sherlock Jr.* Criss-crossing trucks fill a gap in the bridge.

through a variety of vaudevillian magic tricks, which occasionally reconnect with the narrative line of the inner film, yet just as frequently diverge from it. After Buster is apprehended by the Sheik and his gang, he jumps out a window directly through a hoop that contains a lady's dress, which Buster and his assistant, Gillette, had previously placed in the window frame. As the criminals run outside to search for Buster, they see a little old lady in a dress meandering down the street. By dissolving to a cut-away fourth wall before the jump through the window, Keaton converts the view of the building to a theatrical one—with an "invisible fourth wall"—so that he can capture the stunt as it would be performed on a vaudeville stage. The camera is thus able to capture his trajectory through the window in one shot, further emphasizing the actuality of his performance.

The criminals intercept Buster again and the next gags fit loosely into the line of the ensuing chase. Yet once again, we must keep in mind that there is nothing at stake in this chase. Instead, with the crime of the outer film already solved, and with only the union of the lovers remaining, Keaton feels free to create a visual line for the film, using the symmetry of his gags and stunts to unify a film that has strayed from its narrative line. First, Buster appears to be trapped in an alley with the criminals in hot pursuit.

Gillette beckons to Buster to jump into a peddler's case that he holds open in front of his body. Buster faces off with the criminals and then takes a running leap head-first toward Gillette, disappearing through what appears to be an invisible passage in Gillette's stomach.

In the final sequence of the inner film's chase, Buster takes a long ride atop motorcycle handlebars, unaware that Gillette, who had been driving the motorcycle, has been inadvertently knocked off it. Throughout the chase, Buster flirts with death only to find himself miraculously saved by yet again being in the right place at the right time. As he rides down a bridge atop the motorcycle handlebars, he heads toward a large gap in the bridge. Just as he appears to be headed for a fall, two trucks, coming from opposite directions on the ground below, criss-cross precisely at the gap, allowing Buster to ride across their rooftops unharmed (fig. 3.6). As Buster nears the end of the bridge, which stops in mid-air, the bridge collapses, conveying Buster gently to the ground without interrupting the chase.

Yet by this time, the chase is not a chase at all. Buster has lost the criminals and become diverted onto a random path with no driver. As in the cyclone sequence in *Steamboat Bill, Jr.*, we have no idea where Buster is headed. To my mind, these climactic sequences are the most exhilarating in all of Keaton's work, precisely because in these moments Keaton leaves behind all concern for the narrative. It is as if the narrative has allowed him to accumulate enough velocity to veer off onto a trajectory all his own, and this trajectory, which scholars have frequently mistaken for the narrative line, is precisely the opposite: a *visual* line that transcends the narrative through its excess. For these sequences—seen most clearly, oddly enough, when shown as clips in the various documentaries about Keaton—are primarily gags, not comic events.

The climactic sequence of *Sherlock Jr.* continues with several more escapes from near death—as Buster effortlessly avoids massive collisions with a tree, a train, and a car—before Buster's driverless motorcycle leads him right into the wall of the shack where the butler has taken the woman.[74] The impact propels Buster through yet another window and feet-first into the chest of the butler, forcing him out of the shack. In the final car chase that concludes the inner film, Buster derails the criminals' car by throwing the exploding billiard ball, unexpectedly reincorporating this gag from the pool game.[75]

Unlike "Bill Jr.," *Sherlock Jr.* returns to the "real" world of the outer film having gained little knowledge other than the illusion that copying the actions of film heroes might help him to succeed. Ultimately the adventures of the inner film, while echoing the situations and gags of the outer film, have no effect on the outcome of the outer film's plot. While Buster is dreaming of being Sherlock Jr., his girlfriend has been busy solving the crime in the outer film—a crime that would otherwise have kept the two lovers apart. When he awakes from his dream, his girlfriend arrives to tell him of her success. Buster and his girlfriend reconcile with each other, but it is the woman, rather than Buster, who saves the day.

In the final shots of the film Buster stares out through the frame of his projection booth, searching in vain for some last bit of guidance from the inner film. When he sees the hero of the film give a ring to the heroine and kiss her, Buster copies each of these actions successfully. But the next shot shows the hero and heroine with two small children on their laps. Buster looks out at the screen (and out at us in the audience) and scratches his head. By this time, the audience must also ponder which side of which screen they are on—and what happened to the story that seemed so straightforward when the film began.

In *Sherlock Jr.*, the tension between narrative and attractions threatens to pull apart the film at its seams. The similarities between Buster's failed attempts to solve the crime in the outer film and his successful attempts as Sherlock Jr. in the inner film cohere because of his repetition of door and window imagery. The inner film, however, has no effect whatsoever on the story, making it—at twenty-four minutes out of forty-four minutes' total running time for the film—one of the longest narrative disruptions in Hollywood cinema.

The strengths of *Sherlock Jr.*, therefore, do not lie in its narrative, but rather in Keaton's imaginative expansion of the gags, stunts, and magic tricks he learned in vaudeville. As in the cyclone sequence at the end of *Steamboat Bill*, Keaton uses the repetition of gags and imagery to lend coherence to a series of attractions. This suggests an alternative way of viewing Keaton's films. As Jenkins notes in *What Made Pistachio Nuts?*, "Gags may introduce alternative patternings—categorical, spacial, associational—that compete with our interest in causality and plot progression."[76] If we view Keaton's films primarily for their narrative, these alternative patterns seem to disappear in the wake of causality. If, however, we look at Keaton's films for the elements and structures of vaudeville contained in them, different patterns emerge. These patterns—nonlinear, illogical, and often circular—reveal a less classical Keaton, who is as concerned with visual attractions as narrative ones.

All too often, scholars have conflated Keaton's visual attractions with his narrative, interpreting gag symmetry as narrative symmetry. Yet as *Sherlock Jr.* shows, Keaton's imagery often disrupts the actual line of the narrative; he uses gag symmetry to create an alternative unity. By reincorporating two central images—Buster's passing through windows and doors; Buster's narrowly escaping harm through inexplicable coincidences—Keaton is able to weave together a series of vaudeville attractions that had been independent "bits" on stage. By seizing upon film's ability to capture these vaudeville attractions in more realistic environments than the stage provides, Keaton edges the wonder and fantasy of vaudeville closer to believability. Yet by taking advantage of film's capacity to connect a succession of these attractions across vast physical spaces, he simultaneously pushes these vaudeville attractions to the limits of believability. The ensuing blend of the marvelous and the real pushes the boundaries of classical Hollywood cinema to its limits, if not beyond.

From Vaudeville to

Surrealism

$INCE THE 1920s, surrealist film-makers and artists have contended that Keaton's films share aesthetic and thematic concerns with surrealist art of the 1920s and 1930s and paid tribute to him in their work and lives. Keaton's surrealism was achieved without effort or intention; his films exemplify what the surrealists refer to as "involuntary surrealism."[1] They saw involuntary surrealism in the films of many of Keaton's silent-comedy contemporaries—Charlie Chaplin, Harry Langdon, Larry Semon, and Mack Sennett—as well as those of sound-film comedians such as the Marx Brothers. Each of these comedians appealed to the surrealists for different reasons. Most of the surrealists shared political sympathies with Chaplin and respected him for championing the poor and underprivileged;[2] they were divided, however, on the artistic merits of his films. Dalí disapproved of Chaplin's films on the ground that he tried too hard for laughter and instead favored the films of Keaton, Mack Sennett, and the Marx Brothers for their "concrete irrationality."[3] As Hammond explains, Dalí admired these films for their "gratuitous and imaginative use of objects and bodies."[4]

The surrealists' attraction to the films of Keaton, Sennett, Langdon, Semon, and the Marx Brothers stems from the shared means and aims of comedy (particularly slapstick comedy) and surrealism. J. H. Matthews asserts that the surrealists valued comedy for its ability to break the bonds of logic and social decorum: "The comic film impresses [the surrealist] as much more than an amusing movie when it liberates impulses capable of changing life's pattern, nullifying controls exercised in the everyday world by reasonable conjecture."[5] On the surface, Keaton's films may not seem in keeping with the surrealists' interest in comedy. His films frequently close on a positive note that *appears* to reinforce the traditional norms of society.[6] Each of his eleven independent silent features ends with Buster winning the hand of the woman he loves, including *Go West* (although the "woman" in this film is quite literally a cow). I argue, however, that Keaton's surrealism is not contained in the line of his narratives or the norms tentatively reinforced by his films' conclusions, but rather in the gags, stunts, and chases that disrupt the narratives. The logic of the narratives never completely defuses the potent illogic contained in the gag sequences, for although Buster may marry and be invited into society at the end of each film, he still retains his special, illogical way of looking at the world. Unlike Harold Lloyd's character, Buster will never be completely comfortable in mainstream society; he remains an outsider.

The progress of Buster as a character is not merely a question of his maturing in order to fit into society, as Moews suggests,[7] but rather a matter of his learning how to adapt his illogical way of thinking to a world that is revealed as inherently illogical itself. Keaton frequently exposes the irrational lurking beneath the surface of rational society. As Perez observes, "While on earth, he tried his best to do as earthlings do, and thereby made us aware of the peculiar systems by which we rule our lives."[8] Keaton's humor frequently calls into question the rational basis for society's rules of behavior, as in *Seven Chances* (1925) when the conventions of courtship are obliterated by the mad chase of brides and boulders. As Keaton expands the scope of his gags in the final sequences of his films, the physical world takes on an irrational life of its own, as policemen self-destruct (*Cops*), houses spin and fly (*One Week* and *Steamboat Bill, Jr.*), and bulls take over cities (*Go West*). Buster may never quite fit in with society, but in the climactic, nearly apocalyptic conclusions of his films, he finds his niche amidst the chaos of the physical world.

The Surrealists Claim Keaton

The surrealists' regard for Keaton took many forms: criticism; screenings of portions of his films; and poetry and dramatic writing based on his work. They span from the criticism of Robert Desnos, which began in 1924, to Robert Benayoun's critical and pictorial tribute, *The Look of Buster Keaton* (1982).[9] The 1920s were the period of greatest surrealist interest in the silent comedians and Keaton in particular. This should come as no surprise, given that this was a "golden age" for both Keaton and the surrealists. As

Linda Williams observes, two surrealist approaches to film co-existed during the 1920s.[10] The first, typified by Robert Desnos, proposed that film should duplicate the substance of dreams. The second approach, furthered by Jean Goudal, Antonin Artaud, and René Clair, maintained that film should produce the form of the dream rather than its content. As Richard Abel explains, in the latter school of thought "the cinema functioned not as a *representation* [of the dream] but as a *construction*, an approximation of the *form* of unconscious desire."[11] In Keaton's films, surrealists detected both dream form and content.

Desnos wrote most of his criticism of Keaton from 1924 to 1925, focusing on Keaton's short films and early features. He favored the short films for their freedom ("nothing but ease! what apparent absence of method, what seduction, what free imagination, what charming eroticism!") and criticized Keaton for his move from the freedom of these poetic films to the deliberate, overly conscious patience exhibited in *Our Hospitality*.[12] Instead, he preferred the "mechanical comedy" of *One Week*, which he compared favorably to *The Cabinet of Dr. Caligari* (1919), complimenting "the charm and the madness of its poetic excellence."[13] Desnos found *The Three Ages* to be superior to *Our Hospitality*, and with the release of *Sherlock Jr.*, he renewed his praise of Keaton, complimenting his film technique and the poetry of his comedy.[14]

Dalí and Lorca shared an enthusiasm for cinema and a respect for Keaton's work. Near the end of the summer of 1925, Dalí wrote a letter to Lorca in which he elaborated upon Keaton's film of the past year, *The Navigator*, in hyperbolic terms. "It seems that Buster Keaton has made a film on the sea-bed with his straw hat on top of his diver's helmet," wrote Dalí, perhaps inspired by a publicity photograph for the film (fig. 4.1).[15] Although Dalí's written comments on Keaton are brief—his most extensive writings on film comedy embrace the films of the Marx Brothers—a sculpture of his, *The Lobster Telephone* (1938), might reveal that the underwater sequence from *The Navigator* influenced his thinking.[16] The sculpture consists of a telephone in which the receiver has been replaced by a lobster that fits perfectly in its cradle. The connection to Buster's use of a lobster as wire-cutter in *The Navigator* might at first appear to be coincidence, if it were not for Dalí's public tribute to the underwater sequence in 1936, when, dressed up in a deep-sea diver's suit, he delivered a lecture for the 1936 International Surrealist Exhibition in London, a stunt that nearly led to his asphyxiation.[17] Dalí appears to have drawn on the underwater sequence for inspiration for his

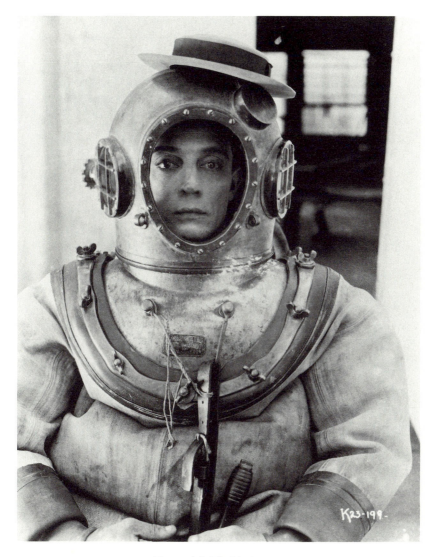

Figure 4.1. *The Navigator.*

sculpture, the common mechanism being the freeing of the lobster from its expected function.[18]

In his short surrealist play *El Paseo de Buster Keaton* (*Buster Keaton's Stroll*, written 1925, published 1928[19]), Federico García Lorca explicitly acknowledges Keaton's influence, creating the first of the surrealist homages to Keaton: derivative works of art that appropriate his character, imagery, or gags. Lorca's short play about Keaton is part of his trilogy of short plays entitled *Teatro breve*. These plays mark the beginning of Lorca's surrealist phase of writing, which culminated in his full-length play *Así que pasen cinco años* (*Once Five Years Pass*, 1929/30).

As the play opens, Buster Keaton leads his four sons onto the stage and kills them with a wooden dagger.[20] He mourns them briefly, counts the bodies, and then rides off on a bicycle. He travels across an odd landscape littered with an eclectic array of objects, animals, and people: tires, gasoline drums, a black man eating a straw hat, a parrot, an owl, an American woman, two butterflies, four seraphim, women pianists, and a wasp-waisted girl with a nightingale's head. At first he delights in his journey, oblivious to his recent murder of his sons, but the play quickly transcends the everyday reality of his bicycle trip when Lorca describes the magical capabilities of Buster Keaton's bicycle in an elaborate stage direction:

> The bicycle is one-dimensional. It can go into books and stretch itself out in bread ovens. . . . It is like any other bicycle, but this is the only one impregnated with innocence. Adam and Eve would run, frightened, across the stage if they should see a glass of water. But they would caress Buster Keaton's bicycle as they passed.[21]

When Buster Keaton falls to the ground, bemoaning a lost love, the bicycle rides off by itself, floating a hair's breadth above the ground.

Philadelphia becomes the backdrop for the rest of the play, seen in the distance. An American woman, "with celluloid eyes," approaches Buster Keaton. He notices her shoes—Lorca describes the shoes as taking "the hide of three crocodiles to make," leading Rupert C. Allen to contend that she wears slapshoes[22]—and he and the woman engage in a bit of slapstick miscommunication: she asks if he has "a sword decorated with myrtle leaves" or "a ring with a poisoned stone," and he replies by lifting first his right foot and then his left foot. Buster Keaton sighs and bemoans his inability to transform himself into a swan: "But I can't, although I would like to be. Where would I leave my hat?"[23]

A girl with the head of a nightingale enters on a bicycle and introduces herself to Buster Keaton. When he bows and offers his name, the girl faints: "Her slender legs tremble upon the lawn like zebras in agony. A gramaphone roars with a thousand simultaneous voices: 'In America there are no nightingales!'" He begs her forgiveness and kisses her, as "the badges of policemen glitter like stars" on the horizon.[24]

El Paseo de Buster Keaton has rarely been produced,[25] and scholars disagree as to Lorca's artistic intentions, alternately suggesting that the piece was an experimental farce skit; a film scenario; criticism in the form of a film scenario; or poetry that uses Buster as a ready-made protagonist and cinema as its language.[26] It stands as a testament to Lorca's vision of Keaton as a symbol of innocence, beauty, and melancholy. Moreover, the fragmented structure of *El Paseo de Buster Keaton*, Lorca's magical transformation of objects, and the disjointed narrative cuts are reminiscent of *Sherlock Jr.* (1924), released the year before Lorca wrote this play. If Lorca does not explicitly consider Keaton to be surrealist, he certainly sees Keaton as worthy of surrealist attention.

Sherlock Jr. attracted the attention of surrealists throughout the 1920s. Writing in 1924, René Clair suggests that *Sherlock Jr.* could be a model for surrealist spectators, "a sort of dramatic critique of that characteristic of the cinema comparable to the one supplied for the theater by Pirandello's *Six Characters in Search of an Author.*"[27] He thus envisions the surrealist film spectator as embarking on a journey into each film that resembles Buster's leap into the inner film of *Sherlock Jr.* Clair pays homage to *Sherlock Jr.* in his 1947 film *Le Silence est d'or* (American release, *Man About Town*), in which he appropriates the graphic-match montage in simplified form by having two characters walk across several stages at a film studio as they converse, thus making them appear to change environments rapidly.[28]

Paul Nougè's *cinépoemè* "D'Or et de Sable" (1927) explicitly appropriates the graphic-match montage from *Sherlock Jr.* He uses the rapid changes in environment that Keaton achieved to create a new version of the sequence, substituting his own set of environments and situations for Keaton's. Nougè keeps the setting inside a movie house, thus emphasizing the self-reflexive commentary on the medium of film that Clair also notes, yet his primary interest appears to be in the film's ability to displace Buster from setting to setting. Nougè displays a central preoccupation with the dream form of this sequence, focusing on the most disruptive moment in the film's narrative, a choice that I examine more closely later in this chapter.

In Antonin Artaud's essay "Cinema and Reality" (1927), which served as the foreword to his screenplay *La Coquille et le clergyman*, Artaud places Keaton's films in the context of a larger discussion of the two paths he saw for the cinema of the future. Artaud argues that the only true cinema straddles the line between "purely linear visual abstraction" and "the fundamentally psychological film."[29] He champions Keaton's and Chaplin's early films for their ability to create ironic images from the raw matter of everyday life:

Figure 4.2. *Go West*. Buster and Brown Eyes.

> The films that are most successful. . . are those dominated by a certain kind of
> humor, like the early Buster Keatons or the less human Chaplins. A cinema
> which is studded with dreams, and which gives you the physical sensation of
> pure life, finds its triumph in the most excessive sort of humor. A certain
> excitement of objects, forms, and expressions can only be translated into the
> convulsions and surprises of a reality that seems to destroy itself with an irony
> in which you can hear a scream from the extremities of the mind.[30]

For Artaud, Keaton's films embrace dream form and content, through a
"collision of objects, forms, repulsions, attractions" that is nonetheless
grounded in reality and life.

In her essay "Sur le film comique et singulièrement sur Buster Keaton"
(1927), Judith Erebé isolates what she sees as the defining elements of Kea-
'ton's style for surrealists, singling out for praise Keaton's short films, particularly *Hard Luck*, as well as *The Three Ages*, *Go West*, *The General*, and
Battling Butler. Erebé's most extensive observations about Keaton's films
center on his preference for unconventional love interests: "In *Go West* we
see Buster, disdained by the pretty girl to whom he's attracted as a lover,
attach himself instead to a cow. . . . The identification with nature, with

animal passivity, this psychological automatism, place him not on an inhuman level, but on a level of an enlarged, delivered humanity"[31] (fig. 4.2). For Erebé, Keaton's "measure cinematographic humor, rhythmic like a ballet" in films like *Battling Butler* distinguishes him from the more sentimental Chaplin.[32] She values Keaton, instead, "for having created a universe where the charm of the absurd is powerful,"[33] and she suggests that most spectators appreciate the radical juxtapositions between character and action that the films contain—"somnambulic beginning and frenetic race, apparent indifference and amassed catastophes"—the very attributes that Erebé sees as creating the absurd world in Keaton's films.[34]

In 1927, before he began making films, Luis Buñuel extolled Keaton's achievement in *College* for its simple cinematic style, in which the technique is so understated that it hardly calls attention to itself.[35] Buñuel focuses on Keaton's lack of sentimentality, his "monochord expression," and his "direct harmony with objects, situations and the other means of his work."[36] Like Dalí, Buñuel sees Keaton's dream content in his transformative work with objects. At least one segment in their classic surrealist film, *Un Chien andalou* (1929), may have been influenced by Keaton. In the introduction to the screenplay, Phillip Drummond notes a physical likeness between Keaton and the protagonist, Batcheff, and suggests that the segment in which Batcheff drags two pianos with dead donkeys in them may have been based on a similar sequence in *One Week*, in which Buster hauls a piano into his new home.[37]

Buñuel arranged showings of the American silent comedians for the Cineclub Español in Madrid beginning in 1930. His first "anthology of comedians," as he termed the screening, included excerpts from films by Ben Turpin, Harold Lloyd, Charlie Chaplin, Harry Langdon, and Keaton.[38] In his program notes for the evening, Buñuel heralded the importance of these films to surrealism: "People are so stupid, with so many prejudices, that they think that *Faust* and *Potemkin* are superior to these lunacies which are not lunacy at all but what I would call the new poetry. The Surrealist equivalent in the cinema is to be found *only in these films*. Much more genuine surrealism than in the films of Man Ray."[39]

In his essay "Films of Revolt" (1929), Robert Aron compares Keaton's films with those of Man Ray and Buñuel.[40] Aron finds Keaton's films to be superior examples of surrealism because they achieve freedom while observing the rules of narrative filmmaking and society, rather than by shunning them as the films of Man Ray and Buñuel do. Aron sees Keaton's films as embracing an anarchic world view by emphasizing the flaws in society:

"Awkwardness triumphant and heedlessness rewarded—these mark a comic spirit and a sense of anarchy that, expressed in the framework of current activity, are all the more aggressive and demoralizing."[41] He examines two of Keaton's features in particular: *Steamboat Bill, Jr.* and *The Navigator*, and praises their endings for the effortless progression from a "hopeless, hierarchical society" to "disorder of nightmarish or hallucinatory proportions."[42]

Surrealist interest in Keaton lay dormant, or at the very least unexpressed, for the next twenty years, until Jacques Brunius's 1949 essay "Experimental Film in France" (1949) ushered in a new era of surrealist writing about the silent comedians. Brunius, observing the influence of the silent comedians on the development of avant-garde film, argues, "American so-called comics, which ought rather to be qualified as poetic or lyric (Mack Sennett, Chaplin, Hal Roach, Al St. John, Larry Semon, Buster Keaton, Harry Langdon), prompted a reconsideration of logic and reason."[43] He notes the particular influence of these comedians on Man Ray and René Clair and compared Clair's *Paris qui Dort* to *Sherlock Jr.* in terms of their "demonstration by the absurd of what the cinema consists of,"[44] thus renewing the surrealists' appreciation of this film.

In his book *Le surréalisme au cinéma* (1963), Ado Kyrou discusses involuntary surrealism in the films of several of the silent comedians, including Keaton, Sennett, Langdon, and Lloyd. He recounts portions of *The Playhouse* and *Sherlock Jr.* in detail, complimenting the latter's "dazzling workmanship" and proclaiming the inner film "one of the most beautiful dreams in the history of cinema." In the graphic-match montage, Kyrou sees "a new mode of thought" in which "the surrealism . . . springs from nonsense."[45]

In the summer of 1966, Robert Benayoun, a surrealist critic, playwright, and filmmaker, published two essays on Keaton in *Positif*, which he later reprinted and expanded upon in his book *The Look of Buster Keaton* (1982). Benayoun goes further than any other critic in drawing parallels between the work of Keaton and the surrealists. Benayoun suggests some of the aesthetic concerns that Keaton shares with surrealism, comparing images from Keaton's films with the work of surrealist visual artists such as René Magritte and Salvador Dalí, the films of Luis Buñuel,[46] as well as the paintings and sculptures of acknowledged precursors of surrealism such as Marcel Duchamp, Giorgio de Chirico, and Francis Picabia. Benayoun contends that Keaton is unconsciously linked with these artists by his fascination with the mechanical and his imperturbable balance between "the serious and the ludicrous."[47]

Like Dalí, Buñuel, and Artaud, Benayoun notes Keaton's ability to transform objects: "Faced with the perverse uncertainty of a shifting, unreliable reality, Keaton merges with things—he becomes football, canoe, bicycle, wooden Indian, target, package."[48] He compares Keaton's use of double images to the paintings of Dalí and Magritte. And he sees Keaton's fascination with labyrinths, particularly in his short films,[49] as evidence of Keaton's world view: "The haunted house, electric house, prefab house, and other trick dwellings in Keaton's shorts are so many crumbling, unbalanced, changeable worlds where traps, vaults, and dungeons are always within reach, where certainty is undermined by some new peril every minute."[50]

In a 1969 essay on Larry Semon, Petr Král suggests that the unstable worlds captured in the films of Mack Sennett and Buster Keaton might be part of the reason they fell out of favor with the general public in the 1930s, when America, in the midst of the Great Depression, preferred the more conformist humor of the films produced by the Hal Roach studio.[51] Král commends "the fragile *fata morganus* of Buster Keaton."[52] His description of what he calls the "centre of gravity" of the silent film comedies is particularly apt for Keaton: "the contenance of the hero as the *lyrical subject* of all the fantastic catastrophes by which he settles his score with objective reality; catastrophes whose explosions colour his cheeks with a reflection of *inner* fire."[53] Within this world, maintains Král, the silent comedians confront audiences with their own sense of solitude and displacement.

Keaton's Affinities with Surrealism

In order to understand more fully the affinities between Keaton and the surrealists, we must first define the surrealist philosophy and aesthetic. In his first *Manifesto of Surrealism* (1924), André Breton declared, "I believe in the future resolution of these two states, dream and reality, which are seemingly so contradictory, into a kind of absolute reality, a *surreality*."[54] Surrealism aims to achieve a *super-reality*—"the semantic force of *surréalisme* is 'superrealism,'" notes Matthews[55]—by blending dream and reality. Surrealism does not advocate escaping reality by dwelling entirely in the realm of the dream; rather, the surrealists seek to reconcile the two states. It is therefore essential to keep in mind the realism in sur-realism.[56]

Surrealists frequently use realism to ground dream images in reality. Judd Chesler points out the role of realistic techniques in creating surrealist imagery: "If you add to the *trompe l'oeil* technique Dalí's highly detailed

graphic and brush style, the result is a characteristic kind of surrealist painting, that of the representation of the irrational as more 'real' than objective
reality."[57] Keaton's settings lend a similar quality of actuality to his most
fantastic gag imagery. Gilberto Perez recognizes the blend of dream and
reality in Keaton's films when he astutely remarks, "Much of the evocative
power of Keaton's films derives from their blend of actuality with a dreamlike strangeness: the dream made all the more haunting for being so convincingly materialized."[58]

Although they value film's ability to capture the disorientation of dreams,
surrealists do not advocate or endorse films that aim to avoid reality.[59] They
distinguish between the *marvelous* and the *fantastic*. The fantastic is the
product of pure fantasy and escapism, while the marvelous is based, in part,
on everyday reality; in the words of Ado Kyrou, "the marvellous explodes *on
earth*."[60] Surrealists attempt to find the marvelous in the everyday and the
everyday in the marvelous, a task for which film is well-suited. As Brunius
contends, "Film enjoys an incomparable facility for passing over the bridge
in both directions, thanks to the extraordinary and sumptuous solidity it
contributes to the creations of the mind, objectifying them in the most convincing fashion, while it makes exterior reality submit in the opposite direction to subjectivization."[61] Keaton's films frequently cross this bridge, particularly when the exquisitely detailed realism of his settings collides with
the inherent theatricality of his acrobatic stunts.[62] As I noted in Chapter 3,
Bermel argues that Keaton shifts his films in and out of farce through the use
of vast and beautiful landscapes, resulting in what Bermel terms "flashes of
lyrical respite."[63] Yet Keaton makes his landscapes such an integral part of
his comedy that his films ultimately do not shift from the farcical to the
lyrical so much as they blend the two modes. By using his landscapes not
just as backdrop for comedy but as a stimulus for it, Keaton grounds his
films in the real world; thus he approaches the surrealist aim of blending the
real world and the dream world, making, as Kyrou urges, the marvelous
explode on earth.

As a director, Keaton draws attention to his settings in contrast to his
silent-film contemporaries, who usually subordinate environment to character and gags in their films. For example, Keaton's *The General*, rather than
Chaplin's *The Gold Rush*, is best known for its detailed re-creation of period
settings. In part this is due to Keaton's painstaking efforts to create a realistic environment. Whereas Chaplin often selected his settings as a pretext for
his gags, characterization, and story, Keaton integrated his settings into the
development and creation of his films, frequently improvising his stories
and gags from the setting.

By selecting primarily long shots and long takes to capture the action, Keaton further focuses our attention on the environments in his films. Keaton may have initially chosen this cinematic style in order to display his "performance virtuosity," as I suggest in Chapter 2, but it quickly became one of the trademarks of his filmmaking style, one that remained consistent throughout his silent feature films regardless of his collaborators. By minimizing his use of fast-paced editing, he accentuates the audience's perception of the action as a single image. We see the visual patterns created by his comic action foregrounded on a single, immovable landscape: the Western plains and city streets in *Go West*; the hills of the boulder sequence in *Seven Chances*; the oceanliner in *The Navigator*. This adds a quality of indelibility to his film imagery. Because he frequently draws on his environment as the source of his gags, the gags become inseparable from the environment. By choosing to capture his gags and stunts in long takes, he creates single images from gags—the falling wall in *Steamboat Bill, Jr.* (fig. 3.2), the wall safe/front door in *Sherlock Jr.*, the waterwheel/treadmill in *Daydreams*. The surrealist quality of these gags comes across even when they are reproduced as still frames because each gag simultaneously fills the entire frame and may be perceived in a single shot from one vantage point. In addition, Keaton frequently captures his environments in classically framed shots: frontal views that are symmetrical and balanced. The classicism of his shots is yet another realistic convention that his gags and stunts undercut through juxtaposition, creating tension between the logic of his shot composition and the illogic of his gags.

Film provided Keaton with the ability to expand the scale of not only his settings, but also his stunts. The Three Keatons' vaudeville routine was constrained by the size of the stage and the limited number of Keaton family members. As I described in Chapter 1, the Three Keatons' best-known and most frequently performed routine was a variation on a chase or a cat-and-mouse game. Buster would follow Joe and try to disturb him, causing Joe to chase him around the stage and literally hurl him into the scenery. In adapting chases to the screen, Keaton expanded their scope far beyond that found in the films of his comic predecessors, the Keystone Cops. He created spectacular chases on a scale that remains unsurpassed to this day. As Keaton enlarges the chase to absurd dimensions, he crosses Brunius's bridge from *reality* to the *marvelous*. Keaton's comic chases begin to share an affinity with surrealism because of the elements of his cinematic style described above. His preference for long shots, long takes, and vast realistic landscapes grounds his chases in strict classical realism, while the progressively larger and larger number of people, objects, and animals in the chases exceeds any reasonable expectations on the part of the audience, becoming dreamlike—a dream made solid and palpable through Keaton's meticulous realism.

In this way, Keaton's realistic environments and his use of the long shot and long take prevent his gags and stunts from slipping over the edge into pure fantasy. The realistic long shots of the church and streets in *Seven Chances*, captured in deep focus, balance the dreamlike quality created by the sheer quantity of brides; the long shots of the hillside prove that several hundred boulders actually "chased" Buster as well. As Keaton places improbable gags such as these in more and more realistic environments, he produces moments that straddle the line between dream and reality—the line that the surrealists call the marvelous.

The underwater sequence in *The Navigator* shows the length to which Keaton would go to capture a gag sequence in the most realistic detail possible. The original plan to film the sequence in a converted swimming pool was dropped when alterations to the pool caused its bottom to collapse. When he tried to shoot on the ocean, he found that the water was too murky, so the entire crew moved to Lake Tahoe. In order to film under water, Keaton had to use a submergible diving bell for the camera and cameramen. Since he was filming in the dead of winter, the water was exceptionally cold. In order to prevent the camera lens from fogging, the crew had to refrigerate the diving bell, causing the bell to grow so cold that the cameramen's health was endangered and shooting had to be limited to increments of only a few minutes. Keaton went to all of this trouble to create a sequence that runs only a few minutes.[64]

The gags in the scene are typical vaudeville fare made strange by their placement in a strikingly new underwater context. Keaton's insistence upon performing the gags under water created the surreality in the scene, for the more real the underwater environment appears, the more surreal Buster's actions become. By actually performing his gags in this environment, Keaton realized the surrealists' goal of breaking down the rigidity of people's perceptions about what is possible and what is impossible, challenging what Breton describes as "this cancer of the mind which consists of thinking all too sadly that certain things 'are,' while others, which well might be, 'are not.' "[65]

Even the simplest gag, a Keaton fall, takes on new meaning under water. As Buster first plummets to the ocean floor, he falls flat on his bottom; his legs are spread wide as in many of his previous falls stretching back to his earliest vaudeville appearances. Yet the change in environment—from the confines of the stage to the depths of the ocean—and the change in costume—from his trademark porkpie hat to a diver's suit—alter our perception of his fall. Dalí's letter to Lorca about *The Navigator* captures the surrealism latent in the incongruous juxtaposition of Keaton's gags with the diving suit and underwater environment.[66] The imaginative disruptions of reality that Buster performs under water become surreal because of the context in which Keaton has placed them. For example, Buster performs two transformation gags in the sequence. In the first, he uses a lobster as a wire-cutter. In the second, he captures a swordfish and uses it to defend himself in a sword fight with another swordfish. In both gags, the comedy stems from using an object (in this case, animals) in an inappropriate or unusual manner. Yet it is Keaton's attention to the realistic execution of these gags in their strange underwater environment that makes them disorienting and hence surreal.

Surrealists employed juxtaposition in a similar manner as a method of removing poetic images from the realm of the rational. In a 1935 lecture in Prague entitled "Surrealist Situation of the Object," Breton summarized the surrealists' investigation of the use of incongruity, juxtaposition, and transformation, a procedure he termed "the cultivation of the effects of a systematic bewildering."[67] In particular, Breton focused on the creation of surrealist objects, which he traced to Lautréamont's phrase, "Beautiful like the fortuitous meeting, on a dissection table, of a sewing machine and an umbrella."[68] Breton's elaboration of the phrase bears quoting at length here:

> A ready-made reality, whose naive purpose seems to have been fixed once and for all (an umbrella), finding itself suddenly in the presence of another very distant and no less absurd reality (a sewing machine), in a place where both must feel *out of their element* (on an operating table) will, by this very fact, escape its naive purpose and lose its identity; because of the detour through what is relative, it will pass from absolute falseness to a new absolute that is true and poetic: the umbrella and the sewing machine will make love. The way this procedure works seems to me to be revealed in this very simple example. A complete transmutation followed by a pure act such as love will necessarily be produced every time that the given facts—*the coupling of two realities which apparently cannot be coupled on a plane which apparently is not appropriate to them*—render conditions favorable.[69]

A similar relationship between two "distant realities" occurs in the underwater sequence of *The Navigator*, in which Keaton places vaudeville humor in an incongruous setting at the bottom of the ocean. In a subsequent sequence the parallels are even more striking. Buster rescues his girlfriend, Betsy, by floating on his back on the water and allowing her to use his body

Figure 4.3. *The Navigator*. Buster as raft.

as a raft (fig. 4.3). Encased in his diving suit and disconnected from his oxygen source, Buster nearly suffocates—shades of Dalí!—in the midst of their attempts to survive. Buster must become an object (a raft) in order to save both their lives through the fortuitous meeting of a diving suit, a woman, and a makeshift paddle atop the ocean.[70]

Keaton's gags in *College* capture the spirit of the surrealists' investigation of the uses of objects, an attribute of his filmmaking that Buñuel championed.[71] Buster cannot throw a javelin properly, but he can throw a lamp like a javelin; he breaks his vaulting pole on the track, but successfully transforms a clothes line support into a pole that he uses to vault into his girlfriend's window and rescue her from his rival. His transformation gags capture the spirit of the surrealists' desire to break free from the bonds of everyday rational thinking, as well as reflecting their obsession with transforming everyday objects into marvelous ones.

The surrealists deployed objects and combinations of objects in the service of the "disruption of objective reality."[72] Surrealist objects take many forms. The found object, the interpreted object, the ready-made object, the assemblage, the incorporated object, the phantom object, and the dreamt object are just a few of the categories that the surrealists and their adherents

Figure 4.4. *Sherlock Jr.* Convertible as sailboat.

devised to describe their bewildering creations.[73] In producing these objects, surrealists aimed to make the marvelous concrete. Regardless of category, the goal of the surrealists' explorations of the object was to challenge its accepted function.[74] The surrealists invented games designed to encourage such explorations:

> Following the lead of Marcel Duchamp's "readymades," the Surrealists would circulate random objects among themselves, posing irrelevant questions about their function. A piece of rose-colored velvet, for example, elicited the question With whom should it meet on a dissection table for it to be beautiful? These games . . . were created as ways of separating the object from its functional connection to a context in order to create new associations emanating from the concrete density of the thing itself.[75]

Keaton's gags frequently exhibit an attitude toward objects akin to that of surrealism. He is forever using objects in unusual and unforeseen ways, as in *Sherlock Jr.* when he turns an automobile into a sailboat by raising its convertible top as a sail (fig. 4.4). Keaton shares the surrealists' interest in transformation: the ability to see things not as they are, but as they may be, must be, or are in the process of becoming. In *One Week*, when Keaton uses

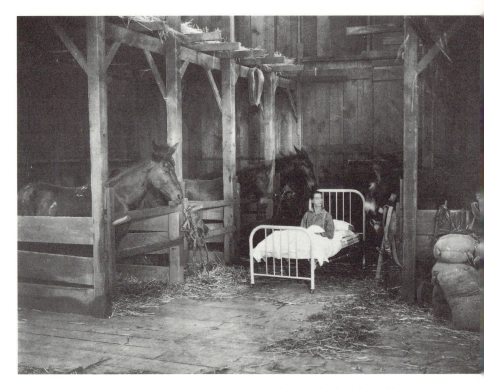

Figure 4.5. *Steamboat Bill, Jr.* Buster's hospital bed in the stable.

the porch railing of the house as a stepladder, he violates our expectations
for such an object. When he transforms a hospital bed into a mobile vehicle
in *Steamboat Bill, Jr.*, he changes our perception of the essential nature and
function of a bed, a perception that is further made strange when the bed
transports Buster to the stables (fig. 4.5). Examples of Keaton's transformation of objects abound: he uses his clip-on tie as a mustache in order to hide
from the police in *Cops*; he uses a bass drum as a boat and a violin as his
paddle in *The Playhouse*. Moreover, because of Keaton's fondness for the
long shot and long take, his object-gags often resemble surrealist images,
especially when reproduced as still photographs. For example, in order to
hide from the police in *Daydreams*, Keaton uses the waterwheel of a boat as
a treadmill (fig. 4.6). As Benayoun observes, Buster "merges with things"[76]
in his films and thus questions the notion that people have rational control
over objects in an inherently orderly universe.

Keaton's most complete merger of man and object occurs during the

Figure 4.6. *Daydreams.* Buster's watermill/treadmill.

graphic-match montage in *Sherlock Jr.* Buster appears to fuse with the celluloid of film itself, as he remains glued in his place throughout the constantly
shifting locales of the montage. The surrealists were most attracted to the
magic of the inner film, yet magic is not inherently surrealist. Chesler observes that magic must possess two qualities in order to appeal to the surrealists: "First, it can be given no logical explanation; and second, it would
have to be presented with a validity at least equal to that of objective reality."[77] Keaton's attention to realistic detail in the magic tricks of *Sherlock Jr.*
makes them so convincingly real that the magic transcends its narrative
justification as a dream sequence and exceeds all "logical explanation" for
how Keaton achieved it.

Inspired by the graphic-match montage in *Sherlock Jr.*, surrealist Paul
Nougé wrote the *cinépoème* "D'Or et de Sable," in which he created his own
version of the sequence:

> Buster Keaton leaves the auditorium to take a hand in what is happening on
> the screen, and suddenly looks at it. He picks a quarrel with the suitor who is
> also the detective, he slaps him in the face, but his fist gets lost in a foun-
> tain. . . . He wants to pick an apple and it is the nose of an old lady that he

pinches disrespectfully, in the middle of a crowd. He runs off, he escapes his pursuers with difficulty, a door opens, he climbs a staircase, another door (which closes behind him), there is an armchair, oops! he falls in a sitting position into a fishing bark lost in the middle of a deserted sea. The bark is empty, no oars, no supplies. . . . There, a scent bottle! He straightens and hands to the elegant lady the bracelet which she is awaiting, smiling. Delighted, Buster Keaton smiles also but at a blind man waiting for charity. Buster Keaton leaves the screen to enter the auditorium again.[78]

Nougé retains the basic premise of the film in his *cinépoème*: from the auditorium, Buster enters the action on the screen in order to fight a rival suitor. From this point, Nougé substitutes his own set of actions for the ones performed by Keaton.[79] What remains consistent, though, is both men's use of instantaneous transformations. In the film, Buster sits on a mound of sand in the desert, only to be surprised by a wave crashing over him when the scene unexpectedly shifts to the ocean. This transformation is equivalent to the section of Nougé's *cinépoème* in which Buster sits down in an armchair only to find himself seated in a fishing bark on the sea. In another section of the sequence, as Buster looks down over the edge of a cliff, the scene shifts and he is surrounded by lions. A similar substitution occurs in the *cinépoème* when Buster returns a lady's smile only to find a blind man in her place.

By basing his *cinépoème* entirely on the graphic-match montage, Nougé places primary emphasis on the most disruptive moment in *Sherlock Jr.*, when Keaton figuratively and literally breaks the bonds of the narrative and crosses from the everyday reality of the outer film to the fantastic dream images of the inner film. Surrealists tend to gravitate to such moments as this one in Keaton's films, where he breaks free from the narrative. Jeremy Cott emphasizes the importance of the dialectic between structure and disruption to Keaton's surrealism when he notes: "Taken as a whole, a Keaton film requires just enough regularity to make fine, structural irregularities meaningful. His realism grades easily into surrealism, then, because surrealism in his films doesn't distort things themselves; it distorts only the relationship between them."[80] While scholars with a classical bias view the triumph and ultimate contribution of Keaton in terms of his ability to integrate gags into classically constructed narratives, those who write of Keaton's surrealism tend to focus their attention on the points at which gags depart from the narrative—the "structural irregularities" to which Cott refers. In her influential study of surrealist film, *Figures of Desire*, Linda Wil-

liams convincingly argues that critics and scholars who claim that surrealists reject all artistic form "confuse an important Surrealist goal—Breton's
famous psychic automatism freed from all *reasoning* controls—with a general freedom from *any* form."[81] Williams locates the surrealists' interest in
form in two places. First, surrealists frequently imitated the "mechanics of
a dream" in their forays into film. Second, surrealists used form to create a
tension between form and content. In the film scenarios of Robert Desnos,
for example, Williams asserts that "surreality arises . . . from the playful way
in which he first sets up and then transgresses the narrative forms that em-
body these contents."[82] Furthermore, in a striking parallel to the feature
films of Keaton and his contemporaries, the narrative that Desnos strives to
disrupt is frequently melodramatic or farcical.[83] Traditional narratives can
serve to ground a film in what audiences perceive as "reality," thus providing a basis for the surrealist journey from reality to the marvelous.[84]

Tom Gunning argues that Keaton's use of moments of unbridled spectacle
cle places him squarely in the tradition of the "cinema of attractions," an
exhibitionist cinema that emphasizes film's ability to show things rather
than tell stories.[85] Gunning argues that the cinema of attractions was the
dominant form of filmmaking until approximately 1906–7, when narrative
film began to dominate filmmaking practice. Yet according to Gunning, the
cinema of attractions remains alive, though dormant, in the films of a few
distinctive filmmakers, including Keaton: "Now in a period of American
avant-garde cinema in which the tradition of contemplative subjectivity has
perhaps run its (often glorious) course, it is possible that this earlier carni-
val of the cinema, and the methods of popular entertainment, still provide
an unexhausted resource—a Coney Island of the avant-garde, whose never
dominant but always sensed current can be traced from Méliès through
Keaton, through *Un Chien andalou* (1928), and Jack Smith."[86] Gunning not
only notes the structural affinities of Keaton's work with the quintessential
surrealist film *Un Chien andalou*, he also perceives the alliance between popular entertainment and the cinema of attractions. By placing Keaton in the
tradition of the cinema of attractions, Gunning directly opposes critics with
a classical bias who dismiss Keaton's attractions as artistic flourishes or narrative excess. It is precisely the disruptiveness of Keaton's attractions that
creates the greatest affinity between his films and those of the surrealists.
This is particularly evident in Keaton's use of multiples: Williams notes that
several surrealist films use the repetition of a single form to disturb narrative
causality, citing the repetition of circular shapes in *Un Chien andalou*, as
well as in Desnos's screenplay *Minuit à quatorze heures*.[87] In the latter, the

final image bears a striking resemblance to several images in Keaton's *Seven Chances*:

> [The narrative] is soon quite literally swallowed up by what at first seem to be inconsequential formal repetitions. These formal repetitions appear first as rings in the water where the old lover drowns, then in circular reflections from the sun, then in the round pupils of the lover's eyes and the round shape of the moon, until gradually, after many intricate variations, both the lovers and their house are swallowed up by a concrete and all-devouring round ball. Thus a purely formal shape existing initially as the form of other objects . . . takes on greater and greater materiality, until it becomes a subject in its own right, swallowing up everything else in the scenario, including (literally) the incipient psychology of the characters.[88]

In a similar way, Keaton's escalation of multiples in *Seven Chances*—from brides to clocks to bees to boulders—eventually "swallows up" the narrative. The final sequence of Buster stuck between hundreds of brides and boulders is so powerful that it stands up as a short film by itself and is frequently shown as an independent excerpt in documentaries on Keaton's life and work. In the cyclone sequence of *Steamboat Bill, Jr.* and the inner film of *Sherlock Jr.*, the repetition of doors and windows exerts a similar force upon the narratives.

Film provided Keaton with the tools to link gag sequences such as these, a linkage that would have been impossible to perform on the vaudeville stage: long shots and takes established the actuality of his performances; editing tied together gags into a trajectory; and location shooting provided the vast realistic landscapes for his films, grounding them in the real world. Yet the vividly captured reality of Keaton's environment inevitably functions in irrational ways. As Keaton expands the illogic of his gags to embrace the operation of the entire world, the world appears to function as a gigantic Rube Goldberg device. In the climactic sequences of his feature films in particular, the world seems to have a mind of its own, as cyclones, driverless motorcycles, and boulders move Buster along a path he cannot see, but nonetheless must follow. In these moments of spectacle and excess, Keaton visually expresses his view of the world with great eloquence. In Keaton's world, anything is possible—objects come to life, people multiply to absurd numbers, humor changes from a way of dealing with life to a way of living— and survival depends on one's acceptance of the existence of the irrational. Each Keaton gag overturns our restrictive assumption that every action causes a logical reaction; each gag sequence displays the overtaking of the world by the mechanisms of chaos. Instead of finding straightforward solutions to his dilemmas, Keaton discovers eccentric resolutions by accepting and harnessing the precarious and volatile nature of the world. By fully exploiting film's ability to give concrete form to the irrational humor of his vaudeville-inspired *Weltanschauung*, Keaton crosses the bridge from vaudeville to surrealism, achieving the surrealists' goal of blending dream and reality in cinema, and thereby expanding our vision of human life in a material world.

·5·

Beyond Surrealism:
Keaton's Legacy

LIKE HIS silent film character, Buster Keaton was a survivor. Despite his dismissal by MGM in 1933, his ongoing battle with alcoholism through much of the 1930s and 1940s, and his relative obscurity until the final years of his life, Keaton continued to make a moderate living as a performer.[1] Though he never regained the budget and artistic control necessary for the realization of the cinematic vision he developed during the 1920s, Keaton always worked, in film and later in television. Yet during these dark days of his career, his influence seemed to wane. Surrealists no longer invoked his name; cinematographers no longer studied his camera techniques. His name, at least in the public eye, became equated with the generic image of the old silent film comedies—that of a pie-thrower, despite the fact that Keaton never threw a single pie in any of the films he directed during the 1920s. Keaton simply used such a misconception to survive, making guest appearances on television variety shows with comedians such as Ed Wynn, in which he threw pies as if he were born to do only that. The lessons in publicity he learned from his father during his childhood ensured his living during the lean years.

Yet in the 1960s, Keaton re-emerged as a living icon of the silent-film era and began to get steady work as a film actor. Seeing Keaton in his last films is alternately exciting and depressing—exciting because he retains much of his earlier vitality and humanity as a performer, yet depressing because he continued to be denied the opportunity to direct his own films and fully control his working process. Nonetheless, to survive at the end of his career, Keaton did not become merely an actor-pawn in other people's films; on the contrary, he survived by holding on to whatever measure of artistic control he could acquire. Fortunately, two of Keaton's last and to my mind most significant film appearances—in Gerald Potterton's *The Railrodder* (1965) and Samuel Beckett's *Film* (1965)—were well-documented, and the records of his working process provide a lucid picture of Keaton's artistic concerns and methods in the more restricted circumstances of his last films.[2]

These films were debuts, of a sort, for both directors: Alan Schneider enjoyed the distinction of having directed the American premieres of Beckett's major plays, but *Film* was to prove his first and last film-directing experience; and although Gerald Potterton was an accomplished young director of animated films (he would go on to create animation for *Yellow Submarine* [1968] and *Heavy Metal* [1981]), *The Railrodder* was his first live action film. For this reason, Keaton might be considered the best or the worst possible actor for these men to employ. Although he brought a wealth of experience to these projects and was, by all accounts, an extremely patient and dedicated performer, Keaton also retained strong ideas about how films should be made, and, as I have described in the previous chapters, he thrived in an environment where he was allowed to improvise. Improvisation and collaboration flourish in an atmosphere of trust, and new film directors, no matter how accomplished in other media, might find it difficult to cede a certain amount of artistic control to a more experienced actor/ director like Keaton.

Gerald Potterton's *The Railrodder*

Gerald Potterton gave Keaton much greater freedom to improvise and collaborate during the filming of *The Railrodder* than Alan Schneider allowed him in *Film*. Potterton originally conceived of the project essentially as an animated film: "Up to that time I had worked mostly in animation, so my initial idea was to place Buster's live-action face on an animated body and send him across Canada."[3] After he discovered that Keaton was still alive— like many people who had seen only Keaton's silent films, Potterton assumed he had died years ago—he contacted Keaton and hired him as a performer. But once on location in Canada, Potterton discovered that Keaton was more than just a live body for his first live action film; he still had an active comic imagination and the desire to contribute to the process of filmmaking.

Several factors led Potterton to allow Keaton more artistic freedom than he had enjoyed since the 1920s. Because Potterton had little more than the germ of an idea for a film when he contacted Keaton about making *The*

Railrodder, much of the film was developed by the two men while they were shooting, and this provided Keaton with the opportunity to suggest and shape gags. By the time filming began in the fall of 1964, Potterton had written a beginning and an ending for the film, a couple of gags, and little else. Intended as a travel film to advertise the beauty of Canada, it would follow Buster on his journey across Canada from the Atlantic Ocean to the Pacific Ocean in a tiny rail car for one. Although Potterton knew little of Keaton's filmmaking methods (none of the critical and biographical books on Keaton had yet been published), he found himself inadvertently working in the Keaton style, collaborating and improvising gags within the sketchy scenario. Moreover, as the film was produced in Canada instead of Hollywood, Potterton and Keaton were not constrained by strict shooting schedules, an oppressive studio hierarchy, or extensive pre-production planning.

Potterton introduced two important elements into *The Railrodder* that were consistent with Keaton's work during the silent film era—a porkpie hat and the miniature rail car. As I discussed in Chapter 2, Keaton's porkpie hat serves as one of the key elements in establishing his screen persona. Age might have changed Keaton's face, added weight to his body, and deprived him of the ability and agility to perform the most dangerous acrobatics of his early films, but his porkpie hat atop his head, framing his face and tipped at a slight angle, remains a telltale sign of his identity. The knowledgeable film-viewing public still identifies the porkpie hat with Buster Keaton, and its mere presence erases the possibility of misidentifying the older Buster in *The Railrodder*. Upon finding himself swiftly speeding across Canada on a small, speeding trolley, Buster looks into the storage compartment and magically finds a porkpie hat and jacket awaiting him. Comforted by his old costume, he dons the hat and heads off down the more than three thousand miles of railroad track that stretch before him.[4]

The second Keatonesque element that Potterton chose for the film—the tiny rail car Buster navigates in the film—was probably an outgrowth of the somewhat limited budget for the film. In retrospect, it might appear to have been an obvious choice on Potterton's part to make one of Keaton's final films a train trip, since by this time Keaton's revived reputation was strongly connected with *The General*, one of his two silent feature films in wide circulation at this time. Yet, strangely enough, no other film had put Keaton on a train since *Around the World in Eighty Days* (1956). Moreover, by choosing, for whatever reason, to have Buster ride a diminutive train, Potterton emulated Keaton's use of miniatures for comic effect, which can be traced all the way back to The Three Keatons (see fig. 2.2). Buster's earliest

Figure 5.1. *The Navigator*. Buster with the tiny cannon.

stage appearances depended upon his dressing up as an identical miniature of his father, an image he invoked in *The Boat* and *The Three Ages* (see fig. 2.3 and fig. 2.4); and in his silent films he frequently battles Lilliputian machines, such as the tiny canon in *The Navigator* that becomes ensnared beneath his feet so that Buster finds himself the perpetual target of this cannon (fig. 5.1). Keaton creates a similar sense of disproportion by placing himself next to enormous objects that dwarf him, as in *The Navigator*, when he eats with oversize utensils (fig. 5.2) and attempts to tow the ocean liner back out to sea with a rowboat.

Potterton's choice of the miniature rail car for *The Railrodder* proved to be an inspired one, for, as the film has come to be identified over the years as Keaton's film as much as, if not more than, Potterton's, film scholars and Keaton fans now view it in the context of Keaton's career and works—Buster, aged but undaunted, steaming once again across the vast panorama

Figure 5.2. *The Navigator*. Buster with oversize utensils.

of North America. The film presents a somewhat romantic view of Buster: no longer locked in perpetual battle with this train, he seems comfortable driving it, as if he has found the perfect fit between the scope of his dreams and the size of the machine that will allow him to fulfill them.

As this was Potterton's first live action film, he proved remarkably open to Keaton's suggestions for gags throughout the project. John Spotton's documentary of the making of the film, *Buster Keaton Rides Again* (1965), captures the evolution of several of Keaton's gags for the film. The first of these gags occurs right after Buster discovers the miniature rail car. As he heads west on the tracks, he finds a full-size train bearing down upon him from the opposite direction. Unperturbed, Buster calmly motions to the train to move out of his way, and, as if following his silent order, the train slips onto a parallel track to his left as Buster's rail car simultaneously shifts onto a track to his right.

The documentary footage of the making of this gag shows the extent of the artistic control over gags Potterton allowed Keaton: Keaton suggests the gag, outlines the camera shots on a sketch pad, and explains how to time the sequence so that the two trains reach the switch point in the tracks at the same moment, revealing the precision of his cinematic vision. At the same

Figure 5.3. *The Railrodder*. Afternoon tea.

time, Keaton demonstrates how his vision has evolved over the decades. In the early parts of most of Keaton's silent films, he struggles with machines; only in the films' climactic sequences does he master them. In *The Railrodder*, Buster confidently handles his small vehicle from the start as if he has retained the knowledge from all his previous cinematic adventures (fig. 5.3).

It might seem as if this is a return to the filmmaking of Keaton's earliest, silent, two-reel shorts—shooting from a simple scenario with no substantial written script, improvising gags, and focusing on gag sequences rather than overall narrative—and in many ways it is reminiscent of Keaton's first release as a director, *One Week*. John C. Tibbetts suggests that *The Railrodder* is "crafted and structured like one of Buster's silent short comedies,"[5] yet beneath the surface of the film lurks a different structure, a vaudeville-inspired assemblage of gags, but one which for the most part refrains from reincorporating gags and studiously avoids a spectacular "topper" at the end of the film. While the film follows Keaton's short films in organizing a series of gags around a single prop, in this case the rail car, Potterton either neglects to escalate, or purposefully avoids escalating, the physical scale of the gags. It is difficult to tell whether this is by choice, or whether the film's budget or Keaton's failing health necessitated it. During the filming of *The Railrodder*, Eleanor Keaton, Buster's wife, explained that Keaton had learned to curtail his more dangerous, larger-scale gags: "He was known as the 'Little Iron Man' around the studio. Nothing stopped him, or there wasn't anything he didn't try. He slowed down and come [sic] around to the line of thinking that he can do other, smaller-type things or less dangerous things that can be almost as funny. Well he may not consider them as funny as falling off the whole top of a building or something, like he might have done earlier, but they're funny enough to get by, let's put it that way."[6]

Although Potterton was in many ways the most generous collaborator with whom Keaton worked in the last part of his career, their working relationship was not without conflict, and they fought most strenuously over the scale of some of the gags in the film. Keaton had been making films before Potterton's birth, but Potterton was not afraid to assert himself with the film legend, and they argued vehemently about one particular gag sequence, which was to be performed on a high, single-track suspension bridge. Initially, the two men developed the gag together, improvising the sequence on paper the night before shooting it, but they disagreed as to the specific actions Buster would perform. In Keaton's version of the gag, he gets tangled up in an enormous map as he approaches the bridge, and the map spreads out over his entire body like a gigantic sail. At the same time, three small, two-seat rail cars approach the bridge from the opposite direction. As the drivers notice Buster speeding blindly toward them, they quickly reverse their direction. Potterton added a small twist to this ending: as the three rail cars leave the bridge, the drivers pull their cars off the tracks and into three small huts beside the tracks, just in time for Buster to pass them as he disentangles himself from the map.

But by the next morning, Potterton began to have reservations about Keaton's safety and substituted a new action for the map business. In Potterton's revised version of the gag, Buster is doing his laundry and remains oblivious to the oncoming traffic. Keaton was understandably bothered by the substitution, and consequently Potterton and Keaton experienced their first major battle for artistic control. As Keaton told John Spotton after shooting the sequence Potterton's way, "I didn't know he shifted gags on me. . . . I thought I was going to be fouled up with the map because I decided that last night. He decided not to and I didn't know it."[7] The statement reveals Keaton's central artistic concerns. Through his choice of words, Keaton exhibits his concern for retaining artistic control over the gag—"I thought I was going to be fouled up with the map because *I decided that last night*."[8] Further, his preference for the map gag displays Keaton's continual focus on making each gag as visually powerful as he could within his somewhat restricted physical capabilities.

After the first set of shots had been filmed, Keaton renewed his arguments with Potterton:

> *Potterton:* Don't forget that there's still two other shots to complete the sequence, Buster. There's a long shot of the bridge, them going over. That's the whole [thing]; the center of the gag . . . is that long shot on that bridge.
>
> *Keaton:* No, the bridge is not your gag. The bridge is only the suspense, a thrill. There's no gag in the bridge at all, doesn't mean a god-damn thing. It's only a dangerous place to be when there is a collision. That's the only thing that's funny.[9]

Much to Potterton's dismay, Keaton would not be dissuaded, and back in the railway car in which the cast and crew traveled, Keaton continued to assert to his wife, Eleanor, that the gag had to be done his way: "Anytime you're shooting gags or laying them out in advance you so often run into guesswork. Well maybe his way's better than doing it mine. Then you try to sell yourself one way or the other because there is a certain amount of guess. Has to be. But every now and then, ain't no guesswork. This is one of them."[10] Keaton's insistence on performing his own stunts compounded the problem. As Potterton told Tibbetts, "It would have been easy to use a double, but Buster insisted on doing it himself. He insisted that everything be real, like everything else in the movie: If he was going to cook an omelet or shave with soapy water then he wanted to really do it. He didn't like to 'cheat' with those kinds of things."[11] In the end, Potterton succumbed to Keaton's arguments, the force of his personality, or perhaps his greater years and experience, and he filmed the sequence Keaton's way.

Their disagreement suggests that Keaton continued to hold strong opinions about filmmaking, opinions he was willing to fight for. Nevertheless, Keaton never questioned Potterton's story construction; he recognized that he could exert a greater influence on *The Railrodder* by suggesting gags than he could by proposing plot ideas. Even in the 1920s, when he had far greater artistic control over his films, Keaton often focused on gags to counteract plots that he disdained, as in *Seven Chances*, when he devoted the entire second half of the film to gags—the rapidly growing hordes of multiple brides and boulders that chase Buster toward his destiny. In *The Railrodder*, Keaton and Potterton started with the same elements that Keaton had used as a foundation for filmmaking since his earliest films—a beginning and an end—and within this framework, the artistic focus of both men remained resolutely on gags. Keaton concentrated on gags, therefore, because gags were the main substance of the film.

The Railrodder's emphasis on gags, however, never threatens its narrative integrity because the film shares a device—a parallel set of train tracks—with one of Keaton's earlier films, *The General*. But the similarity between the two films ends at this point. In *The Railrodder*, the tracks provide Buster with a destination and a route and thus prevent the gags from straying too far from the simple narrative line. Nonetheless, Buster's excursion in *The Railrodder* has none of the drive of his journey in *The General*, which gains momentum by virtue of the escalating stakes (the rescue of his train and girlfriend) of the chase sequence. Moreover, the symmetry of the chase in *The General* allows Buster to revisit and amend on the return trip all of his comic failings from his trip north. What is missing in *The Railrodder*, then, are the key elements of classical Hollywood cinema—narrative economy, causality, and momentum—that Keaton balanced in varying proportions with elements of vaudeville in his silent features.

By excluding these elements from the film, Potterton shifts the structure of his film closer to that of Keaton's early short films. But perhaps because Potterton and Keaton worked together only once, the film lacks the vaudeville elements that Keaton traditionally used in his films to create structural cohesiveness. There is little to bind together the separate gag sequences of *The Railrodder* beyond the railroad tracks and the final gag of the film. In the final sequence, Buster has reached his goal—the Pacific Ocean—and steps off the rail car to gaze at the ocean. As he strolls leisurely toward the water, an Asian man emerges from the Pacific, unseen by Buster, wearing a hat and suit identical to the one Buster wore at the beginning of the film.[12] Mirroring Buster's actions, the man examines the rail car and rides off. When Buster turns around, he finds that the car has vanished, and bravely begins his three thousand mile return trip down the tracks on foot.

The gag embraces some key elements from Keaton's past work—the use of a mirror image of Buster, the reincorporation of an earlier gag—yet the payoff seems meek by Keaton standards because of the small physical scale of the gag. Compared to Keaton's early work, this "topper" falls short and fails to provide a sense of closure to the film. Yet, on another level, the gag seems a fittingly dry final joke at the end of Keaton's career. His railroad trip has become a casual sightseeing tour; his destination has no concrete goal or deadline; there is no woman to be won at the end of the tracks. And since he performs all of his tasks admirably on the trip west, there is no need to prove himself on the way back east. He can simply walk home.

Samuel Beckett's *Film*

In June 1964, shortly before he acted in *The Railrodder*, Keaton began work on *Film*, Samuel Beckett's only script written expressly for the cinema. An independent short film commissioned by Evergreen Theatre as part of a trilogy of films by avant-garde playwrights (the other scripts, written by Eugene Ionesco and Harold Pinter, were not produced), *Film* represented the movie-directing debut of Alan Schneider. Keaton found himself paired with a cinematic novice again, albeit one with an impressive list of theater credentials. Worse yet, Keaton had not been Schneider's or Beckett's first choice for the project. In his essay "On Directing *Film*," Schneider reveals that Keaton was at best their fourth choice, suggested by Beckett as an eleventh-hour replacement for veteran Beckett actor Jack MacGowran:

> During a transatlantic call one day (as I remember) [Beckett] shattered our desperation over the sudden casting crisis by calmly suggesting Buster Keaton. Was Buster still alive and well? (He was.) How would he react to acting in Beckett material? (He'd been offered the part of Lucky in the original American *Godot* some years back, and had turned it down.) Would this turn out to be a Keaton film rather than a Beckett film?[13]

After reading the script, Keaton met with Schneider and expressed his reservations about the project; he was, in Schneider's words, "not sure what could be done to fix it up."[14] Schneider's account of their meeting is nothing short of contemptuous; he rejects Keaton's appraisal of the script along with his offer of help as hopelessly dated, "From 1927."[15] From this inauspicious beginning developed the unlikely collaboration between Samuel Beckett and Buster Keaton entitled *Film*.

Keaton plays "O," a character Beckett describes in the original screenplay as an object being pursued by "E," the eye and alter ego of O, played by the motion picture camera. Throughout the film, O attempts to avoid the piercing stare of E by running and hiding, one aspect of O's overall fear of being perceived. O shuns the curious gazes of passersby on the street, attempts to hide his face from a tenant inside his mother's apartment building, and, once safely inside the apartment, rids the room of all possible eyes that could see him—those in photographs, those belonging to a cat and dog, even objects that are shaped like eyes. Having safely completed this task, he begins to fall asleep, only to be awakened by the eye of the camera. In the revealing climactic shot, the camera finally registers O's face, and a reverse shot divulges E's true identity—E is O. O can hide from the world, but he cannot hide from himself.

Unlike his experience collaborating with Gerald Potterton on *The Railrodder*, for a variety of reasons Keaton found little space to exert artistic influence working with Beckett and Schneider on *Film*. First, Beckett wrote detailed directions for both the director and actor in his screenplay, upon which he and Schneider elaborated in pre-production conferences before Keaton joined the cast; nowhere is this more evident than in the restriction that the camera not capture O's face until the final shots. Consequently, Schneider worried that they might have trouble finding a big-name actor who would be willing to perform in the project: "What actor of star stature would be willing to play a part in which we would almost never see his face?"[16] Moreover, Schneider was known as a playwright's director, someone who was willing to subordinate his artistic vision in the service of the playwright's vision; he was not an *auteur* director who re-envisioned theatrical texts. Schneider admitted as much about his work on *Film* when he introduced his essay on the movie by proclaiming, "With every new wavelet of contemporary cinema turning directors, in effect, into authors, it took the surprising author of *Film*, playwright Samuel Beckett, to become, not too surprisingly, its real director."[17]

Whereas *The Railrodder* was largely unscripted and therefore provided Keaton with ample opportunity to improvise, *Film* had a detailed and precise screenplay by Beckett with which Schneider saw little reason to trifle. Schneider saw himself as the conduit for Beckett's vision; in his own words, "It was exactly that faithful translation of intention we were all after."[18] Given this conception of his role in the film, Schneider set similar limitations on his collaborators, particularly Keaton—to serve the text, not augment it. In Schneider's report of his first meeting with Keaton, he makes no effort to hide his amusement over Keaton's suggestions of comic business: "He suggested some special business with his walk, or perhaps a bit where he could keep sharpening a pencil and it would get smaller and smaller. I said that we didn't normally pad Beckett's material."[19]

In his defense, Schneider should not be taken to task too strenuously for ignoring Keaton's expertise. Although by the time the film was shot, in the summer of 1964, Keaton was experiencing the start of his rediscovery as a classic filmmaker and actor, most of his silent films were not in wide circulation. The only Keaton films to which Schneider refers in his essay are *The Navigator* and *The General*, which were shown by film societies across the United States following the publication of James Agee's landmark essay "Comedy's Greatest Era" in 1949, so he cannot be faulted for his limited knowledge and appreciation of Keaton's work. Perhaps because Beckett had seen many of Keaton's films when they were released and was by his own admission a big fan, the dramatist was somewhat more open to Keaton's input than Schneider was. As Beckett controlled the vision, tone, and content of *Film*, Keaton needed his support to contribute something beyond his body and name to the project.

Once on the set, Keaton quickly discovered that his gag ideas were not appreciated. The only exception to this was the dog-and-cat sequence, in which O, having arrived at the apartment, proceeds to rid the space of all perceiving eyes; anything that reminds him of eyes must be expelled before he can relax. His chief antagonistic perceivers are a cat and a dog, sitting peacefully in a basket near a rocking chair. Beckett's original script did not indicate any comic business at this point in the action: "He turns towards dog and cat still staring at him. He puts them out of room."[20] Yet from his first reading of the script, Keaton saw this as an opportunity for comedy,[21] and eventually Beckett capitulated and allowed Keaton to build a gag sequence with the dog and cat. In the final cut, O carries the cat outside, but when he tries to do the same with the dog, the cat scampers back in; when O closes the door behind the dog he discovers the cat back in the basket. O repeats the sequence several times—first the cat, then the dog, then the cat—and in each repetition the gag is based upon the Keaton take, his body freezing as he returns from depositing an animal on the other side of the door, only to find the other animal back in the basket.

Beckett expressed disappointment with this sequence in its final form: "Because I don't feel the animal gag at all funny, I find it too long."[22] Yet close study of the sequence, which represents the only attempt at a gag in the twenty-two-minute film, reveals that the gag failed because of Schneider's direction rather than Keaton's performance. Putting aside for the moment the obvious observation that a take depends upon the audience's seeing the face of the performer, Schneider's deeper error resulted from his lack of awareness of editing rhythm and the nature of a comic take. In film, the take depends upon the camera's staying on the performer for at least a beat before cutting to another shot; otherwise the punch line to the gag—the performer's reaction—disappears. Schneider literally cut the gag out from under Keaton by cutting on the take instead of a moment after it, limiting the shot to a split-second view of O's back. Keaton would never have shot the sequence this way, and Beckett and Schneider, extraordinary theater-makers but novice filmmakers, failed to utilize the shot, the building block of film, to the gag's advantage. Beckett failed to detect the problem with the sequence when he said it was too long. On the contrary, the sequence *seems* too long because it is about three seconds too short—three seconds of vintage Buster takes.

Within the constraints Keaton found in working with Beckett and Schneider, he managed to exert his influence in a small, but even more significant way that influences the perception of *Film* to this day: at the end of his first meeting with Beckett, he suggested that he wear a porkpie hat. As Schneider recounted,

> Oh, yes, just before we left, Keaton made some comment about his old flattened-down Stetson being his trademark . . . and mentioned that he'd brought several of them along in different colors to use in the film. (The script called for slightly different headgear.) While I was figuring out how to react to this choice between Scylla and Charybdis, Sam replied—to my surprised delight—that he didn't see why Buster couldn't wear his own hat in this one.[23]

With this one small contribution, Keaton changed *Film* irrevocably, for the porkpie hat clearly marks the actor whom Beckett and Schneider otherwise studiously avoided identifying within the film. With O transformed into Buster, Beckett lost primary ownership of *Film*, and it became a Keaton film.

This was immediately apparent to Schneider, who found that Keaton's name, and not Beckett's, provided the major opportunities for exhibiting the film. The first major screening of *Film*, at the New York Film Festival, came in the summer of 1965:

> Amos Vogel had seen a print somewhere and thought it was worth showing—as part of a Keaton revival series. Already the film was becoming Keaton's and not Beckett's. I fought another losing battle to keep it from getting sandwiched in between two Keaton shorts, a standard one he'd made some years earlier

and a new railroad commercial he'd just completed [*The Railrodder*]. . . . I dreaded what would happen when the unexpected Keaton came on.[24]

As Schneider feared, the initial audience of film critics and Keaton fans at the New York Film Festival roundly rejected the film, but interest grew, and over the next year *Film* was shown at several European film festivals, garnering awards at festivals in Venice (1965), London (1965), Oberhausen (1966), and Tours (1966).[25] Schneider found himself both the beneficiary and victim of the revived interest in Keaton. He and Beckett sought a major, if faded, film star to attract an audience for *Film*, yet they discovered that the choice of Keaton soon dominated audiences' perception of their work.

As Keaton struggles to avoid the camera in *Film*, he appears as an icon from the bygone era of silent film comedy, his performance "an ironic echo" of his past physical virtuosity.[26] This sense of him as an icon—as a symbol standing in for himself and his era—is only heightened by the fact that the primary indicator of his identity is his porkpie hat. Despite Beckett's strict directions to avoid revealing Keaton's face in *Film*, his identity shines through nonetheless; as Tom Milne observes, "he cannot be reduced to a meaningless object."[27] Yet the film fails to satisfy beyond its appeal as a curiosity, even though the pairing of Keaton and Beckett seems, on its face, to be an inspired combination. Like Keaton, Beckett treaded the line between low and high culture, between vaudeville and surrealism. In 1932, long before he began writing drama, Beckett contributed several translations of surrealist works (by Breton, Tzara, Eluard, Péret, and Crevel) to the publication *This Quarter*,[28] and his plays evince the continuing influence of surrealism.[29] Keaton and Beckett each blended the low art of popular entertainment and the high art of the avant-garde; black comedy and nonclassical structures allowed them to explore the place of man in an indifferent or malevolent universe. Moreover, they shared an aesthetic interest in the fusion of the fantastic and the everyday, a concern that links them to surrealism. Though he is writing of Beckett, Bernard Beckerman's appraisal applies as well to Keaton: "It is by being fantastically literal that Beckett's images produce so insistent a visual effect."[30]

In his essay on Beckett and Keaton, Andrew Sarris notes that despite their apparent kinship, each developed his aesthetic from a completely different background and set of experiences: "What Keaton arrived at intuitively out of a combination of a relatively rootless childhood, a fantastic physical adaptability, and a suitably uninhibited medium still in the midst of its birth pains, Beckett formulated intellectually out of his confrontation with the nightmare of modern history."[31] While Beckett enjoyed full intellectual freedom in conceiving and writing *Film*, Keaton lacked the artistic freedom to contribute his knowledge of physical comedy and filmmaking technique. Though Keaton's films and Beckett's plays might seem to have something in common in terms of their use of vaudeville, the two men found little common ground for artistic collaboration, and ultimately Beckett's rigid control of the process stifled Keaton's ability to contribute to *Film* as a comedian or filmmaker. Ultimately, because Beckett remained unwilling to subordinate form and theme to gags for more than a moment, he sacrificed the comic atmosphere that he desired and Keaton could have provided, and therefore failed to find the fusion of high-brow intellect and low-brow comedy that both men created in their other work.

Afterlife: New Vaudeville, Jackie Chan, and Coming Attractions

Beyond Keaton's influence on these two short films from the 1960s, his strongest contemporary legacy has emerged on the stage, in the subgenre of performance art dubbed New Vaudeville, and in foreign film, in the comedy-action films of Hong Kong's Jackie Chan.[32] The term "New Vaudeville" was coined in the 1980s to describe a wide range of theatrical acts, from circus performers to performance artists, that employed physical comedy, improvisation, and a direct relationship with the audience in the service of anarchistic comedy and irreverence. Little attempt has been made to define the genre; instead, much like Supreme Court Justice Potter Stewart's famous dictum in a case about pornography, theater critics claim to know it when they see it. Consequently, most New Vaudevillians reject the term as being overly broad.[33] While I recognize that the New Vaudevillians draw their inspiration from a wide range of vaudeville, circus, mime, and avant-garde predecessors, I believe that in many ways Keaton is the spiritual father of this movement, for his blend of vaudeville and unconscious surrealism comes closest to the avant-garde sensibility of New Vaudeville.

Of the New Vaudevillians, the performer who has consistently attracted the greatest public attention is Bill Irwin. Irwin has acknowledged Keaton's influence many times and has singled him out as the performer whom he most admires. As a student at the Ringling Brothers and Barnum & Bailey Clown College in Sarasota, Florida in 1974, Irwin watched the films of the silent comedians every night, and Keaton's movies figured prominently in these showings.[34] In a recent tribute to Keaton in *The New York Times*, Irwin complimented Keaton's ability to balance physical comedy with narrative: "What's the blend that makes Buster Keaton's physical comedy so wild and so visceral but at the same time so finished, so sure? For one thing, he was one of his era's finest actors *and* one of the best acrobats ever captured on film: As an acrobat he had a particular—and very rare—actor's knowledge of how to harness the story-telling potential of acrobatic movement.[35]

After performing with the Pickle Family Circus from 1975 to 1978, Irwin developed several theater pieces, most notably *The Regard of Flight* (1982), *Largely New York* (1989), and his collaborative effort with David Shiner, *Fool Moon* (1993), that display the signs of Keaton's influence in their varied use of vaudeville structure and narrative as well as in the appropriation and revision of some of Keaton's imagery and gags.[36] In *The Regard of Flight*, Irwin draws inspiration from *The Playhouse*. Whereas in the second reel of *The Playhouse* stagehands awaken Buster from the nightmare of the first reel by taking down the flats of the stage room in which he has been sleeping, in *The Regard of Flight* a piano player enters and announces over the public address system, "Places for the opening dance," rousing Irwin from slumber into nightmarish misadventures. The piano player continually interrupts Irwin's attempts to sleep with periodic announcements over the public address system, which propel him from one routine to the next: "Warning: costume change"; "Places for dance segment"; "Obscene monologue." The pianist also doubles as resident scholar, analyzing Irwin's gags after he performs them. In one sequence, Irwin executes a "lean," tilting forward at a forty-five degree angle—a move Buster uses in the cyclone sequence in *Steamboat Bill, Jr.*—only to have the piano player explain in dry detail how weighted shoes provide the means for the stunt. Later, a more abusive critic dresses up in a costume identical to Irwin's and periodically chases him around the stage, eventually joining him in a two-man eccentric dance that closely resembles Buster's dance with a duplicate of himself in *The Playhouse*. The piano player-scholar self-conciously notes the vaudeville roots of this imagery over the address system—"The recurrent image and lack of narrative structure show the decline of the role of the playwright and the rise of the actor-poet."[37] By incorporating these critics into the show, Irwin constantly draws attention to the mechanics of his own performance, demystifying his work while dryly satirizing the scholars' need to analyze performance.

In his first Broadway show, *Largely New York*, Irwin combines the vaudevillian "interrupted act"[38] with a love interest, as Keaton did in all of his silent feature films. Throughout the show, Irwin attempts to perform an eccentric dance—as in *The Regard of Flight*, it resembles Buster's dance in *The Playhouse*—only to be disrupted by mechanical malfunctions, two break-dancers, a band of college graduates in robes and mortar boards, and a modern dance troupe. The dance troupe's lead dancer is Irwin's love interest, and he follows her throughout the play, eagerly trying to please her by dancing in her style and demonstrating his own steps, much to her chagrin. At the same time, Irwin shares steps with the break dancers and the graduates attempt to please Irwin by copying his movements.

This structure produces a blend of vaudeville and narrative that resembles Keaton's silent features. By choosing different styles of dance for his supporting cast, Irwin achieves the vaudevillian ideal of variety, while his love interest offers his character an achievable goal, providing the show with a stronger throughline than his previous pieces. Moreover, Irwin appears to have drawn several individual gag sequences from Keaton's films. He demonstrates the forward lean to the adoring graduates, and they all lean together in the same direction. Not only does Irwin adopt Keaton's use of multiples in this sequence, but his use of graduates in black robes directly appropriates Keaton's use of this image in *College*. In Keaton's version of the gag, Buster gives the valedictorian speech at his high school graduation. As he decries the dominance of sports in school life, leaning to the right and then the left, the teachers in graduation robes seated behind him lean with him, literally "swayed" by the power of his rhetoric.

Irwin appears to have drawn the central image for *Largely New York* from *Sherlock Jr.* In this gag sequence, which Irwin used for publicity and which was used as the photograph accompanying most of the production reviews, a video camera appears to suck Irwin into its interior, so that his head appears enlarged on the monitor, but his body is left flapping like an eccentric vaudeville dancer as he tries to extract himself. In the resulting image, Irwin seems to be part human, part television—atop his actual body sits a large, video close-up of his head. After extracting himself from the television, Irwin reaches a tentative truce with the video monitor, which now offers him a video clone of himself with whom he can dance. During the climax of *Largely New York*, Irwin finally performs his eccentric dance to "Tea for Two" with his electronic double on the video monitor, occasionally disrupting their otherwise perfectly mirrored movement to improvise his own variations on the softshoe dance, which incorporate new moves he has learned from the modern dancer and the break dancers.[39]

Irwin's inspiration for the gag sequence combines the graphic-match montage from the inner film of *Sherlock Jr.*, in which the movie screen appears to consume Buster and project him into the inner film's plot, with the multiple Busters in *The Playhouse*, particularly the two-man eccentric dance by identical Busters.[40] As I discussed in Chapter 4, the graphic-match montage was a favorite of the surrealists and the basis for Paul Nougé's *cinépoème*, "D'Or et de Sable"; Irwin's common interest in the sequence suggests that a similar sensibility pervades his work. While Nougé focused on the transformations that he imagined might occur between cuts in the sequence, Irwin expands upon the moment of crossing over from outer film to inner film, which he redefines as the line between life and television. While Keaton examined what might happen if life functioned like a film, Irwin investigates the significance of the line between life and television, and, by clinging to both worlds at the same time, he consciously or unconsciously creates a surreal image of the fusion of man and machine, updating Keaton's imagery to the technological age.

Irwin's recent adaptation with Mark O'Donnell of Molière's *Scapin*, which he directed as well as starred in at Seattle Repertory company (1995) and the Roundabout Theatre (1996), exhibits his debt to Keaton in the balance he finds between narrative and spectacular gags. *Scapin* is a farce in the style of *commedia dell'arte*, and as such it provides numerous opportunities for gags or *lazzi* to disrupt the linearity of the narrative. Irwin and O'Donnell's adaptation simplifies Molière's text (and adds numerous contemporary touches from popular culture) to make room for even more physical comedy than the original text suggests. This is most evident in the climax of the production, to which Irwin added a long chase sequence reminiscent of, if not drawn directly from, Keaton's chase at the end of *The High Sign*.[41] Irwin's incorporation of the extended chase sequence adds a physical climax to the production without unduly disturbing the narrative line of the plot, and shows that Irwin has studied Keaton's films not only for gags but for the relationship of these gags to the narrative. In his *Scapin*, Irwin further emphasizes the silent-film roots of the chase by having a musician accompany the action of the chase sequence on a large pipe organ.

While Irwin seeks a blend of gags and narrative, Blue Man Group, in their long-running Off-Broadway show *Tubes*, eschews narrative in favor of a montage of off-beat "attractions." Three men—Matt Goldman, Phil Stanton, and Chris Wink—perform the show silently, dressed in identical black clothes, their skin uniformly cobalt blue, including their apparently bald, earless heads. From the start, the image of these three identical men recalls the multiple Busters in *The Playhouse*, which I have traced back to the identical stage Irishmen of The Three Keatons. Throughout the production, the Blue Men maintain poker faces, limiting themselves to the smallest range of facial reaction to their often confusing surroundings, and, although the three performers have never publicly acknowledged the influence of Keaton, he is certainly the best-known poker-faced comedian of the twentieth century. Moreover, *Tubes* presents the Blue Men as aliens attempting to find their way in a world they fail to understand—the basic premise of most, if not all, of Keaton's silent films.

Film actor and director Jackie Chan extends Keaton's influence into the realm of Hong Kong action cinema; he acknowledges his debt to Keaton for many of his most dangerous stunts in almost every interview he gives. The roots of his affinity with Keaton originate in Chan's early childhood training in Peking opera, the most popular and well-known Chinese theater form.[42] His parents enrolled him in the Chinese Opera Research School at the age of seven and a half, where he trained with Master Yu Jim-yuen and performed with the Seven Little Fortunes Opera Group, a traveling children's troupe. The training was rigorous and students worked on dance, acrobatics, stage combat, and singing from 5 a.m. to midnight.[43] Over the years Peking opera performers, including several of Chan's fellow performers from the Seven Little Fortunes, have influenced the development of the Hong Kong action cinema by providing a large number of its actors, fight choreographers, and directors.[44]

Vaudeville and Peking opera share a surprising number of aesthetic elements. Both forms developed out of the fusion of other forms, blending comedy, acrobatics, singing, and music. Like vaudeville, Peking opera follows a variety format, using a skeletal script based on excerpts from longer plays and operas, interspersed with comic and acrobatic interludes.[45] It replaces the more traditional Western structure of a single, dominant narrative line with an escalation of rhythm and tempo based on improvisation and the dynamism of the performers. And it is also an actor's theater, developed and sustained by the virtuosity of its performers.[46]

By the time Chan graduated from the Chinese Opera Research School, though, Peking opera was no longer in vogue in Hong Kong, and Chan was forced to look for work elsewhere. Chan found employment as a stunt man and fight choreographer in the emerging Hong Kong film industry, which grew rapidly with the international popularity of Bruce Lee's kung fu films. After Lee's sudden death in 1973, the Hong Kong studios searched for a successor. Chan was one of several actor-fighters who attempted to make films in the style of Bruce Lee, working with a variety of producers and directors, yet he found little success in this vein.

It was not until Chan started to incorporate comedy into his action films that he achieved commercial success. Although some kung fu films had included humor before Chan's films, he is generally credited with popularizing the subgenre of Hong Kong comedy-action, beginning with *Snake in the Eagle's Shadow* (1978) and *Drunken Master* (1978).[47] These films established kung fu comedy as the "next wave of the genre," and dispensed with any pretense of realism in their fight sequences, which instead incorporate the more stylized combat and acrobatics of Peking opera.[48]

In 1983 Chan discovered the films of the silent comedians and Keaton in particular, and he began to incorporate elements of Keaton's work into his own. *Project A* (1983) was the first Chan film to display the influence of the silent comedians, appropriating elements of the clock tower sequence from Harold Lloyd's *Safety Last*. By the time he directed *Project A II* (1987), Chan had firmly settled on Keaton as his favorite source for inspiration. In *Project A II*, Chan appropriates the falling-wall sequence from *One Week* and *Steamboat Bill, Jr.*, as well as performing several ladder tricks reminiscent of Keaton's use of the front porch rail as a ladder in *One Week*. In subsequent films, Chan performs his own versions of Keaton's battle against the wind in *Steamboat Bill, Jr.*, his flight through the air attached to a crane in *Seven Chances*, and his stunt with a waterspout in *Sherlock Jr.*[49] Although Chan employs fast cutting in his fight sequences, shooting them in small segments, he studiously avoids cutting when he performs his most dangerous, Keaton-inspired stunts, retaining Keaton's practice of using long shots and long takes to prove that he actually performs his stunts. Moreover, Chan further emphasizes his physical virtuosity as a performer by frequently including up to three takes of the same stunt in rapid succession and including outtakes of his failed attempts at his stunts during the final credits of most of his films.

By incorporating Keaton's stunts into Hong Kong action cinema, Chan brings this style of stunt work to a new audience, fusing the variety aesthetics of vaudeville and Peking opera in Hong Kong action cinema. Chan's popularity is growing; he is currently the most popular film star in the world, a position he is likely to retain now that New Line Cinema and Miramax are distributing his films in the United States. Yet after a brief attempt at making films in the United States in the mid-1980s, Chan continues to make most of his films in Hong Kong, in part because Hollywood studios will not allow him to perform his own stunts or work in the improvisational, non-scripted style he shares with Keaton. His popularity suggests that Keaton's aesthetic and working methods are still commercially viable, though perhaps not in Hollywood.

The large audiences, enormous budgets, and monolithic economic system of Hollywood prevent directors who might follow in Keaton's footsteps
from finding the artistic means to do so, and thwart physical comedians,
such as Irwin, Martin Short, and Michael Richards, who might work in Keaton's improvisatory style.[50] At the same time, the genius of Keaton's death-
defying cinematic stunts has been rendered virtually obsolete by the development of computer-generated special effects. As audience members see
more and more spectacular special effects, all stunts lose credibility as believable, actual occurrences. In such a viewing climate, it is only on the stage
that extraordinary physical comedy and stuntwork can regain its visceral
impact on audiences. Perhaps this is one reason why a gifted physical performer such as Jackie Chan chooses to include multiple takes and outtakes
of his most daring stunts in his films—only by repeating a stunt, or even
showing a failed stunt, can Chan display the sense of performance virtuosity
that he developed in Peking opera.

Paradoxically, the use of video has figured prominently in Keaton's renewed influence on the contemporary stage; Bill Irwin's *Largely New York*
and Blue Man Group's *Tubes* make extensive use of video cameras and mon-
itors. Keaton's successors have not reverted to the simpler form of vaudeville, but instead have found new amalgams of theater and film. Keaton
appeals to contemporary artists who wish to explore how they can expand
the vision and scope of theater through the use of current technology. They
share with him an ambivalent relationship to that technology: although
they are drawn to video for its ability to expand stage space and illusion,
they insist upon the inclusion of physically present human beings, avoid-
ing the trap of allowing video to replace people. Irwin and Blue Man Group
pursue marvelous imagery that nevertheless remains based in everyday reality, and the presence of a live audience confirms that these images are real
and immediate.

If Keaton's legacy can be found in his preservation and adaptation of the
vaudeville aesthetic, then how does this affect the evaluation of his films?
Film scholars initially granted Keaton admission into the canon of "great
films" in the 1960s on the basis of his classicism, favoring films such as *The
General* and *Our Hospitality*. If we re-evaluate his work, foregrounding the
influence of the vaudeville aesthetic, do we risk forfeiting Keaton's place
within the established cultural hierarchy?[51] By extending the investigation
of Keaton's films beyond the safe confines of classical Hollywood cinema to
include his roots in vaudeville and his influence on subsequent artists (from
Beckett to Jackie Chan), we arrive at a more complete picture of his films

and filmmaking process, as well as his cultural and aesthetic significance. In Keaton's films, we see vestiges of older theatrical forms finding new expression; through his influence on other artists, we might find new models for future work. Film scholarship often tries to create clear-cut distinctions between high art and low art, vaudeville and classical Hollywood cinema. But there is more interplay between these realms than might previously have been suggested. By examining Keaton's films from multiple points of view, rather than through a single lens such as vaudeville, classical Hollywood cinema, or surrealism, we detect trends in popular stage entertainment, Hollywood, and the avant-garde, clashing, mixing, and evolving toward new forms.

Notes

Introduction

1. Bordwell and Thompson, *Film Art*, 173–79; Giannetti, *Understanding Movies*, 314–17. See also Cook, *History of Narrative Film*, 217–24.

2. Buñuel, "Keaton's *College*," 64.

3. Henry Jenkins recognizes this when he observes that *Sherlock Jr.* has replaced *The General* as "the canonical Keaton film for the 1980s and 1990s" because of changes in critical perspectives and taste within film studies. "Interrupted Performance," 31.

4. Jakobson, "The Dominant," 82. See also Bordwell, Staiger, and Thompson, *Classical Hollywood Cinema*, 12.

5. Patterson, *Cinema Craftsmanship*, 5.

6. Bordwell, Staiger, and Thompson, *Classical Hollywood Cinema*, 17.

7. Karnick and Jenkins, "Golden Eras and Blind Spots," in *Classical Hollywood Comedy*, 3.

8. See also Sweeney, "Dream of Disruption," 104–20. Sweeney argues that the structure of *Sherlock Jr.* is an extension of the three-part gag structure that Keaton derived from vaudeville. Yet Sweeney still perceives this structure as ultimately serving the narrative and suggests that even this departure from classical Hollywood cinema is an exception in Keaton's works. According to Sweeney, "Except for parts of *Seven Chances* (1925) and *Go West* (1925), Keaton in the later features comes to accept romantic narrative as the contextual basis for his comedy" (118). Thus, Sweeney falls short of suggesting that Keaton's films can be viewed through the lens of vaudeville, instead arguing for the unique structural qualities of *Sherlock Jr.*

9. McCaffrey, *Four Great Comedians*, 91.

10. Moews, *Keaton: Silent Feature Close Up*, 246.

11. Ibid.

12. See ibid., 1. Moews claims that Keaton's films all follow the same structure: "He made one good movie and released it under nine different titles." Not only is this argument reductive, but, if true, it would obviate the need for the repeated analysis of Keaton's narratives in which Moews engages.

13. Ibid., 44.

14. Mast, *Comic Mind*, 135–39. For an opposing view, see Rapf, "Moral and Amoral Visions," 335–45.

15. Bordwell, Staiger, and Thompson, *Classical Hollywood Cinema*, 43.

16. Throughout the book, I use "Keaton" to denote him as director and "Buster" to signify his film character.

17. Brownlow, *Parade's Gone By*, 487.

18. Matthews, *Surrealism and Film*, 6.

19. Moews, *Keaton: Silent Features Close Up*, 3–4.

20. Bordwell, Staiger, and Thompson, *Classical Hollywood Cinema*, 50–51.

21. Ibid., 51.

22. Robinson, *Buster Keaton*, 90. See also Dardis, *Man Who Wouldn't Lie Down*, 138–45. Dardis judges *The General* to be Keaton's masterpiece on the basis of its logic, structure, symmetry, and the blend of gags and story. When Dardis discovers that *The General* was a box-office and critical failure at the time of its release, all he can muster in its defense is that "it was just too good."

23. Bordwell, Staiger, and Thompson, *Classical Hollywood Cinema*, 54.

24. Ibid., 63.

25. Keaton created at least one entire film around a prop. When offered the opportunity to rent the *S.S. Buford*, an ocean liner scheduled to be junked, Keaton immediately accepted and built an entire movie around the enormous ship.

26. Bordwell, Staiger, and Thompson, *Classical Hollywood Cinema*, 59.

27. See Jenkins, "Interrupted Performance," 46–47, on the difference between tricks Keaton performs "for the camera" and "with the camera" in *Sherlock Jr.* In the former, "Keaton wants us to watch his performance unfold in continuous space and time so that there can be no escaping our awareness of his mastery" (46).

28. Bordwell, Staiger, and Thompson, *Classical Hollywood Cinema*, 62.

29. Ibid., 60. Bordwell further observes that whereas Douglas Fairbanks's and Harold Lloyd's films use a larger than average number of short shots, Keaton routinely used a larger than average number of long takes (62).

30. Perhaps this assumption is premised on the poor quality of Keaton's MGM sound films. At MGM, Keaton had very little control over the stories chosen for his films. Keaton's lack of artistic control was not limited to stories, however, and therefore it seems premature to attribute the flaws of the MGM films solely to narrative construction.

31. See Rheuban, *Harry Langdon*, for a similar thesis applied to Langdon.

32. Sarris, *American Cinema*, 62.

33. See Crafton, "Pie and Chase," 106–19; Gunning, "Response to 'Pie and Chase'," 120–22. For the application of gag/narrative analysis to Keaton's films, see Sweeney, "Dream of Disruption," 104–20; and Kramer, "Derailing the Honeymoon Express," 101–16.

34. Karnick and Jenkins, "Funny Stories," in *Classical Hollywood Comedy*, 85. See also Sweeney, "Dream of Disruption," 104–20.

35. For a discussion of Keaton's "admixture" of melodrama and farce, see Kauffmann, "Melodrama and Farce," 169–72.

36. Although it can be argued that the influence of vaudeville on circus is minimal because circus predates vaudeville, circus performers still study the vaudeville routines in silent film comedy for inspiration and instruction. Ringling Brothers' clown school, for example, assigns the films of Keaton, Chaplin, and Laurel and Hardy to its students.

37. Jenkins, *What Made Pistachio Nuts?*

38. Jenkins discusses Keaton's various approaches to incorporating the vaudeville aesthetic into his films, examining *Back Stage*, *The Playhouse*, *Sherlock Jr.*, and *Speak Easily*, in his essay in Andrew Horton's *Buster Keaton's Sherlock Jr.*, "Interrupted Performance," 29–66.

39. Jenkins, *What Made Pistachio Nuts?*, 5. Italics added.

40. Lebel, *Buster Keaton*.

41. Ibid., 102.

42. Agee, "Comedy's Greatest Era," 15.

43. Crafton, "Pie and Chase," 107.

44. Jenkins, *What Made Pistachio Nuts?*, 79.

45. Ibid., 79. See also Jenkins, "Interrupted Performance," 44.

46. Jenkins, *What Made Pistachio Nuts?*, 79.

47. See Krämer, "Slapstick Comedian at Crossroads," 133–46, on the reasons for Keaton's transition from vaudeville to film.

48. Lebel, *Buster Keaton*, 66–68.

49. Keaton convinced Thalberg to allow him to improvise extensively—and put aside the studio's script—during the filming of *The Cameraman* (1928), and the result was Keaton's most critically acclaimed film for MGM. See Keaton with Samuels, *Wonderful World of Slapstick*, 207–14.

50. See John Spotton's documentary, *Buster Keaton Rides Again*, on the filming of *The Railrodder*; Alan Schneider, "On Directing *Film*," 63–94. See also Kramer, "Keaton and *The Saphead*," 190–210. Kramer argues that although Keaton did not direct *The Saphead*, his first feature film as an actor, he exerted significant artistic control over the film as a performer.

51. See also Jenkins, "Interrupted Performance," 29–66, on the vaudeville aesthetic in Keaton's films.

52. Jenkins, *What Made Pistachio Nuts?*, 61.

53. See Vardac, *Stage to Screen*. Vardac argues that the drive toward greater scenic realism and spectacle in nineteenth-century stage melodrama influenced the development and structure of early silent film.

54. Matthews, *Surrealism and Film*, viii.

55. Ibid., viii.

56. Ibid., 29.

57. Translated and quoted in Matthews, *Surrealism and Film*, 52.

58. Breton, "As in a Wood," 81.

59. Aranda, *Luis Buñuel: Critical Biography*, 51–53. On one program, for exam-

ple, Buñuel included segments from films by Ben Turpin, Harold Lloyd and Snub Pollard, Chaplin, Keaton (*The Navigator*), and Harry Langdon.

60. Matthews, *Surrealism and Film*, 2.

61. See "The Surrealists Claim Keaton," in Chapter 4.

Chapter 1
The Evolution of Keaton's Vaudeville

1. Blesh, *Keaton*, 45. Three biographies of Keaton have been published since Blesh's book, as well as Keaton's autobiography with Charles Samuels. Tom Dardis uncovered a wealth of economic information about Keaton's filmmaking career in *Keaton: The Man Who Wouldn't Lie Down*. Recently, Marion Meade published a more in-depth account of the personal side of Keaton's life in *Buster Keaton: Cut to the Chase*. See also Larry Edwards, *Buster Keaton: A Legend in Laughter*.

2. Myra Keaton's scrapbook, 155 (hereafter "Scrapbook"). A less generous reviewer stated, "As a matter of fact Joe, a gaunt Irishman, doesn't figure in the show except to furnish the muscle, while Myra, who is 'Buster's' mother, is positively in the way." Scrapbook, 79. Because most of the clippings in the scrapbook are unattributed, page notations indicate the scrapbook page number. Where possible I provide additional citation information. Access to Myra Keaton's scrapbook was graciously provided to me by Mrs. Eleanor Keaton and Ron Pesch. Copies of the Keaton scrapbook are available for viewing through the Academy of Motion Picture Arts and Science and the American Film Institute in Los Angeles.

3. For the remainder of this chapter, I will refer to Keaton as "Buster" in order to distinguish him from his father.

4. The newspaper clippings in the Keaton scrapbook, in particular the extensive clippings from vaudeville programs, indicate that The Three Keatons were often the headline act when they toured, but usually held a lower spot on the bill in New York.

5. Blesh, *Keaton*, 21.

6. Ibid., 21.

7. Ibid., 26.

8. Ibid., 17.

9. Ibid., 4.

10. Scrapbook, 32. *Dramatic Mirror*, 23 January 1904.

11. See Saunders and Lieberfeld, "Dreaming in Pictures," 14–28. Saunders and Lieberfeld argue that Keaton's melancholy quality derived from the fierce beatings his father inflicted upon him, both on the stage and off. Such psychoanalytic readings of Keaton's work are based on scant evidence and ultimately sacrifice understanding of Keaton's films as art in order to attempt to get closer to Keaton the person. As such, they lend little to our understanding of Keaton's filmmaking and instead reveal much more about the authors' own agendas.

12. Blesh, *Keaton*, 72.

13. See Scrapbook, 156–57; Dardis, *Man Who Wouldn't Lie Down*, 4.

14. Blesh, *Keaton*, 38.

15. Scrapbook, 26.

16. Ibid., 24.

17. Ibid., 49. "In Vaudeville Houses," *New York Times*, 21 May 1903.

18. Blesh, *Keaton*, 12.

19. Ibid., 32.

20. Scrapbook, 129.

21. Ibid.

22. Blesh, *Keaton*, 22.

23. Keaton with Samuels, *Wonderful World of Slapstick*, 33; Scrapbook, 66. A photograph in the scrapbook from an uncredited Boston newspaper dated September 24, 1904, shows a vaudeville poster billing Buster Keaton as "The Greatest of All Midget Comedians."

24. Keaton with Samuels, *Wonderful World of Slapstick*, 32.

25. In 1907, all five Keatons played a benefit at the Grand Opera House in Manhattan. According to Keaton, the manager had promised there would be no resistance from the Gerry Society, but the Keatons were prosecuted for violation of child labor laws nonetheless and the manager refused to corroborate their story: "We were fined $250 and The Three Keatons were banned from the New York stage. The ban remained in force for two years and was a cruel setback." Ibid., 68.

26. Scrapbook, 60.

27. Ibid., 24.

28. Keaton with Samuels, *Wonderful World of Slapstick*, 34.

29. Blesh, *Keaton*, 31.

30. For a history of the Bluffton actors' colony, see Okkonnen, *Muskegon Connection*.

31. Blesh, *Keaton*, 68.

32. See Johnstone, *Impro*, 116–18.

33. Scrapbook, 75. Although the clipping is uncredited, the attached advertisement and Myra's note indicate that this clipping is a review of a vaudeville bill at The Farm in Toledo, Ohio, the week of August 6, 1905.

34. Buster Keaton, interview, ed. Joan and Bob Franklin, 11–12.

35. Scrapbook, 32.

36. Ibid., 51.

37. Ibid., 78.

38. Ibid., 21, 110, 145.

39. Ibid., 127.

40. Ibid., 55, 56, 85, 86.

41. Blesh, *Keaton*, 330–34.

42. Keaton with Samuels, *Wonderful World of Slapstick*, 36.

43. Ibid., 62–63.

44. Blesh, *Keaton*, 41–42.

45. Keaton with Samuels, *Wonderful World of Slapstick*, 26. See also Scrapbook 73: "He is a born mimic and has only to see a full-grown actor go through his performance once in order to be able to reproduce his mannerisms to perfection."

46. The "Original Aboriginal Splash" and Keaton's performing monkey show up in *The Playhouse*, while Keaton performs sharpshooting tricks in the first short film he made after the Arbuckle shorts, *The High Sign*.

47. Scrapbook, 82. The review is uncredited, but Myra's attached note indicates that The Three Keatons shared the bill with Colonel Bordeverry at Proctor's in New York City in 1905, when Buster was nine or ten years old.

48. Keaton with Samuels, *Wonderful World of Slapstick*, 26.

49. In refusing Hearst's offer, Joe reputedly told him, "We work for years perfecting an act, and you want to show it, a nickel a head, on a dirty sheet?" Blesh, *Keaton*, 69–71.

50. Ibid., 35–36; Slide, ed., *Encyclopedia of Vaudeville*, 406, 515.

51. Blesh, *Keaton*, 59.

52. Ibid., 85.

53. Keaton with Samuels, *Wonderful World of Slapstick*, 93.

54. Their move to Hollywood was part of what became a mass exodus of filmmaking companies from New York to California. The primary impetus for the move was economic: land was cheap in California and it had yet to be developed extensively. Film companies, therefore, could build sets inexpensively on lots in the desert, as well as find locations that could be easily cleared for shooting. Ibid., 95.

55. Meade, *Cut to the Chase*, 91.

56. Blesh, *Keaton*, 139–44.

57. Ibid., 150.

58. The early comic features were much shorter than the standard two-hour film of today. *The Kid* was about one hour long, and the average feature-length comedy during the silent era ran about sixty to seventy minutes.

59. Blesh, *Keaton*, 217.

60. Dardis, *Man Who Wouldn't Lie Down*, 155.

61. Keaton probably could have gotten a contract as an actor, but the financial failure of his recent films foreclosed the possibility of making his own films. Ibid., 156.

62. Ibid., 148.

63. The coming of sound films raised production costs rapidly, causing MGM to severely limit Keaton's improvisation in favor of controlled shooting schedules, complete shooting scripts, and formulaic plots. Ibid., 166.

64. Keaton with Samuels, *Wonderful World of Slapstick*, 208, 213.

65. Ibid., 205.

66. Dardis, *Man Who Wouldn't Lie Down*, 200.

67. Blesh, Keaton, 310.

68. Ibid.

69. Dardis, *Man Who Wouldn't Lie Down*, 240.

70. Blesh, *Keaton*, 329. The land yacht, a thirty-foot-long vehicle equipped with all the conveniences of a home, could sleep six.

71. For accounts of Keaton's work at Educational and Columbia, see Maltin, *Great Movie Shorts*, 155–61.

72. Meade, *Cut to the Chase*, 240–41.

73. Schneider, "On Directing *Film*," 67–68.

Chapter 2
From Stage to Film:
The Transformation of Keaton's Vaudeville

1. Jenkins, *What Made Pistachio Nuts?*, 107.

2. Robinson, *Buster Keaton*, 18. See Jenkins, *What Made Pistachio Nuts?*, 75.

3. Keaton with Samuels, *Wonderful World of Slapstick*, 33.

4. Dardis, *Man Who Wouldn't Lie Down*, 38.

5. Brownlow, *Parade's Gone By*, 270.

6. Keaton, interview, ed. Joan and Bob Franklin, 19–20.

7. Early silent film was shot almost entirely in long shots, reflecting the influence of theater on film. Bordwell, Staiger, and Thompson, *Classical Hollywood Cinema*, 214.

8. Blesh, *Keaton*, 214.

9. Chinoy, "Emergence of the Director," 22–31.

10. Jenkins, *What Made Pistachio Nuts?*, 67.

11. Ibid., 61.

12. Ibid., 73–77.

13. Page, *Writing for Vaudeville*, 86.

14. Jenkins, *What Made Pistachio Nuts?*, 79.

15. As vaudeville grew as an economic institution, the demand for variety within each act increased too. Performers were required to incorporate more and more specialties within their acts in order to distinguish themselves from competing acts. See Jenkins, *What Made Pistachio Nuts?*, 69–70. The Keatons followed this trend, blending knockabout comedy with eccentric dancing, imitations, songs, and music.

16. McNamara, *American Popular Entertainments*, 17.

17. I will look at these films more closely in Chapter 3 in the context of the gag/narrative debate in silent film theory.

18. See Oldham, *Keaton's Silent Shorts*, for a descriptive analysis of the nineteen short films Keaton directed from 1920 to 1923.

19. Meade, *Cut to the Chase*, 96.

20. It was customary at the time to toss old shoes following a wedding as a token of good luck.

21. Seidman, *Comedian Comedy*, 40–53.

22. See Jenkins, *What Made Pistachio Nuts?*, 63–71, on the centrality of the performer's virtuosity to the vaudeville aesthetic.

23. Kerr, *Silent Clowns*, 123. Italics in original.

24. See Chapter 3 of this book for an extended analysis of the falling-wall sequence in *Steamboat Bill, Jr.* Patty Tobias notes two other examples of this gag, in *The Blacksmith* and in Keaton's last short film, *The Scribe.* "History of a Keaton Gag," 6–7.

25. Within the context of the bath scene, the milk scene may also possess sexual overtones. As with the pie fights for which silent film comedians were known, this scene's humor derives from our pleasure in seeing someone get dirty, a type of comedy that derives on one level from an implied sexual or scatological reference. For a closer reading of scatological and anal humor in silent comedy, see Paul, "Annals of Chaplin," 109–30.

26. This type of gag may also be called a "metamorphosis gag" or a "visual pun." Kamin, *Chaplin's One-Man Show*, 37. Kamin breaks down transformation gags into eight different types. Although the categories are somewhat imprecise for the purpose of film analysis, they provide valuable insights into how transformation gags function.

27. Jenkins, *What Made Pistachio Nuts?*, 79.

28. For a smaller-scale version of this gag, see *The Garage* (1920), directed by Arbuckle and co-starring Keaton and Al St. John.

29. The year listed is the release date. *The High Sign* was filmed in 1920, but Keaton withheld it from circulation. See filmography for the release dates of Keaton's films.

30. See Chapter 1.

31. Vardac, *Stage to Screen*, 20–88.

32. Critics have variously claimed that Keaton withheld the release of *The High Sign* because he believed it was not funny enough (Meade, *Cut to the Chase*, 94), not as good as *One Week* (Dardis, *Man Who Wouldn't Lie Down*, 68), or a complete failure (Blesh, *Keaton*, 139).

33. See Chapter 3 of this book for an extended treatment of the gag/narrative debate in film theory.

34. On Schenck's business sense, see Kramer, "Making of a Comic Star," 190–210.

35. In the chariot race toward the end of the film, Buster drives a chariot through the snow on sleigh runners pulled by a team of sled dogs.

36. For a different view, see Jenkins, "Interrupted Performance," 48. Jenkins suggests that the inner film, particularly at the moment in which Buster enters it, invokes the vaudeville device of the disrupted act.

37. See Sweeney, "Dream of Disruption," 104–20. Sweeney notes the structural similarities between the inner and outer film, yet neglects the differences in gag/narrative emphasis.

38. Ibid. Sweeney argues that Keaton is playing with a new form of full-length film comedy in *Sherlock Jr.*, one that balances gag structure and narrative structure. His analysis of individual "tripartite gags" is thorough, yet he fails to demonstrate how this tripartite structure is extended to the overall structure of the film.

39. Ibid., 110.

40. On Keaton's use of magic in *Sherlock Jr.*, see Parshall, "Houdini's Protégé," 67–88.

41. Buñuel, "Keaton's *College*," 64–65.

42. Moews, *Silent Features Close Up*, 246–47.

43. Rapf and Green, *Keaton: Bio-Bibliography*, 5.

44. Keaton with Samuels, *Wonderful World of Slapstick*, 174.

45. Bentley, "Farce," 241.

46. Bermel, *Farce*, 180.

47. Ibid., 180.

48. Parshall, "Keaton and Space of Farce," 41.

49. For the use of multiples in the Keatons' vaudeville act, see Chapter 1.

50. Seidman, *Comedian Comedy*, 15.

51. Ibid., 40. Italics in original.

52. Chaplin also had his trademark, though he depended upon a more complex assembly of clothing and props: baggy trousers, a tight coat, a bowler hat, a mustache, and a cane. Moreover, to a greater extent than Lloyd or Keaton, Chaplin's characterization depended upon his movement. The exaggeration of his movements, combined with the all-encompassing nature of his costume, made imitating Chaplin much easier, one reason why Chaplin's popularity spawned numerous impersonation contests.

53. Other films in which the porkpie hat draws attention to Keaton's screen persona include *Go West*, in which he attempts to put his hat over the horns of a devil's costume; *The Paleface* (1922), in which he wears a feather in his porkpie hat; and Beckett's *Film* (1965), in which, because Keaton is filmed only from behind, his porkpie hat is the only characteristic identifying him until the last shot of the film.

54. Keaton publicity photographs, Film Stills Archive, Museum of Modern Art, New York.

55. See Jenkins, "Interrupted Performance," 40–44, on the vaudeville aesthetic in *The Playhouse*.

56. Kerr, *Silent Clowns*, 134.

57. Similarly, Keaton and cameraman Elgin Lessley used a metronome and a banjo player to synchronize the nine-man minstrel show to the tune of "Darktown Strutters' Ball." Blesh, *Keaton*, 168.

58. In *Moonshine*, Keaton used a primitive version of the shuttered lens he built

for *The Playhouse*—he simply taped off half of the lens at a time so that it appeared as if over fifty tax agents stepped out of one automobile. By covering the left side of the lens, he was able to hide the fact that the actors stepped into the car from the other side. When another film company attempted to copy the trick, it was unable to do so. Keaton realized that the car would move when the actors climbed through it, therefore he put the car up on jacks to keep it still in both shots. Unlike Keaton, the rival company never solved this technical problem. Blesh, *Keaton*, 107–8.

59. Ibid., 264.

60. During the first half of the twentieth century, "bull" was also slang for a policeman. *Webster's New Twentieth Century Dictionary*, 2nd ed.

61. Blesh, *Keaton*, 258–60.

62. The references are to the following films, in order: *The Boat, The Playhouse, The Three Ages, Cops, Go West,* and *Seven Chances.*

63. Gunning, "Crazy Machines," 103.

64. Ibid., 101–2.

65. Keaton uses the Rube Goldberg–style kitchen again in *The Navigator.*

66. Bentley, "Psychology of Farce," xx.

67. Kerr, *Silent Clowns*, 145.

68. Bentley, "Farce," 245.

69. See Baker, *Aesthetics of Farce*, 51–54.

70. I use the term "graphic-match montage" to describe the two layers that make up this sequence: the *montage* of brief, unrelated shots of environments achieves continuity only through the *graphic match* of Buster from shot to shot. I am indebted to Charles Maland and Bert Cardullo for their suggestions in coining this composite term.

71. Jenkins sees this sequence as an outgrowth of the vaudevillian "interrupted act," comparing it to Buster's disruption of his father in The Three Keatons' vaudeville routines. "Interrupted Performance," 62–63.

72. For the most comprehensive explanation of how Keaton created the sequence, see Bishop, "Interview with Keaton," 17–18.

73. For a discussion of the mathematics of Keaton's gags, see Goodwin, "Mathematics in *Sherlock Jr.*," 118–129.

74. See Bordwell, Staiger, and Thompson, *Classical Hollywood Cinema*, on the first chase films in 1903–4 (160) and the incorporation of chases into longer narratives in the early teens (175).

75. See Crafton, "Pie and Chase," 106–19. Crafton uses the terms "pie" and "chase" metaphorically, to capture the disruptive impact of the gag (the pie) and the linearity of the narrative (the chase), but this does not mean that a specific chase cannot function as one of his metaphorical "pies" (111).

76. See also the waterwheel sequence in *Daydreams*, in which Buster jogs inside a waterwheel, trying to keep pace with its revolutions.

77. Perez, "Bewildered Equilibrist," 344.

78. Ibid.

79. For an analysis of the shifting meanings of the terms "spectacle" and "excess," see Grindon, "Role of Spectacle," 35–43.

80. "Biography: Buster Keaton," Arts & Entertainment Network.

Chapter 3
Keaton Re-Viewed:
Beyond Keaton's Classicism

1. Gunning, "Cinema of Attraction" 63–70.

2. Bordwell, Staiger, and Thompson, *Classical Hollywood Cinema*, 157.

3. Neale and Krutnik, *Popular Film and Television Comedy*, 5.

4. Furthermore, the production history of each film reveals the evolution of Keaton's economic and artistic relationship with Schenck. *Sherlock Jr.* was made in 1924, when Keaton enjoyed almost unlimited artistic control over his films. Keaton's account of the shooting in 1928 of *Steamboat Bill, Jr.*, his last film for Schenck, betrays the artistic constraints that Schenck placed on Keaton in the wake of *The General*'s box-office failure.

5. See Bordwell, Staiger, and Thompson, *Classical Hollywood Cinema*, 158. "The term 'primitive' is in many ways an unfortunate one, for it may imply that these films were crude attempts at what would later become classical filmmaking. While I use the word because of its widespread acceptance, I would prefer to think of primitive films more in the sense that one speaks of primitive art, either produced by native cultures (e.g., Eskimo ivory carving) or untrained individuals (e.g., Henri Rousseau). That is, such primitive art is a system apart, whose simplicity can be of a value equal to more formal aesthetic traditions."

6. Gunning, "Cinema of Attraction," 64.

7. Bordwell, Staiger, and Thompson, *Classical Hollywood Cinema*, 157.

8. Ibid., 159. See also Allen, *Vaudeville and Film*, on the economic interaction between the two media from the advent of film until 1912.

9. Ibid., 160.

10. Ibid., 159.

11. Ibid., 160.

12. Ibid., 160.

13. Ibid., 162.

14. Koszarski, *Evening's Entertainment*, 174.

15. Ibid., 175.

16. Arbuckle starred in features produced by Adolf Zukor starting with *The Round Up* (1920), but the films were hastily made and unsuited for him, particularly in their emphasis on dialogue titles over slapstick. See Koszarski, *Evening's Entertainment*, 178.

17. Although I have kept references to other film comedians to a minimum throughout this book, I feel that it is necessary to compare Keaton to his contemporaries at this point in order to isolate the particular qualities of Keaton's blend of vaudeville and film. Most scholars of silent film comedy limit themselves to discussing Keaton in the context of the films of his two or three most famous rivals: Charlie Chaplin, Harold Lloyd, and occasionally Harry Langdon. I will follow this tradition for the following reasons. First, few if any slapstick comedians other than the "big four" had demonstrable artistic control over their films. Roscoe Arbuckle, for example, lost almost all artistic control over his films when he began making features for Paramount in 1920. Many of the next tier of comedians (in terms of box-office success) never made feature films, and although I do not mean to equate running time with quality, short films necessarily curtail the extent of our inquiry into the gag-narrative relationship. Langdon will also be excluded from my comparisons, for, despite the influence he exerted on his films as a comic performer, they were directed by the strong-willed Frank Capra, and it is therefore difficult to attribute any cinematic innovations solely to Langdon. For a detailed analysis of Langdon's influence on the mise-en-scène of his films, see Rheuban, *Harry Langdon*.

18. Krutnik, "Spanner in the Works?," 19. Italics in original. In his tribute to Larry Semon, Petr Král contrasts the nonconformism of Semon's films with Lloyd's films, which he characterizes as "healthy, classically balanced *white* humour," crediting Lloyd's style to Roach. Král, "Larry Semon's Message," 177. Král attributes Roach's commercial success in the 1930s to his essential conformism, asserting that Roach's films provided a sense of stability for audiences living in the economic uncertainty of the Depression.

19. See McCaffrey, *Four Great Comedians*, 165.

20. Buñuel, "Buster Keaton's *College*," 64.

21. Kamin, *Chaplin's One-Man Show*.

22. See ibid., for a detailed analysis of the mechanics of Chaplin's work as a mime.

23. Kerr, *Silent Clowns*, 198.

24. Bordwell, Staiger, and Thompson, *Classical Hollywood Cinema*, 17.

25. See ibid., 19–23, on the four types of motivation—compositional, realistic, intertextual, and artistic—and their function within classical Hollywood cinema.

26. See Chapter 2.

27. Moews, *Silent Feature Close Up*, 118.

28. Ibid., 118.

29. Bordwell and Thompson, *Film Art*, 178.

30. Bordwell, Staiger, and Thompson, *Classical Hollywood Cinema*, 81.

31. Crafton notes the inherent difficulty of defining the term "gag": "There can be no concrete definition of a gag because it is marked by affective response, not set forms or clear logic." Crafton, "Pie and Chase," 109. See also Gunning, "Crazy Machines," 89.

32. Crafton, "Pie and Chase," 107.

33. Ibid., 107.

34. Ibid., 111.

35. Gunning, "Response to 'Pie and Chase,'" 121.

36. Gunning, "Crazy Machines," 97.

37. Gunning, "Response to 'Pie and Chase,'" 121.

38. Neale and Krutnik, *Popular Film and Television Comedy*, 44–57.

39. See Keaton, "Why I Never Smile," 173, in which Keaton defines gags and their relationship to action: "A gag in comedy is what they call a piece of business in the theater. It is the handling of a property. It is not like a situation which arises out of the action, though it may help the action."

40. Thompson, *Neoformalist Film Analysis*, 259. See also Grindon, "Role of Spectacle," 35–43. Grindon convincingly argues that the distinction between spectacle and excess is ambiguous and "has hindered precision in thinking about the cinema" (42).

41. Gunning, "Crazy Machines," 97. Italics added.

42. Gunning, "Cinema of Attraction," 64. Italics in original.

43. See Eisenstein, "Montage of Attractions," 77–84.

44. Gunning, "Cinema of Attraction," 66.

45. Blesh, *Keaton*, 268–70.

46. See Kishpaugh, "Real General," 1–2.

47. See Moews, *Silent Features Close Up*, 212–45.

48. Giannetti, *Understanding Movies*, 315.

49. Ibid., 317.

50. See Carroll, "*General* and Visible Intelligibility," 125–40.

51. Moews, *Silent Features Close Up*, 245.

52. Ibid., 221.

53. Blesh, *Keaton*, 258.

54. Ibid.

55. Megrue, *Seven Chances*, 7–47.

56. Moews argues that *Seven Chances* contains a social commentary, which he characterizes as "an unfeeling expression of a then-dominant male chauvinism" (129). By failing to examine the play, however, Moews misunderstands Keaton's contribution to the film.

57. The servant is played in blackface, a convention that Keaton uses in several films. Though it is easy to criticize Keaton with 20/20, politically correct hindsight, it must be remembered that blackface was still a common convention in film and on stage in the 1920s.

58. Megrue, *Seven Chances*, 82–85.

59. Bordwell, Staiger, and Thompson, *Classical Hollywood Cinema*, 45.

60. See Chapter 2.

61. Blesh, *Keaton*, 258–60.

62. Compare to Mast, *Comic Mind*, 141–42; and Deleuze, *Cinema 1*, 174.

63. Crafton, "Pie and Chase," 107.

64. The hat sequence also functions as a self-reference to Buster's trademark porkpie hat. See Chapter 2.

65. Keaton, interview, ed. Joan and Bob Franklin, 28.

66. See Pearson, "Playing Detective," 140–57, for a playful investigation of the production history of *Sherlock Jr.*

67. See Jenkins, "Interrupted Performance," 62–63, on the vaudeville origins of this disruption.

68. Stewart, "Keaton Through the Looking Glass," 353.

69. Brownlow, *Parade's Gone By*, 487.

70. Ibid., 487. See also Bishop, "Interview with Buster Keaton," 17–18.

71. Jenkins observes that the excesses of the inner film are ultimately "constrained by classical norms." "Interrupted Performance," 49. Horton stresses that the anarchistic comedy of the inner film provides the majority of the comedy, within the form provided by the romantic comedy of the outer film. Introduction to *Buster Keaton's Sherlock Jr.*, 11–13.

72. "Biography: Buster Keaton," Arts & Entertainment Network.

73. See Sweeney, "Dream of Disruption," 108.

74. I discuss Buster's ride on the driverless motorcycle in Chapter 2, in the context of Keaton's creation of a world that functions like a Rube Goldberg invention.

75. Jenkins astutely observes that the long delay in reincorporating the billiard ball "renders the whole concept of narrative economy an absurd joke, resolving an enigma that the audience has long since forgotten." "Interrupted Performance," 51.

76. Jenkins, *What Made Pistachio Nuts?*, 102.

Chapter 4
From Vaudeville to Surrealism

1. Matthews, *Surrealism and Film*, 30; Williams, "Buñuelian Cinema," 200. See also Erebé, "Sur le film comique," 10.

2. The surrealists also rallied to Chaplin's side when the newspapers criticized him for his sexual exploits during his divorce from Lita Grey. In 1927, thirty-two surrealists signed a declaration entitled "Hands Off Love," published in *La Révolution surréaliste*, in defense of Chaplin's behavior. Bédouin, et al., 183–92.

3. Dalí, "Critical History of Cinema," 73. See also Král, "Larry Semon's Message," 175–82.

4. Hammond, "Available Light," 14.

5. Matthews, *Surrealism and Film*, 30.

6. Rapf and Green contend that Keaton's parody of narrative conventions and

closure frequently undercuts Buster's success at the end of his films. Rapf and Green, *Keaton: Bio-Bibliography*, 43–44.

7. Moews, *Keaton: Silent Features*, 2–18.

8. Perez, "Bewildered Equilibrist," 339.

9. On the importance of Desnos's film criticism within the surrealist movement, see Kovács, *Enchantment to Rage*, 48.

10. Williams, *Figures of Desire*, 14–17, 26. See also Abel, *French Film Theory*, 337–39.

11. Abel, *French Film Theory*, 338. Italics in original. See also Williams, *Figures of Desire*, 18; and Kovács, *Enchantment to Rage*, 251–53.

12. Desnos, *Cinéma*, 117, translation by Pamela Waxman. Desnos praised Chaplin's films as well: "The logic which these ups and downs of life obey is related to that of dreams." Desnos, *Cinéma*, 124, translated and quoted in Kovács, *Enchantment to Rage*, 53.

13. Desnos, *Cinéma*, 126. Translation by Pamela Waxman. The nearest translation of the French title for this film would be *The Collapsible House of Malec* (Malec being the French name for Keaton). Although this title could refer to *The Electric House*, it seems more fitting for *One Week*.

14. Ibid., 132.

15. Translated in Gibson, *Lorca: A Life*, 151, from *Santos Tottoella* (1987) 19. See also Finkelstein, "Nature of a Collaboration," 129–30. In another letter, he sent Lorca a collage of publicity photographs of Keaton and Natalie Talmadge, supplemented by his own additions. The surrealists were fond of using photographs from press clippings for illustrations; in December 1924 Louis Aragon used a publicity photograph of Buster Keaton and Sybil Seeley from *One Week*, in which Buster gazes at his wife in the shower, to embellish his essay "L'Ombre de l'Inventeur" ("Shadow of the Inventor," *La Révolution surréaliste*, 22–24). See also Benayoun, *Look of Buster Keaton*, 105.

16. I first saw this sculpture at the Tate Gallery in London, though other versions exist.

17. Gibson, *Lorca: A Life*, 151.

18. Both Keaton and Dalí employed this mechanism repeatedly. For examples in Keaton's films, see the car as sailboat at the end of *Sherlock Jr.*; the bed as car during the cyclone sequence in *Steamboat Bill, Jr.*; the lamp as javelin at the end of *College*. For examples in Dalí's work, see the lips as couch, nose as mantel, and hair as drapes in *Mae West* (1934–36); the leg as table in *The Ghost of Vermeer van Delft, which can be used as a table* (1934); and the woman's torso as a "chest" of drawers in *The City of Drawers* (1936). See Matthews, *Introduction to Surrealism*, 130, and Benayoun, *Look of Buster Keaton*, 177, on Dalí's use of double imagery.

19. See Havard, "Lorca's *Buster Keaton*" 19, footnote 1. Each translator of the play has furnished a different version of the title of this play: *Keaton's Promenade* (Rey-

nolds), *Buster Keaton's Spin* (Hutchison), *Buster Keaton Takes a Walk* (Lloyd), and *Buster Keaton's Ride* (Spicer).

20. Lorca uses the full name "Buster Keaton" throughout his text. I retain that distinction in this passage to differentiate Lorca's character from Keaton's film character, Buster.

21. Lorca, *Buster Keaton's Promenade*, 132.

22. Allen, "Commentary on Lorca's *El Paseo*," 25.

23. *Buster Keaton's Promenade*, 133.

24. Ibid., 133.

25. A version of *El Paseo de Buster Keaton* was presented recently at the Festival Grec de Barcelona, Spain (21 June–31 July 1998), staged by Joan Baixes, with music by Sordi Sabatés.

26. Davis, "Teatro Breve," 98; Allen, "Lorca's *El Paseo*," 23; Higginbotham, "Experimental Farces," 100–101; Havard, "Lorca's *Buster Keaton*," 13. For a discussion of surrealist film scenarios within the context of post–World War I French film practice, see Abel, "Surrealist Scenario Text," 58–71.

27. Clair, *Cinema Yesterday and Today*, 103.

28. McGerr, *René Clair*, 162–63. On the relationship between the Sennett chase and Clair's *Entr'acte*, see Noël Carroll, "Entr'acte, Paris and Dada," 5–11.

29. Artaud, "Cinema and Reality," 150.

30. Ibid., 152.

31. Erebé, "Sur le film comique," 12. Translation by Pamela Waxman.

32. Ibid.

33. Ibid.

34. Ibid.

35. Buñuel, "Keaton's *College*," 65.

36. Ibid., 64–65.

37. Drummond, "Introduction," *Un Chien andalou*, xvi. Drummond notes that Dalí contributed more to filming this segment than to any other portion of the film (xii). See also Horton, Introduction to *Buster Keaton's Sherlock Jr.*, 26.

38. Aranda, *Buñuel: Critical Biography*, 52. The films screened included excerpts from Ben Turpin's *News*, Chaplin's *Sunnyside*, Langdon's *Long Pants*, and Keaton's *The Navigator*. Despite the inclusion of Chaplin, Buñuel and Dalí preferred Keaton over Chaplin, who they felt was overly sentimental. See Aranda, *Buñuel*, 53, 268–69.

39. Ibid. Italics in original.

40. Aron discusses Man Ray's *Emak Bakia* (1927), *L'Etoile de mer* (1928), and *Les Mysteres du Chateau du Dé* (1929), Buñuel's *Un Chien andalou* (1929), and Keaton's *The Navigator* (1924), *Steamboat Bill, Jr.* (1926), and *The Cameraman* (1928). Aron, "Films of Revolt," 432–36.

41. Ibid., 434.

42. Ibid.

43. Brunius, "Experimental Film in France," 77.

44. Ibid., 89.

45. Kyrou, *Le Surréalisme au cinéma*, 94–95.

46. Benayoun suggests that the cow in *Go West* "could have been the inspiration for the more provocative symbol in Buñuel's *Golden Age* (1930)." Benayoun, *Look of Keaton*, 56. This essay was originally published as "Le Collose de silence," *Positif* (summer 1966), 18–24.

47. Ibid., 101.

48. Benayoun, *Look of Keaton*, 19. This essay was originally published as "Le Regard de Buster Keaton," *Positif* (summer 1966), 1–17. Although not, strictly speaking, a surrealist journal, *Positif* published a good deal of work by surrealists. Benayoun began writing for *Positif* in 1954; he took over as editor of the journal in May 1962.

49. Ibid., 176.

50. Ibid., 55.

51. Král, "Larry Semon's Message," 177.

52. Ibid.

53. Ibid., 175. Italics in original.

54. Breton, *Manifestoes of Surrealism*, 14. Italics in original.

55. Matthews, *Surrealism and Film*, 4. Italics in original.

56. See Kuenzli, Introduction to *Dada and Surrealist Film*, 10, on the surrealists' use of realistic effects, narratives, and characters in their films.

57. Chesler, *Surrealist Film Aesthetic*, 42.

58. Perez, "Bewildered Equilibrist," 347.

59. See Matthews, *Surrealism and Film*, 2.

60. Kyrou, "The Fantastic—The Marvellous," 167–68.

61. Translated in Matthews, *Surrealism and Film*, 3.

62. See also Breton's *Second Manifesto of Surrealism*, in which he articulates the role of realistic settings in his novels: "The verisimilitude of the setting will, for the first time, stop concealing from us the strange symbolic life which objects, the most commonplace as well as the most clearly defined, have only in dreams." *Manifestoes of Surrealism*, 163.

63. Bermel, *Farce*, 180.

64. Blesh, *Keaton*, 256–57.

65. Breton, *Manifestoes of Surrealism*, 187.

66. See "The Surrealists Claim Keaton," above.

67. Breton, *Manifestoes of Surrealism*, 275.

68. Quoted in Balakian, *Surrealism: Road to Absolute*, 154. See Kuenzli, Introduction to *Dada and Surrealist Film*, 9, on the relationship of this phrase to filmic montage.

69. Breton, *Manifestoes of Surrealism*, 275. Italics in original.

70. See Chesler, *Surrealist Film Aesthetic*, 88–89, who contends that the surrealists valued American slapstick for its combination of unreal events with realistic settings.

71. See Buñuel, "Keaton's *College*," 64–65, and Chapter 2.

72. Chesler, *Surrealist Film Aesthetic*, 43.

73. Alexandrian, *Surrealist Art*, 140–50.

74. See Matthews, *Introduction to Surrealism*, 147.

75. Williams, *Figures of Desire*, 12. For a description of other surrealist games, including the "Exquisite Corpse," see Ray, *Avant-Garde Finds Andy Hardy*, 40–73.

76. Benayoun, *Look of Keaton*, 19.

77. Chesler, "Surrealist Film Aesthetic," 56.

78. Translated in Matthews, *Surrealism and Film*, 75. Originally published in Nougé, *L'Expérience Les Lèvres continue* (Brussels, 1966), 175–76. In his analysis of "D'Or et de Sable," Matthews fails to recognize that Nougé based it on *Sherlock Jr.* He therefore mistakenly attributes the imaginative impulse of the film to Nougé.

79. Nougé's *cinépoème* is an example of another surrealist game—"the irrational enlargement of a film scene"—in which a small moment or circumstance from a film is used as a jumping off point for poetic imagery. For examples of this type of work, see Bèdouin, et al., "Irrational Enlargement," 128–37; and Ray, *Avant-Garde Finds Andy Hardy*, 48–73.

80. Cott, "Limits of Silent Comedy," 101.

81. Williams, *Figures of Desire*, 24–25. Italics in original.

82. Ibid., 26.

83. Ibid., 28. "Three of the four Desnos scenarios published . . . begin either as melodrama or farce, which before the end is transformed into surreal visions."

84. See ibid., 9, on Apollonaire's early use of this technique in his first film scenario, *La Bréhatine* (1917).

85. Gunning, "Cinema of Attraction," 64.

86. Ibid., 70.

87. Williams, *Figures of Desire*, 27. See also Matthews, *Surrealism and Film*, 56–58.

88. Williams, *Figures of Desire*, 27.

Chapter 5
Beyond Surrealism:
Keaton's Legacy

1. In *Sunset Boulevard* (1950), Keaton has a cameo role as a former Hollywood star who has fallen from grace, who plays in a weekly bridge game with Norma Desmond and two other former stars from the silent era. Although Keaton appears briefly and utters only one line—"Pass . . . pass"—his appearance contributes to the film's satiric commentary on how Hollywood discarded some of its most talented stars. See Kline, *Complete Films*, 193–95.

2. John Spotton's documentary *Buster Keaton Rides Again* (1965) captures Keaton

at work during the filming of *The Railrodder*. Alan Schneider's essay "On Directing *Film*" provides a revealing look at the working relationship among Keaton, Beckett, and Schneider during the making of *Film*.

3. Tibbetts, "Last Ride of Keaton," 5.

4. Potterton was not the only filmmaker to incorporate the porkpie hat into his film—Keaton wears a porkpie in many of his films from the 1960s. He wears a porkpie hat with a feather atop it (à la *The Paleface*) in a series of cameo appearances in the Frankie Avalon and Annette Funicello beach movies, such as *Beach Blanket Bingo* (1965) and *How to Stuff a Wild Bikini* (1965). In his final film, *War Italian Style* (1967), Keaton plays a Nazi general, but when his Italian captors release him at the end of the film, they give him his porkpie hat and jacket for his last walk off into the sunset. Finally, as I describe later in this chapter, Keaton suggested that he wear a porkpie hat in *Film* and Beckett agreed.

5. Tibbetts, "Last Ride of Keaton," 5.

6. Spotton, *Buster Keaton Rides Again*.

7. Ibid.

8. Ibid. Italics added.

9. Ibid.

10. Ibid.

11. Tibbetts, "Last Ride of Keaton," 6.

12. The sequence bears a striking similarity to the final gag in *Hard Luck* (1921), in which Buster attempts a high dive into a swimming pool, but misses the pool, only to emerge years later from the hole he made in the ground dressed as a stereotypical "Chinaman" with a Chinese wife and two kids.

13. Schneider, "On Directing *Film*," 66–67. McGowan was third choice. Beckett originally wanted Chaplin or Zero Mostel.

14. Ibid., 67.

15. Ibid., 68.

16. Ibid., 66.

17. Ibid., 63.

18. Ibid.

19. Ibid., 68.

20. Beckett, *Film*, 27–28.

21. Schneider, "On Directing *Film*," 68.

22. Quoted in Gontarski, *Beckett's Dramatic Texts*, 108.

23. Schneider, "On Directing *Film*," 72. See Hale, *Beckett's Dramatic Perspective*, 85.

24. Schneider, "On Directing *Film*," 90–93.

25. Ironically, in the summer of 1997, in the wake of the second surge of interest in Keaton on the 100th anniversary of his birth, Blue Moon Books released *Film* on videotape.

26. Perlmutter, "Beckett's *Film*," 91.

27. Milne, "Festivals '65: Venice," 207.

28. Brater, *Beckett at 80*, 8–9.

29. See Brater, "Dada, Surrealism, and *Not I*," 49–59.

30. Beckerman, "Act of Listening," 150.

31. Sarris, "Keaton and Beckett," 42–43.

32. Horton notes the influence of Keaton on several recent films, including *Cinema Paradiso*, *Last Action Hero*, and *Benny and Joon*. Introduction to *Buster Keaton's Sherlock Jr.*, 26–27.

33. For more on the development of New Vaudeville, see Harrison, *New Vaudeville*, 1–35.

34. Gussow, "Profiles: Clown," 63.

35. Irwin, "Beauty in the Form," 1.

36. In *Fool Moon* Irwin uses a more characteristic vaudeville structure, alternating his solo performance with duets with and solos by his partner, David Shiner, and the accompanying band, the Red Clay Ramblers, as well as varying their performance modes from slapstick and dance to audience-participation clowning.

37. Theatre on Film and Video Collection, Lincoln Center Library for the Performing Arts.

38. See Jenkins, "Interrupted Performance."

39. See Barr, review of *Largely New York*, 242–44.

40. See Chapters 2 and 4 on *The Playhouse* and *Sherlock Jr.*, respectively.

41. See Chapter 2.

42. Scott, "Classical Theater," 118.

43. Gentry, *Inside the Dragon*, 6–7.

44. Logan, *Hong Kong Action Cinema*, 11.

45. Scott, "Classical Theater," 133–34.

46. Ibid., 118–19.

47. Chan directed his first comic kung fu film, *Half a Loaf of Kung Fu* (1978) before the success of *Snake in the Eagle's Shadow*, but his producer, Lo Wei, withheld it from circulation because he felt it was inferior to Chan's other films. In 1980, after the success of Chan's early comedies, Lo Wei released *Half a Loaf of Kung Fu* and it did well at the box office. Gentry, *Inside the Dragon*, 13–15.

48. Logan, *Hong Kong Action Cinema*, 63.

49. In *Operation Condor* (1991) and *Supercop* (1992).

50. I write this with full recognition that these comedians might not be capable of creating a successful, Keaton-inspired film. On the basis of Rowan Atkinson's British television shows, I had high hopes for *Bean* (1997), only to find Atkinson embracing the more infantile side of his humor. Nevertheless the lack of opportunity for physical comedians to make films in an improvisational style in Hollywood limits Keaton's influence on the contemporary American film industry.

51. To some extent, the shift in the prevalent view of Keaton's films has already begun, resulting in a rift between the changing evaluation of his films and main-

stream recognition of this fact. On the one hand, Cambridge University Press selected *Sherlock Jr.*, and not *The General*, as the representative Keaton film for its
series of books on classic films, indicating that film scholars are beginning to perceive the significance of the vaudeville aesthetic in his work. On the other hand, as
many have decried in editorials, not a single Keaton film appears on the American
Film Institute's recently proclaimed list of "100 Great American Films." In all the
controversy about the omission, no one has noticed that the only Keaton film considered for the list was *The General*, which suggests that AFI has yet to acquiesce to
the reevaluation of his films.

Filmography

THIS FILMOGRAPHY includes all of Keaton's short and feature-length silent films, his sound features for MGM, his subsequent appearances in feature films, and a few significant short films at the end of his career. For a complete annotated Keaton filmography, see Jim Kline, *The Complete Films of Buster Keaton*. Films marked with an asterisk are believed to be lost.

Arbuckle Silent Shorts

The Butcher Boy (1917). Released on April 23, 1917. Produced by the Comique Film Corporation. Distributed by Paramount Pictures. Director/ Writer: Roscoe Arbuckle. Story: Joe Roach. Editor: Herbert Warren. Photography: Frank D. Williams. Length: 2 reels.
> CAST: Roscoe "Fatty" Arbuckle, Buster Keaton, Al St. John, Josephine Stevens, Arthur Earle, Agnes Neilson, Joe Bordeau, Luke the Dog.

A Reckless Romeo (1917)*. Released on May 21, 1917. Produced by the Comique Film Corporation. Distributed by Paramount Pictures. Director/ Writer: Roscoe Arbuckle. Story: Joe Roach. Editor: Herbert Warren. Photography: Frank D. Williams. Length: 2 reels.
> CAST: Roscoe "Fatty" Arbuckle, Buster Keaton, Al St. John, Alice Lake, Corinne Parquet, Agnes Neilson.

The Rough House (1917). Released on June 25, 1917. Produced by the Comique Film Corporation. Distributed by Paramount Pictures. Director/ Writer: Roscoe Arbuckle. Story: Joe Roach. Editor: Herbert Warren. Photography: Frank D. Williams. Length: 2 reels.
> CAST: Roscoe "Fatty" Arbuckle, Buster Keaton, Al St. John, Alice Lake, Agnes Neilson, Glen Cavender.

His Wedding Night (1917). Released on August 20, 1917. Produced by the Comique Film Corporation. Distributed by Paramount Pictures. Director/Writer: Roscoe Arbuckle. Story: Joe Roach. Editor: Herbert Warren. Photography: George Peters. Length: 2 reels.

CAST: Roscoe "Fatty" Arbuckle, Buster Keaton, Al St. John, Alice Mann, Arthur Earle, Jimmy Bryant, Josephine Stevens.

Oh, Doctor! (1917).* Released on September 30, 1917. Produced by the Comique Film Corporation. Distributed by Paramount Pictures. Director/Writer: Roscoe Arbuckle. Scenario: Jean Havez. Editor: Herbert Warren. Photography: George Peters. Length: 2 reels.

CAST: Roscoe "Fatty" Arbuckle, Buster Keaton, Al St. John, Alice Mann.

Fatty at Coney Island [a.k.a. *Coney Island*] (1917). Released on October 29, 1917. Produced by the Comique Film Corporation. Distributed by Paramount Pictures. Director/Writer: Roscoe Arbuckle. Editor: Herbert Warren. Photography: George Peters. Length: 2 reels.

CAST: Roscoe "Fatty" Arbuckle, Buster Keaton, Al St. John, Alice Mann, Agnes Neilson, Jimmy Bryant, Joe Bordeau.

A Country Hero (1917).* Released on December 10, 1917. Produced by the Comique Film Corporation. Distributed by Paramount Pictures. Director/Writer: Roscoe Arbuckle. Editor: Herbert Warren. Photography: George Peters. Length: 2 reels.

CAST: Roscoe "Fatty" Arbuckle, Buster Keaton, Al St. John, Alice Lake, Joe Keaton, Stanley Pembroke.

Out West (1918). Released on January 20, 1918. Produced by the Comique Film Corporation. Distributed by Paramount Pictures. Director/Writer: Roscoe Arbuckle. Scenario: Natalie Talmadge. Editor: Herbert Warren. Photography: George Peters. Length: 2 reels.

CAST: Roscoe "Fatty" Arbuckle, Buster Keaton, Al St. John, Alice Lake, Joe Keaton.

The Bell Boy (1918). Released on March 18, 1918. Produced by the Comique Film Corporation. Distributed by Paramount Pictures. Director/Writer: Roscoe Arbuckle. Editor: Herbert Warren. Photography: George Peters. Length: 2 reels.

CAST: Roscoe "Fatty" Arbuckle, Buster Keaton, Al St. John, Alice Lake, Joe Keaton, Charles Dudley.

Moonshine (1918). Released on May 13, 1918. Produced by the Comique Film Corporation. Distributed by Paramount Pictures. Director/Writer: Roscoe Arbuckle. Editor: Herbert Warren. Photography: George Peters. Length: 2 reels.

CAST: Roscoe "Fatty" Arbuckle, Buster Keaton, Al St. John, Alice Lake, Charles Dudley, Joe Bordeau.

Good Night, Nurse (1918). Released on July 6, 1918. Produced by the Comique Film Corporation. Distributed by Paramount Pictures. Director/ Writer: Roscoe Arbuckle. Editor: Herbert Warren. Photography: George Peters. Length: 2 reels.

CAST: Roscoe "Fatty" Arbuckle, Buster Keaton, Al St. John, Alice Lake, Joe Bordeau.

The Cook (1918).* Released on September 15, 1918. Produced by the Comique Film Corporation. Distributed by Paramount Pictures. Director/ Writer: Roscoe Arbuckle. Editor: Herbert Warren. Photography: George Peters. Length: 2 reels.

CAST: Roscoe "Fatty" Arbuckle, Buster Keaton, Al St. John, Alice Lake, Glen Cavender, Luke the Dog.

Back Stage (1919). Released on September 7, 1919. Produced by the Comique Film Corporation. Distributed by Paramount Pictures. Director/ Writer: Roscoe Arbuckle. Scenario: Jean Havez. Photography: Elgin Lessley. Length: 2 reels.

CAST: Roscoe "Fatty" Arbuckle, Buster Keaton, Al St. John, Molly Malone, John Coogan.

The Hayseed (1919). Released on October 26, 1919. Produced by the Comique Film Corporation. Distributed by Paramount Pictures. Director/ Writer: Roscoe Arbuckle. Scenario: Jean Havez. Photography: Elgin Lessley. Length: 2 reels.

CAST: Roscoe "Fatty" Arbuckle, Buster Keaton, Molly Malone, John Coogan, Luke the Dog.

The Garage [a.k.a. *Fire Chief*] (1920). Released on January 11, 1920. Produced by the Comique Film Corporation. Distributed by Paramount Pictures. Director/Writer: Roscoe Arbuckle. Scenario: Jean Havez. Photography: Elgin Lessley. Length: 2 reels.

CAST: Roscoe "Fatty" Arbuckle, Buster Keaton, Molly Malone, Harry McCoy, Daniel Crimmins, Luke the Dog.

Keaton Silent Shorts

One Week (1920). Released: September 1, 1920. Presented by the Comique Film Corporation. Distributed by Metro Pictures. Producer: Joseph M. Schenck. Director/Script: Buster Keaton and Eddie Cline. Photography: Elgin Lessley. Length: 2 reels.

CAST: Buster Keaton, Sybil Seely, Joe Roberts.

Convict 13 (1920). Released on October 27, 1920. Presented by the Comique Film Corporation. Distributed by Metro Pictures. Producer: Joseph M. Schenck. Director/Script: Buster Keaton and Eddie Cline. Photography: Elgin Lessley. Length: 2 reels.

CAST: Buster Keaton, Sybil Seely, Joe Roberts, Eddie Cline, Joe Keaton.

The Scarecrow (1920). Released on November 17, 1920. Presented by the Comique Film Corporation. Distributed by Metro Pictures. Producer: Joseph M. Schenck. Director/Script: Buster Keaton and Eddie Cline. Photography: Elgin Lessley. Length: 2 reels.

CAST: Buster Keaton, Sybil Seely, Joe Roberts, Eddie Cline, Joe Keaton, Luke the Dog.

Neighbors (1920). Released on December 22, 1920. Presented by the Comique Film Corporation. Distributed by Metro Pictures. Producer: Joseph M. Schenck. Director/Script: Buster Keaton and Eddie Cline. Photography: Elgin Lessley. Length: 2 reels.

CAST: Buster Keaton, Virginia Fox, Joe Roberts, Joe Keaton, Eddie Cline, James Duffy, The Flying Escalantes.

The Haunted House (1921). Released on February 10, 1921. Presented by the Comique Film Corporation. Distributed by Metro Pictures. Producer: Joseph M. Schenck. Director/Script: Buster Keaton and Eddie Cline. Photography: Elgin Lessley. Length: 2 reels.

CAST: Buster Keaton, Virginia Fox, Joe Roberts, Joe Keaton, Eddie Cline.

Hard Luck (1921). Released on March 16, 1921. Presented by the Comique Film Corporation. Distributed by Metro Pictures. Producer: Joseph M. Schenck. Director/Script: Buster Keaton and Eddie Cline. Photography: Elgin Lessley. Length: 2 reels.

CAST: Buster Keaton, Virginia Fox, Joe Roberts, Bull Montana.

The High Sign (1921). Released on April 12, 1921. Presented by the Comique Film Corporation. Distributed by Metro Pictures. Producer: Joseph M. Schenck. Director/Script: Buster Keaton and Eddie Cline. Photography: Elgin Lessley. Length: 2 reels.

CAST: Buster Keaton, Bartine Burkett, Al St. John (cameo).

The Goat (1921). Released on May 18, 1921. Presented by the Comique Film Corporation. Distributed by Metro Pictures. Producer: Joseph M. Schenck. Director/Script: Buster Keaton and Mal St. Clair. Photography: Elgin Lessley. Length: 2 reels.

CAST: Buster Keaton, Virginia Fox, Joe Roberts, Mal St. Clair, Eddie Cline, Jean Havez.

The Playhouse (1921). Released on October 6, 1921. Presented by the Comique Film Corporation. Distributed by First National. Producer: Joseph M. Schenck. Director/Script: Buster Keaton and Eddie Cline. Photography: Elgin Lessley. Technical Director: Fred Gabourie. Length: 2 reels.

CAST: Buster Keaton, Virginia Fox, Joe Roberts.

The Boat (1921). Released in November 1921. Presented by the Comique Film Corporation. Distributed by First National. Producer: Joseph M. Schenck. Director/Script: Buster Keaton and Eddie Cline. Photography: Elgin Lessley. Technical Director: Fred Gabourie. Length: 2 reels.

CAST: Buster Keaton, Sybil Seely, Eddie Cline.

The Paleface (1922). Released in January 1922. Presented by the Comique Film Corporation. Distributed by First National. Producer: Joseph M. Schenck. Director/Script: Buster Keaton and Eddie Cline. Photography: Elgin Lessley. Technical Director: Fred Gabourie. Length: 2 reels.

CAST: Buster Keaton, Virginia Fox, Joe Roberts.

Cops (1922). Released in March 1922. Presented by the Comique Film Corporation. Distributed by First National. Producer: Joseph M. Schenck. Director/Script: Buster Keaton and Eddie Cline. Photography: Elgin Lessley. Technical Director: Fred Gabourie. Length: 2 reels.

CAST: Buster Keaton, Virginia Fox, Joe Roberts, Eddie Cline.

My Wife's Relations (1922). Released in May 1922. Presented by the Comique Film Corporation. Distributed by First National. Producer: Joseph M. Schenck. Director/Script: Buster Keaton and Eddie Cline. Photography: Elgin Lessley. Technical Director: Fred Gabourie. Length: 2 reels.

CAST: Buster Keaton, Kate Price, Monty Collins, Joe Roberts, Tom Wilson, Wheezer Dell.

The Blacksmith (1922). Released on July 21, 1922. Presented by the Comique Film Corporation. Distributed by First National. Producer: Joseph M. Schenck. Director/Script: Buster Keaton and Mal St. Clair. Photography: Elgin Lessley. Technical Director: Fred Gabourie. Length: 2 reels.

CAST: Buster Keaton, Virginia Fox, Joe Roberts.

The Frozen North (1922). Released in August 1922. Presented by Buster Keaton Productions, Inc. Distributed by First National. Producer: Joseph M. Schenck. Director/Script: Buster Keaton and Eddie Cline. Photography: Elgin Lessley. Technical Director: Fred Gabourie. Length: 2 reels.

CAST: Buster Keaton, Bonnie Hill, Freeman Wood, Joe Roberts, Sybil Seely, Eddie Cline, Robert Parker.

The Electric House (1922). Released in October 1922. Presented by Buster Keaton Productions, Inc. Distributed by Associated First National. Pro-

ducer: Joseph M. Schenck. Director/Script: Buster Keaton and Eddie
Cline. Photography: Elgin Lessley. Technical Director: Fred Gabourie.
Length: 2 reels.

CAST: Buster Keaton, Joe Roberts, Virginia Fox, Joe, Myra, and Louise
Keaton.

Daydreams (1922). Released in November 1922. Presented by Buster Kea-
ton Productions, Inc. Distributed by First National. Producer: Joseph M.
Schenck. Director/Script: Buster Keaton and Eddie Cline. Photography:
Elgin Lessley. Technical Director: Fred Gabourie. Length: 3 reels.

CAST: Buster Keaton, Renee Adoree, Joe Roberts, Joe Keaton, Eddie
Cline.

The Balloonatic (1923). Released on January 22, 1922. Presented by Buster
Keaton Productions, Inc. Distributed by Associated First National. Pro-
ducer: Joseph M. Schenck. Director/Script: Buster Keaton and Eddie
Cline. Photography: Elgin Lessley. Technical Director: Fred Gabourie.
Length: 2 reels.

CAST: Buster Keaton, Phyllis Haver.

The Love Nest (1923). Released in March 1923. Presented by Buster Keaton
Productions, Inc. Distributed by Associated First National. Producer: Joseph M. Schenck. Director/Script: Buster Keaton and Eddie Cline. Photography: Elgin Lessley. Technical Director: Fred Gabourie. Length: 2
reels.

CAST: Buster Keaton, Joe Roberts, Virginia Fox.

Keaton Silent Features

The Saphead (1920). Released on October 18, 1920. Produced and distrib-
uted by Metro Pictures. Director: Herbert Blache. Producer: Winchell
Smith. Script: June Mathis, based on *The New Henrietta* by Winchell
Smith and Victor Mapes, and *The Henrietta*, a play by Bronson Howard.
Photography: Harold Wenstrom. Length: 7 reels.

CAST: Buster Keaton, William H. Crane, Irving Cummings, Carol Hol-
loway, Beulah Booker, Edward Alexander, Jeffrey Williams, Edward
Jobson, Jack Livingston, Helen Holte, Odette Taylor, Edward Connelly,
Katherine Albert, Alfred Hollingsworth, Henry Clauss.

The Three Ages (1923). Released in September 1923. Presented by Buster
Keaton Productions, Inc. Distributed by Metro Pictures. Producer: Joseph
M. Schenck. Directors: Buster Keaton and Eddie Cline. Script: Clyde

Bruckman, Joseph Mitchell, and Jean Havez. Photography: William McGann and Elgin Lessley. Technical Director: Fred Gabourie. Length: 6 reels.

CAST: Buster Keaton (Boy), Margaret Leahy (Girl), Wallace Beery (Rival), Joe Roberts (Girl's Father), Lillian Lawrence (Girl's Mother), Blanche Payson (Amazon), Horace Morgan (Emperor), Lionel Belmore.

Our Hospitality (1923). Released on November 19, 1923. Presented by Buster Keaton Productions, Inc. Distributed by Metro Pictures. Producer: Joseph M. Schenck. Directors: Buster Keaton and Jack C. Blystone. Script: Clyde Bruckman, Joseph Mitchell, and Jean Havez. Photography: Gordon Jennings and Elgin Lessley. Technical Director: Fred Gabourie. Electrician: Denver Harmon. Costumes: Walter Israel. Length: 7 reels.

CAST: Buster Keaton (Willie McKay, age twenty-one), Buster Keaton, Jr. (Willie, age one), Kitty Bradbury (Aunt Mary), Joe Keaton (Lem Doolittle), Natalie Talmadge (Virginia Canfield), Joe Roberts (Joseph Canfield), Leonard Clapham (James Canfield), Ralph Bushman and Craig Ward (Clayton and Lee Canfield), Edward Coxen (John McKay), Jean Dumas (Mrs. McKay), James Duffy (Sam Gardner), Monty Collins (Rev. Benjamin Dorsey).

Sherlock Jr. (1924). Released on April 21, 1924. Presented by Buster Keaton Productions, Inc. Distributed by Metro Pictures. Producer: Joseph M. Schenck. Director: Buster Keaton. Script: Clyde Bruckman, Joseph Mitchell, and Jean Havez. Photography: Byron Houck and Elgin Lessley. Costumes: Clare West. Technical Director: Fred Gabourie. Length: 5 reels.

CAST: Buster Keaton (Sherlock Jr.), Kathryn McGuire (Girl), Ward Crane (Rival), Joe Keaton (Girl's Father), Erwin Connelly, Jane Connelly, Ford West, George Davis, John Patrick, Ruth Holley, Horace Morgan.

The Navigator (1924). Released on October 13, 1924. Presented by Buster Keaton Productions, Inc. Distributed by Metro-Goldwyn Pictures Corp. Producer: Joseph M. Schenck. Directors: Buster Keaton and Donald Crisp. Script: Clyde Bruckman, Joseph Mitchell, and Jean Havez. Photography: Byron Houck and Elgin Lessley. Electrician: Denver Harmon. Technical Director: Fred Gabourie. Length: 6 reels.

CAST: Buster Keaton (Rollo Treadway), Kathryn McGuire (Betsy O'Brien), Frederick Vroom (John O'Brien), Clarence Burton and H. M. Clugston (Spies), Noble Johnson (Cannibal Chief).

Seven Chances (1925). Released on March 11, 1925. Presented by Buster Keaton Productions, Inc. Distributed by Metro-Goldwyn Pictures Corp. Producer: Joseph M. Schenck. Director: Buster Keaton. Script: Clyde

Bruckman, Joseph Mitchell, and Jean Havez, based on the play by Roi Cooper Megrue, originally produced by David Belasco. Photography: Byron Houck and Elgin Lessley. Electrician: Denver Harmon. Technical Director: Fred Gabourie. Length: 6 reels.

CAST: Buster Keaton (Jimmie Shannon), T. Roy Barnes (Billy Meekin), Snitz Edwards (Lawyer), Ruth Dwyer (Mary Brown), Frankie Raymond (Mrs. Brown), Jules Cowles (Hired Hand), Erwin Connelly (Clergyman), Jean Arthur (Receptionist), Loro Bara, Marion Harlan, Hazel Deane, Pauline Toler, Judy King, Eugenie Burkette, Edna Hammon, Barbara Pierce, Connie Evans, Rosalind Mooney.

Go West (1925). Released on November 1, 1925. Presented by Buster Keaton Productions, Inc. Distributed by Metro-Goldwyn. Producer: Joseph M. Schenck. Director: Buster Keaton, assisted by Lex Neal. Story: Buster Keaton. Script: Raymon Cannon. Photography: Bert Haines and Elgin Lessley. Technical Director: Fred Gabourie. Length: 7 reels.

CAST: Buster Keaton (Homer Holiday), Howard Truesdale (Ranch Owner), Kathleen Myers (Ranch Owner's Daughter), Ray Thompson (Ranch Foreman), Brown Eyes (Cow), Joe Keaton, Roscoe Arbuckle (in drag), and Babe London (cameos).

Battling Butler (1926). Released on September 19, 1926. Presented by Buster Keaton Productions, Inc. Distributed by Metro-Goldwyn-Mayer. Producer: Joseph M. Schenck. Director: Buster Keaton. Script: Ballard Mac-Donald, Paul Gerard Smith, Albert Boasberg, Lex Neal, and Charles Smith, based on the musical comedy by Stanley Brightman, Austin Melford, Philip Brabham, Walter L. Rosemont, and Douglas Furber. Photography: Dev Jennings and Bert Haines. Electrician: Ed Levy. Technical Director: Fred Gabourie. Length: 7 reels.

CAST: Buster Keaton (Alfred Butler), Snitz Edwards (Valet), Sally O'Neil (Mountain Girl), Walter James (Her Father), Bud Fine (Her Brother), Francis McDonald (Alfred "Battling" Butler), May O'Brien (His Wife), Tom Wilson (His Trainer), Eddie Borden (His Manager).

The General (1927). Released on February 5, 1927. Presented by Buster Keaton Productions, Inc. Distributed by United Artists. Producer: Joseph M. Schenck. Director: Buster Keaton and Clyde Bruckman. Script: Buster Keaton and Clyde Bruckman, based on the book *The Great Locomotive Chase* by William Pittinger (1863). Adaptation: Al Boasberg and Charles Smith. Photography: Dev Jennings and Bert Haines. Technical Director: Frank Barnes. Production Manager: Fred Gabourie. Electrician: Denver Harmon. Editors: J. Sherman Kell and Buster Keaton. Assistant Editor:

Harry Barnes. Wardrobe and Makeup; Bennie Hubbel, J. K. Pitcairn and Fred C. Ryle. Length: 8 reels.

CAST: Buster Keaton (Johnnie Gray), Marion Mack (Annabelle Lee), Charles Smith (Mr. Lee), Frank Barnes (His Son), Glen Cavender (Captain Anderson), Frederick Vroom (Confederate General), Jim Farley (General Thatcher), Edward Hearn (Union Officer), Frank Hagney (Recruiter), Ray Thomas, Bud Fine, Jimmy Bryant, Red Rial, Ross McCutcheon, Red Thompson, Ray Hanford, Charles Phillips, Al Hanson, Tom Moran, Anthony Harvey (Raiders), and Joe Keaton, Mike Donlin, Tom Nawn (Union Generals).

College (1927). Released on September 10, 1927. Presented by Buster Keaton Productions, Inc. Distributed by United Artists. Producer: Joseph M. Schenck. Director: James W. Horne. Script: Carl Harbaugh and Bryan Foy. Photography: Dev Jennings and Bert Haines. Technical Director: Fred Gabourie. Editor: J. S. Kell. Lighting: Jack Lewis. Production Supervisor: Harry Brand. Length: 6 reels.

CAST: Buster Keaton (Ronald), Florence Turner (Ronald's Mother), Ann Cornwall (Mary Haines), Harold Goodwin (Jeff Brown), Snitz Edwards (Dean Edwards), Carl Harbaugh (Rowing Coach), Sam Crawford (Baseball Coach), Flora Bramley (Mary's Friend), Buddy Mason and Grant Withers (Jeff's Friends).

Steamboat Bill, Jr. (1928). Released on May 12, 1928. Presented by Buster Keaton Productions, Inc. Distributed by United Artists. Producer: Joseph M. Schenck. Director: Charles F. Reisner. Assistant Director: Sandy Roth. Script: Carl Harbaugh. Photography: Dev Jennings and Bert Haines. Technical Director: Fred Gabourie. Editor: J. S. Kell. Supervisor: Harry Brand. Length: 7 reels.

CAST: Buster Keaton (Willie Canfield), Ernest Torrence ("Steamboat Bill" Canfield), Tom Lewis (Tom Carter), Tom McGuire (John James King), Marion Byron (Mary King), Louise Keaton (stunt double).

The Cameraman (1928). Released on September 22, 1928. A Metro-Goldwyn-Mayer Production. Distributed by MGM. Producer: Lawrence Weingarten (uncredited). Director: Edward M. Sedgwick. Story: Clyde Bruckman and Lew Lipton. Script: Richard Schayer. Titles: Joseph Farnham. Photography: Elgin Lessley and Reggie Lanning. Editors: Hugh Wynn and Basil Wrangell. Technical Director: Fred Gabourie. Length: 8 reels.

CAST: Buster Keaton (Luke Shannon), Marceline Day (Sally Richards), Harold Goodwin (Harold Stagg), Sidney Bracy (Edward J. Blake), Harry

Gribbon (Officer Hennessey), William Irving (Photographer), Edward Brophy (Man in Dressing Room), Vernon Dent (Man in Tight Bathing Suit), Dick Alexander (The Big Sea Lion), Ray Cooke (Office Worker), Josephine (Monkey).

Spite Marriage (1929). Released on April 6, 1929. A Metro-Goldwyn-Mayer Production. Distributed by MGM. Producer/Director: Edward M. Sedgwick. Script: Lew Lipton and Ernest S. Pagano. Continuity: Richard Schayer. Titles: Robert Hopkins. Photography: Reggie Lanning. Supervisor: Lawrence Weingarten. Editor: Frank Sullivan. Art Director: Cedric Gibbons. Costumes: David Cox. Length: 9 reels.

CAST: Buster Keaton (Elmer Edgemont), Dorothy Sebastian (Trilby Drew), Edward Earle (Lionel Benmore), Leila Hyams (Ethyle Norcrosse), Willian Bechtel (Frederick Nussbaum), John Byron (Giovanni Scarzi), Hank Mann (Stage Manager), Pat Harmon (Ship Captain).

MGM Sound Features

The Hollywood Revue of 1929 (1929). Released on November 23, 1929. A Metro-Goldwyn-Mayer Production. Distributed by MGM. Producer: Harry Rapf. Director: Charles Riesner. Dialogue: Al Boasberg and Robert E. Hopkins. Photography: John Arnold, Irving G. Reis, Maximillian Fabian and John M. Nickolaus. Editors: William S. Gray and Cameron K. Wood. Art Directors: Cedric Gibbons and Richard Day. Recording Engineer: Douglas Shearer. Sound Technician: Russell Franks. Dances and Ensembles: Sammy Lee and George Cunningham. Orchestral Arrangements: Arthur Lange. Music: Gus Edwards. Lyrics: Joe Goodwin. Interpolations: Nacio Herb Brown, Arthur Freed, Dave Snell, Jesse Greer, Ray Klages, Martin Broones, Fred Fisher, Andy Rice. Costumes: David Cox. Length: 130 minutes.

CAST: Buster Keaton, Joan Crawford, Norma Shearer, John Gilbert, Jack Benny, Cliff Edwards, Conrad Nagel, Laurel and Hardy, Bessie Love, Lionel Barrymore, Marion Davies, Marie Dressler, William Haines, Charles King.

Free and Easy (1930). Released on March 22, 1930. A Metro-Goldwyn-Mayer Production. Distributed by MGM. Producer/Director: Edward Sedgwick. Scenario: Richard Schayer. Dialogue: Al Boasberg. Adaptation: Paul Dickey. Photography: Leonard Smith. Editors: William LeVanway and George Todd. Art Director: Cedric Gibbons. Recording Engineer:

Douglas Shearer. Songs: Roy Turk and Fred E. Ahlert. Dances: Sammy Lee. Length: 92 minutes.

CAST: Buster Keaton (Elmer Butts), Anita Page (Elvira Plunkett), Trixie Friganza (Ma Plunkett), Robert Montgomery (Larry Mitchell), Fred Niblo (Director), Edward Brophy (Stage Manager), Edgar Dearing (Officer), David Burton (A Director), and Gwen Lee, John Miljan, Lionel Barrymore, William Collier, Sr., William Haines, Dorothy Sebastian, Karl Dane, Jackie Coogan, Cecil B. DeMille (as themselves).

Doughboys (1930). Released on August 30, 1930. A Metro-Goldwyn-Mayer Production. Distributed by MGM. Producer: Buster Keaton. Director: Edward Sedgwick. Scenario: Richard Schayer. Dialogue: Al Boasberg and Richard Schayer. Story: Al Boasberg and Sidney Lazarus. Photography: Leonard Smith. Editor: William LeVanway. Art Director: Cedric Gibbons. Recording Engineer: Douglas Shearer. Wardrobe: Vivian Baer. Songs: Edward Sedgwick, Joseph Meyer, and Howard Johnson. Dances: Sammy Lee. Length: 81 minutes.

CAST: Buster Keaton (Elmer Stuyvesant), Sally Eilers (Mary Rogers), Cliff Edwards (Cliff Nescopeck), Edward Brophy (Sergeant Brophy), Victor Potel (Svendenburg), Arnold Korff (Gustave), Frank Mayo (Captain Scott), Pitzy Katz (Abie Cohn), William Steele (Lieutenant Randolph), Ann Sothern (WAC), Edward Sedgwick (Guggelheimer, Camp Cook), John Carroll (Soldier/Singer).

Parlor, Bedroom and Bath (1931). Released on February 28, 1930. A Metro-Goldwyn-Mayer Production. Distributed by MGM. Producer: Buster Keaton. Director: Edward Sedgwick. Adaptation: Richard Schayer and Robert Hopkins, from the play by Charles W. Bell and Mark Swan. Photography: Leonard Smith. Editor: William LeVanway. Art Director: Cedric Gibbons. Recording Engineer: Karl Zint. Wardrobe: Rene Hubert. Length: 73 minutes.

CAST: Buster Keaton (Reginald Irving), Charlotte Greenwood (Polly Hathaway), Reginald Denny (Jeffery Haywood), Dorothy Christy (Angelica Embry), Joan Peers (Nita Leslie), Sally Eilers (Virginia Embry), Cliff Edwards (Bellhop), Natalie Moorhead (Leila Crofton), Edward Brophy (Detective), Walter Merrill (Frederick Leslie), Sidney Bracy (Butler).

Sidewalks of New York (1931). Released on September 26, 1931. A Metro-Goldwyn-Mayer Production. Distributed by MGM. Producer: Lawrence Weingarten (uncredited). Directors: Jules White and Zion Myers. Story/Scenario: George Landy and Paul Gerard Smith. Dialogue: Robert E. Hopkins and Eric Hatch. Photography: Leonard Smith. Editor: Charles

Hochberg. Art Director: Cedric Gibbons. Recording Engineer: Douglas Shearer. Length: 70 minutes.

CAST: Buster Keaton (Homer Van Dine Harmon), Anita Page (Margie), Cliff Edwards (Poggle), Norman Phillips, Jr. (Clipper), Frank Rowan (Butch), Frank La Rue (Police Officer), Oscar Apfel (Judge), Syd Saylor (Mulvaney), Clark Marshall (Lefty).

The Passionate Plumber (1932). Released on February 6, 1932. A Metro-Goldwyn-Mayer Production. Distributed by MGM. Producer: Harry Rapf (uncredited). Director: Edward Sedgwick. Adaptation: Laurence E. Johnson, from the play *Her Cardboard Lover* by Jacques Deval. Dialogue: Ralph Spence. Photography: Norbert Brodine. Editor: William S. Gray. Art Director: Cedric Gibbons. Recording Engineer: Douglas Shearer. Length: 73 minutes.

CAST: Buster Keaton (Elmer Tuttle), Jimmy Durante (McCracken), Irene Purcell (Patricia Alden), Polly Moran (Albine), Gilbert Roland (Tony Lagorce), Mona Maris (Nina), Maude Eburne (Aunt Charlotte), Henry Armetta (Bouncer), Paul Porcasi (Paul Le Maire), Jean Del Val (Chauffeur), August Tollaire (General Bouschay), Edward Brophy (Pedestrian).

Speak Easily (1932). Released on August 13, 1932. A Metro-Goldwyn-Mayer Production. Distributed by MGM. Producer: Lawrence Weingarten (uncredited). Director: Edward Sedgwick. Adaptation: Ralph Spence and Laurence E. Johnson, from the story "Footlights" by Clarence Budington Kelland. Photography: Harold Wenstrom. Editor: William Le Vanway. Art Director: Cedric Gibbons. Recording Engineer: Douglas Shearer. Costumes: Arthur Appell. Length: 80 minutes.

CAST: Buster Keaton (Professor Timoleon Zanders Post), Jimmy Durante (James), Ruth Selwyn (Pansy Peets), Thelma Todd (Eleanor Espere), Hedda Hopper (Mrs. Peets), William Pawley (Griffo), Sidney Toler (Stage Manager), Lawrence Grant (Dr. Bolton), Henry Armetta (Tony), Edward Brophy (Reno).

What! No Beer? (1933). Released on February 10, 1933. A Metro-Goldwyn-Mayer Production. Distributed by MGM. Producer: Lawrence Weingarten (uncredited). Director: Edward Sedgwick. Story: Robert E. Hopkins. Script: Carey Wilson. Additional Dialogue: Jack Cluett. Photography: Harold Wenstrom. Editor: Frank Sullivan. Art Director: Cedric Gibbons. Recording Engineer: Douglas Shearer. Costumes: Arthur Appell. Length: 80 minutes.

CAST: Buster Keaton (Elmer J. Butts), Jimmy Durante (Jimmy Potts),

Roscoe Ates (Schultz), Phyllis Barry (Hortense), John Miljan (Butch Lorado), Henry Armetta (Tony), Edward Brophy (Spike Moran), Charles Dunbar (Mulligan), Charles Giblyn (Chief).

Educational Sound Shorts

The Gold Ghost (1934). Released on March 16, 1934. An Educational Pictures Production. Presented by E. W. Hammons. Distributed by 20th Century Fox. Producer: E. H. Allen. Director: Charles Lamont. Story: Ewart Adamson and Nick Barrows. Adaptation/Continuity: Ernest Pagano and Charles Lamont. Photography: Dwight Warren. Length: 2 reels.

    CAST: Buster Keaton, Dorothy Dix, William Worthington, Lloyd Ingraham, Warren Hymer, Joe Young, Billy Engle, Al Thompson, Leo Willis.

Allez Oop (1934). Released on May 25, 1934. An Educational Pictures Production. Presented by E. W. Hammons. Distributed by 20th Century Fox. Producer: E. H. Allen. Director: Charles Lamont. Story: Ewart Adamson and Ernest Pagano. Photography: Dwight Warren. Length: 2 reels.

    CAST: Buster Keaton, Dorothy Sebastian, Harry Myers, George Lewis, The Flying Escalantes.

Palooka from Paducah (1935). Released on January 11, 1935. An Educational Pictures Production. Presented by E. W. Hammons. Distributed by 20th Century Fox. Producer: E. H. Allen. Director: Charles Lamont. Story: Glen Lambert. Photography: Dwight Warren. Length: 2 reels.

    CAST: Buster Keaton, Joe Keaton, Myra Keaton, Louise Keaton, Dewey Robinson, Bull Montana.

One Run Elmer (1935). Released on February 22, 1935. An Educational Pictures Production. Presented by E. W. Hammons. Distributed by 20th Century Fox. Producer: E. H. Allen. Director: Charles Lamont. Story: Glen Lambert. Photography: Dwight Warren. Length: 2 reels.

    CAST: Buster Keaton, Harold Goodwin, Dewey Robinson, Lon Andre, Jim Thorpe.

Hayseed Romance (1935). Released on March 15, 1935. An Educational Pictures Production. Presented by E. W. Hammons. Distributed by 20th Century Fox. Producer: E. H. Allen. Director/Story: Charles Lamont. Dialogue/Continuity: Glen Lambert. Photography: Gus Peterson. Length: 2 reels.

    CAST: Buster Keaton, Jane Jones, Dorothea Kent.

Tars and Stripes (1935). Released on May 3, 1935. An Educational Pictures

Production. Presented by E. W. Hammons. Distributed by 20th Century Fox. Producer: E. H. Allen. Director/Story: Charles Lamont. Adaptation: Ewart Adamson. Photography: Dwight Warren. Length: 2 reels.

CAST: Buster Keaton, Vernon Dent, Dorothea Kent, Jack Shutta.

The E-flat Man (1935). Released on August 9, 1935. An Educational Pictures Production. Presented by E. W. Hammons. Distributed by 20th Century Fox. Producer: E. H. Allen. Director: Charles Lamont. Story: Charles Lamont and Glen Lambert. Photography: Dwight Warren. Sound: Karl Zint. Length: 2 reels.

CAST: Buster Keaton, Dorothea Kent, Si Jenks, Fern Emmett, Broderick O'Farrell, Charles McAvoy, Jack Shutta.

The Timid Young Man (1935). Released on October 25, 1935. An Educational Pictures Production. Presented by E. W. Hammons. Distributed by 20th Century Fox. Producer: Mack Sennett. Director: Mack Sennett. Photography: Dwight Warren. Sound: Karl Zint. Length: 2 reels.

CAST: Buster Keaton, Lona Andre, Kitty McHugh, Tiny Sandford, Harry Bowen.

Three on a Limb (1936). Released on January 3, 1936. An Educational Pictures Production. Presented by E. W. Hammons. Distributed by 20th Century Fox. Producer: E. H. Allen. Director: Charles Lamont. Story: Vernon Smith. Photography: Gus Peterson. Length: 2 reels.

CAST: Buster Keaton, Lona Andre, Harold Goodwin, Grant Withers, Barbara Bedford, John Ince, Fern Emmett, Phyllis Crane.

Grand Slam Opera (1936). Released on February 21, 1936. An Educational Pictures Production. Presented by E. W. Hammons. Distributed by 20th Century Fox. Producer: E. H. Allen. Director: Charles Lamont. Story: Buster Keaton and Charles Lamont. Photography: Gus Peterson. Length: 2 reels.

CAST: Buster Keaton, Harold Goodwin, Diana Lewis, John Ince, Bud Jamison, Eddie Fetherstone, Melrose Coakley.

Blue Blazes (1936). Released on August 21, 1936. An Educational Pictures Production. Presented by E. W. Hammons. Distributed by 20th Century Fox. Producer: E. H. Allen. Director: Raymond Kane. Story: David Freedman. Photography: George Webber. Length: 2 reels.

CAST: Buster Keaton, Arthur Jarrett, Rose Kessner, Patty Wilson, Marlyn Stuart.

The Chemist (1936). Released on October 9, 1936. An Educational Pictures Production. Presented by E. W. Hammons. Distributed by 20th Century Fox. Producer/Director: Al Christie. Story: David Freedman. Photography: George Webber. Length: 2 reels.

CAST: Buster Keaton, Marlyn Stuart, Earl Gilbert, Donald McBride, Herman Lieb.

Mixed Magic (1936). Released on November 20, 1936. An Educational Pictures Production. Presented by E. W. Hammons. Distributed by 20th Century Fox. Producer: E. H. Allen. Director: Raymond Kane. Story: Arthur Jarrett and Marcy Klauber. Photography: George Webber. Length: 2 reels.

CAST: Buster Keaton, Marlyn Stuart, Eddie Lambert, Eddie Hall, Jimmie Fox, Walter Fenner, Pass Le Noir, Harry Myers.

Jail Bait (1937). Released on January 8, 1937. An Educational Pictures Production. Presented by E. W. Hammons. Distributed by 20th Century Fox. Producer: E. H. Allen. Director: Charles Lamont. Story: Paul Gerard Smith. Photography: Dwight Warren. Length: 2 reels.

CAST: Buster Keaton, Harold Goodwin, Mathew Betz, Bud Jamison, Betty Andre.

Ditto (1937). Released on February 21, 1937. An Educational Pictures Production. Presented by E. W. Hammons. Distributed by 20th Century Fox. Producer: E. H. Allen. Director: Charles Lamont. Story: Paul Gerard Smith. Photography: Dwight Warren. Length: 2 reels.

CAST: Buster Keaton, Harold Goodwin, Gloria and Barbara Brewster, Lynton Brent, Al Thompson, Bob Ellsworth.

Love Nest on Wheels (1937). Released on March 26, 1937. An Educational Pictures Production. Presented by E. W. Hammons. Distributed by 20th Century Fox. Producer: E. H. Allen. Director: Charles Lamont. Story: William Hazlett Upson. Adaptation: Paul Gerard Smith. Photography: Dwight Warren. Length: 2 reels.

CAST: Buster Keaton, Myra Keaton, Louise Keaton, Harry Keaton, Lynton Brent, Al St. John, Diana Lewis, Bud Jamison.

Columbia Sound Shorts

Pest from the West (1939). Released on June 16, 1939. A Columbia Pictures Production. Producer: Jules White. Director: Del Lord. Script: Clyde Bruckman. Length: 2 reels.

CAST: Buster Keaton, Lorna Gray, Richard Fiske, Gino Corrado, Bud Jamison, Eddie Laughton, Ned Glass, Forbes Murray.

Mooching Through Georgia (1939). Released on August 11, 1939. A Columbia Pictures Production. Producer/Director: Jules White. Script: Clyde Bruckman. Length: 2 reels.

CAST: Buster Keaton, Bud Jamison, Ned Glass, Monty Collins, Jill Martin, Lynton Brent, Jack Hill, Stanley Mack.

Nothing but Pleasure (1940). Released on January 19, 1940. A Columbia Pictures Production. Producer/Director: Jules White. Script: Clyde Bruckman. Photography: Henry Freulich. Lenth: 2 reels.

CAST: Buster Keaton, Dorothy Appleby, Beatrice Blinn, Bud Jamison, Jack Randall, Richard Fiske, Robert Sterling, Johnny Tyrell, Eddie Laughton, Victor Tremers, Lynton Brent.

Pardon My Berth Marks (1940). Released on March 22, 1940. A Columbia Pictures Production. Producer/Director: Jules White. Script: Clyde Bruckman. Photography: Benjamin Kline. Length: 2 reels.

CAST: Buster Keaton, Dorothy Appleby, Vernon Dent, Dick Curtis, Eva McKenzie, Bud Jamison, Richard Fiske, Billy Gilbert, Clarice the Parrot.

The Taming of the Snood [a.k.a. *Four-Thirds Off*] (1940). Released on June 28, 1940. A Columbia Pictures Production. Producer/Director: Jules White. Script: Ewart Adamson and Clyde Bruckman. Photography: Henry Freulich. Length: 2 reels.

CAST: Buster Keaton, Dorothy Appleby, Elsie Ames, Richard Fiske, Bruce Bennett.

The Spook Speaks (1940). Released on September 20, 1940. A Columbia Pictures Production. Producer/Director: Jules White. Script: Ewart Adamson and Clyde Bruckman. Photography: Henry Freulich. Length: 2 reels.

CAST: Buster Keaton, Elsie Ames, Dorothy Appleby, Lynton Brent, Bruce Bennett, Don Beddoe, Orson the Penguin.

His Ex Marks the Spot (1940). Released on December 13, 1940. A Columbia Pictures Production. Producer/Director: Jules White. Script: Felix Adler. Photography: Benjamin Kline. Length: 2 reels.

CAST: Buster Keaton, Elsie Ames, Dorothy Appleby, Matt McHugh.

So You Won't Squawk (1941). Released on February 21, 1941. A Columbia Pictures Production. Producers: Del Lord and Hugh McCollum. Director: Del Lord. Script: Elwood Ullman. Photography: Benjamin Kline. Length: 2 reels.

CAST: Buster Keaton, Matt McHugh, Eddie Fetherstone, Hank Mann, Bud Jamison, Edmond Cobb, Vernon Dent.

General Nuisance [a.k.a. *The Private General*] (1941). Released on September 18, 1941. A Columbia Pictures Production. Producer/Director: Jules White. Script: Felix Adler and Clyde Bruckman. Length: 2 reels.

CAST: Buster Keaton, Elsie Ames, Dorothy Appleby, Monty Collins, Nick Arno, Bud Jamison, Lynton Brent, Harry Semels.

She's Oil Mine (1941). Released on November 20, 1941. A Columbia Pictures Production. Producer/Director: Jules White. Script: Felix Adler. Length: 2 reels.

CAST: Buster Keaton, Elsie Ames, Monty Collins, Eddie Laughton, Jacqueline Dalya, Bud Jamison.

Appearances in Other Sound Features

Le Roi des Champs-Elysees [*The King of the Champs-Elysees*] (1934). Released in December 1934 (no U.S. release). A Nero Films Production. Distributed in France by Paramount. Producer: Seymour Nebenzal. Director: Max Nosseck. Supervisor: Robert Siodmak. Script: Arnold Lipp. Dialogue: Yves Mirande. Photography: Robert Le Febvre. Art Directors: Hugues Laurent and Jacques-Laurent Atthalin. Music: Joe Hajos. Length: 70 minutes.

CAST: Buster Keaton (Buster Garnier/Jim LeBalafre), Paulette Dubost (Germaine), Colette Darfeuil (Simone), Madeline Guitty (Madame Garnier), Jacques Dumesnil, Pierre Pierade, Gaston Dupray, Paul Clerget, Frank Maurice, Pitouto, Lucien Callamand.

An Old Spanish Custom [a.k.a. *The Intruder*] (1935). Released on January 2, 1935. A British Continental Production (MGM). Released in the U.S. by J. H. Hoffberg. Producers: Sam Spiegel and Harold Richman. Director: Adrian Brunel, assisted by Pelham Leigh Aman. Script: Walter Greenwood. Photography: Eugene Schufftan and Eric L. Gross. Editor: Dan Birt. Music: John Greenwood and George Rubens. Recording Engineer: Denis Scanlan. Length: 61 minutes.

CAST: Buster Keaton (Leander Proudfoot), Lupita Tovar (Lupita Malez), Esme Percy (Jose), Lyn Harding (Gonzalo Gonzalez), Andrea Malandrinos (Carlos), Hilda Moreno (Carmita), Clifford Heatherly (David Cheesman), Webster Booth (Serenader).

Hollywood Cavalcade (1939). Released on October 13, 1939. A 20th Century-Fox Production. Producer: Darryl F. Zanuck. Director: Irving Cummings. Script: Ernest Pascal. Story: Hilary Lynn and Brown Holmes, based on an idea by Lou Breslow. Photography: Allen M. Davey and Ernest Palmer. Editor: Walter Thompson. Technical Advisor: Mack Sennett and Buster Keaton (uncredited). Technicolor. Length: 96 minutes.

CAST: Buster Keaton, Alice Faye, Don Ameche, Stuart Erwin, Mary Forbes, Chester Conklin, Mack Sennett, Al Jolson, Ben Turpin, Harold Goodwin, Willie Fung.

The Villain Still Pursued Her (1940). Released on October 11, 1940. A Franklin-Blank Production. Distributed by RKO Pictures. Producer: Harold B. Franklin. Director: Edward Cline. Script: Elbert Franklin, based on the play *The Fallen Saved*, also known as *The Drunkard*. Additional Dialogue: Ethel La Blanche. Photography: Lucien Ballard. Editor: Arthur Hilton. Music: Frank Tours. Length: 96 minutes.

CAST: Buster Keaton (William Dalton), Anita Louise (Mary Wilson), Richard Cromwell (Edward Middleton), Alan Mowbray (Silas Cribbs), Hugh Herbert (Frederick Healy), Maragaret Hamilton (Widow Wilson), Joyce Compton (Hazel Dalton), Billy Gilbert (Emcee), Diane Fisher (Julia Wilson), Charles Judels (Pie Vendor), Jack Norton (Pie Customer), Vernon Dent (Police Officer), Carlotta Monti (Streetwalker).

Li'l Abner (1940). Released on November 1, 1940. A Vogue-RKO Pictures Production. Distributed by RKO. Producers: Lou Ostrow and Herman Schlom. Director: Albert S. Rogell. Script: Charles Kerr and Tyler Johnson, based on the comic strip by Al Capp. Musical Director: Lud Gluskin. Art Director: Ralph Berger. Editors: Otto Ludwig and Donn Hayes. Photography: Harry Jackson. Length: 75 minutes.

CAST: Buster Keaton (Lonesome Polecat), Granville Owen (Li'l Abner), Martha O'Driscoll (Daisy Mae), Mona Ray (Mammy Yokum), Johnnie Morris (Pappy Yokum), Billie Seward (Cousin Delightful), Kay Sutton (Wendy Wilecat), Maude Eburne (Granny Scraggs), Edgar Kennedy (Cornelius Cornpone), Charles A. Post (Earthquake McGoon), Bud Jamison (Hairless Joe), Dick Elliott (Marryin' Sam), Johnny Arthur (Montague), Walter Catlett (Barber), Chester Conklin (Mayor Gurgle), Doodles Weaver (Hannibal Hoops), Al St. John (Joe Smithpan), Hank Mann (Bachelor), Blanche Payson (Large Spinster), Louise Keaton (Small Spinster), Lucien Littlefield (Sheriff/Old Timer), Mickey Daniels (Cicero Grunts).

Forever and a Day (1943). Released on March 26, 1943. An Anglo-American/RKO Pictures Production. Distributed by RKO. Production Supervisor: Lloyd Richards. Directors: René Clair, Edmund Goulding, Cedric Hardwicke, Frank Lloyd, Victor Saville, Robert Stevenson, and Herbert Wilcox. Script: Charles Bennett, C. S. Forester, Lawrence Hazard, Michael Hogan, W. P. Lipscomb, Alice Duer Miller, John Van Druten, Alan Campbell, Peter Godfrey, S. M. Herzig, Christopher Isherwood, Gene Lockhart, R. C. Sherriff, Claudine West, Norman Corwin, Jack Hatfield, James Hilton, Emmett Lavery, Frederick Lonsdale, Donald Ogden Stewart, and Keith Winter. Photography: Robert De Grasse, Lee Garmes, Russell Metty, Nicholas Musuraca. Music Director: Anthony Collins. Editors: Elmo J. Williams and George Crone.

CAST: Buster Keaton (Plumber), Brian Aherne, Robert Cummings, Ida Lupino, Charles Laughton, Herbert Marshall, Ray Milland, Anna Neagle, Merle Oberon, Claude Rains, Victor McLaglen, Roland Young, C. Aubrey Smith, Edward Everett Horton, Elsa Lanchester, Edmund Gwen, Cedric Hardwick.

San Diego, I Love You (1944). Released on September 29, 1944. A Universal Pictures Production. Producers/Script: Michael Fessier and Ernest Pagano, based on a story by Ruth McKenney and Richard Branstein. Director: Reginald LeBorg. Photography: Hal Mohr and John P. Fulton. Editor: Charles Maynard. Length: 83 minutes.

CAST: Buster Keaton (Bus Driver), Jon Hall, Louise Allbritton, Edward Everett Horton, Eric Blore, Irene Ryan, Rudy Wissler, Chester Clute, Hobart Cavanaugh.

That's the Spirit (1945). Released on June 1, 1945. A Universal Pictures Production. Producers/Script: Michael Fessier and Ernest Pagano. Director: Charles Lamont. Photography: Charles Van Enger and John P. Fulton. Editor: Fred R. Feitshans, Jr. Songs: Inez James, Sidney Miller, Jack Brooks, Richard Wagner, and Hans J. Salter. Length: 93 minutes.

CAST: Buster Keaton (Head of Complaint Department in Heaven), Peggy Ryan, Jack Oakie, June Vincent, Gene Lockhart, Johnny Coy, Andy Devine, Arthur Treacher, Irene Ryan.

That Night with You (1945). Released on September 28, 1945. A Universal Pictures Production. Producers/Script: Michael Fessier and Ernest Pagano, based on a story by Arnold Belgard. Director: William A. Seiter. Photography: Charles Van Enger and John P. Fulton. Editor: Fred R. Feitshans, Jr. Songs: Jack Brooks and Hans J. Salter. Choreography: Leslie Horton, George Moro, and Louis Dapron. Length: 84 minutes.

CAST: Buster Keaton (Sam), Franchot Tone, Susanna Foster, David Bruce, Louise Allbritton, Jacqueline de Wit, Irene Ryan.

God's Country (1946). Released in April 1946. An Action Pictures and Screen Guild Production. Producer: William B. David. Director/Screenplay: Robert Tansey. Photography: Carl Webster. Cinecolor. Length: 62 minutes.

CAST: Buster Keaton (Mr. Boone), Robert Lowery, Helen Gilbert, William Farnum, Stanley Andrews, Trevor Bardette, Si Jenks, Estelle Zarco, Juan Reyes, Al Ferguson.

El Moderno Barba Azul [*The Modern Bluebeard/Boom in the Moon*] (1946). Release on August 2, 1946. An Alsa Film Production (Mexico). Producer: Alexander Salkind. Director: Jaime Salvador. Scenario: Victor Trivas. Photography: Agustin Jiminez. Length: 90 minutes.

CAST: Buster Keaton, Angel Garasa, Virginia Seret, Luis Barreiro, Fernando Soto, Jorge Mondragon, Luis Mondragon.

The Lovable Cheat (1949). Released on May 11, 1949. A Skyline Pictures Production. Distributed by Film Classics, Inc. Producers/Script: Richard Oswald and Edward Lewis, based on the play *Mercadet le Falseur* by Honore de Balzac. Director: Richard Oswald. Photography: Paul Wang. Editor: Douglas Bagier. Length: 74 minutes.

CAST: Buster Keaton, Charles Ruggles, Peggy Ann Garner, Richard Ney, Alan Mowbray, Iris Adrian, Ludwig Donath, Fritz Feld, John Wengraf, Edna Holland, Minerva Urecal, Helen Servis, Jody Gilbert, Judith Trafford.

In the Good Old Summertime (1949). Released on July 29, 1949. A Metro-Goldwyn-Mayer Production. Producer: Joe Pasternak. Director: Robert Z. Leonard. Screenplay: Samson Raphaelson. Adaptation: Albert Hackett, Frances Goodrich, and Ivan Tors, based on the play *Parfumerie* by Miklos Laszlo. Photography: Harry Stradling. Editor: Adrienne Fazan. Length: 102 minutes.

CAST: Buster Keaton (Hickey), Judy Garlan, Van Johnson, S. Z. Sakall, Spring Byington, Clinton Sundberg, Macia Van Dyke, Lillian Bronson, Liza Minnelli.

Sunset Boulevard (1950). Released in August 1950. A Paramount Pictures Production. Producer: Charles Brackett. Director: Billy Wilder. Script: Charles Brackett, Billy Wilder, and D. M. Marshman, Jr., based on the short story "A Can of Beans." Photography: John F. Seitz. Editors: Doane Harrison and Arthur Schmidt. Music: Franz Waxman. Length: 110 minutes.

CAST: Buster Keaton (as himself), Gloria Swanson, William Holden, Erich Von Stroheim, Fred Clark, Jack Webb, Hedda Hopper, Cecil B. De Mille, Anna Q. Nilsson, H. B. Warner, Nancy Olson.

Limelight (1952). Released on February 6, 1952. A Celebrated Films Corporation Production. Distributed by United Artists. Producer/Director/Script/Music: Charles Chaplin. Photography: Karl Struss. Editor: Joe Inge. Length: 145 minutes.

CAST: Buster Keaton (Piano Accompanist), Charles Chaplin, Claire Bloom, Nigel Bruce, Sydney Chaplin, Norman Lloyd, Marjorie Bennett, Wheeler Dryden, Barry Bernard, Stapleton Kent, Mollie Blessing, Leonard Mudie, Julian Ludwig, Snub Pollard, Loyal Underwood, Andre Eglevsky, Melissa Hayden, Charley Rogers, Geraldine Chaplin, Michael Chaplin, Josephine Chaplin, Charles Chaplin, Jr., Edna Purviance.

Around the World in Eighty Days (1956). Released on October 17, 1956. A

United Artists Release. Producer: Michael Todd. Director: Michael Anderson. Script: James Poe, John Farrow, and S. J. Perelman, based on the novel by Jules Verne. Photography: Lionel Lindon. Editors: Gene Ruggiero, Howard Epstein, and Paul Weatherwax. Music: Victor Young. Todd-AO and Eastman Color. Length: 168 minutes.

CAST: Buster Keaton (Train Conductor), David Niven, Cantinflas, Shirley MacLaine, Robert Newton, cameo appearances by many stars.

The Adventures of Huckleberry Finn (1960). Released on June 17, 1960. A Metro-Goldwyn-Mayer Production. Producer: Samuel Goldwyn, Jr. Director: Michael Curtiz. Script: James Lee, from the novel by Mark Twain. Photography: Ted McCord. Editor: Frederic Steinkamp. Music: Jerome Moross. Art Directors: George W. Davis and McClure Capps. Cinema-Scope and MetroColor. Length: 107 minutes.

CAST: Buster Keaton (Lion Tamer), Eddie Hodges, Archie Moore, Tony Randall, Patty McCormack, Neville Brand, Judy Canova, Mickey Shaughnessy, Andy Devine, Josephine Hutchinson, Finlay Currie, Royal Dano, John Carradine, Sterling Holloway, Sherry Jackson.

It's a Mad, Mad, Mad, Mad World (1963). Released on November 7, 1963. A United Artists Production. Producer/Director: Stanley Kramer. Script: William and Tania Rose. Photography: Ernest Laszlo. Music: Ernest Gold. Editor: Fred Knudtson. Production Design: Rudolph Sternad. Ultra Panavision and Technicolor. Length: 154 minutes.

CAST: Buster Keaton (Jimmy the Crook), Spencer Tracy, Milton Berle, Sid Caesar, Buddy Hackett, Ethel Merman, Mickey Rooney, Jimmy Durante, Jonathan Winters, Dick Shawn.

Pajama Party (1964). Released on November 11, 1964. An American-International Pictures Production. Producers: James H. Nicholson and Samuel Z. Arkoff. Director: Don Weis. Script: Louis M. Heyward. Photography: Floyd Crosby. Editors: Fred Feitshans and Eve Newman. Music: Les Baxter. Panavision and Pathecolor. Length: 85 minutes.

CAST: Buster Keaton (Chief Rotten Eagle), Tommy Kirk, Annette Funicello, Elsa Lanchester, Harvey Lembeck, Jesse White, Jody McCrea, Susan Hart, Bobbi Shaw, Don Rickles, Frankie Avalon, Dorothy Lamour.

Beach Blanket Bingo (1965). Released on April 15, 1965. An American-International Pictures Production. Producers: James H. Nicholson and Samuel Z. Arkoff. Director: William Asher. Script: William Asher and Leo Townsend. Photography: Floyd Crosby. Editors: Fred Feitshans and Eve Newman. Music: Les Baxter. Panavision and Pathecolor. Length: 98 minutes.

CAST: Buster Keaton, Annette Funicello, Harvey Lembeck, Deborah Walley,

Linda Evans, Bobbi Shaw, Don Rickles, Timothy Carey, Paul Lynde, Earl Wilson, John Ashley.

How to Stuff a Wild Bikini (1965). Released on July 14, 1965. An American-International Pictures Production. Producers: James H. Nicholson and Samuel Z. Arkoff. Director: William Asher. Script: William Asher and Leo Townsend. Photography: Floyd Crosby. Editors: Fred Feitshans and Eve Newman. Music: Les Baxter. Panavision and Pathecolor. Length: 90 minutes.

CAST: Buster Keaton (Bwana the Witch Doctor), Annette Funicello, Frankie Avalon, Dwayne Hickman, Harvey Lembeck, Mickey Rooney, Brian Donlevy, Beverly Adams, Bobbi Shaw, John Ashley, Jody McCrea, Marianne Gaba, Irene Tsu, Elizabeth Montgomery (cameo).

Sergeant Deadhead (1965). Released on August 18, 1965. An American-International Pictures Production. Producers: James H. Nicholson and Samuel Z. Arkoff. Director: Norman Taurog. Script: Louis M. Heyward. Photography: Floyd Crosby. Editors: Ronald Sinclair, Fred Feitshans and Eve Newman. Music: Les Baxter. Panavision and Pathecolor. Length: 90 minutes.

CAST: Buster Keaton (Private Blinken), Frankie Avalon, Deborah Walley, Fred Clark, Eve Arden, Cesar Romero, Gale Gordon, Reginald Gardiner, Harvey Lembeck, Bobbi Shaw, John Ashley, Donna Loren, Norman Grabowski, Pat Buttram, Patti Chandler.

A Funny Thing Happened on the Way to the Forum (1966). Released on October 16, 1966. A United Artists/Quadrangle Production. Producer: Melvin Frank. Director: Richard Lester. Script: Melvin Frank and Michael Pertwee, based on the stage play produced by Harold S. Prince. Music/Lyrics: Stephen Sondheim. Book: Burt Shevelove and Larry Gelbart. Photography: Nicolas Roeg. Editor: John Victor Smith. DeLuxe Color. Length: 99 minutes.

CAST: Buster Keaton (Erronius), Zero Mostel, Phil Silvers, Jack Gilford, Michael Crawford, Michael Hordern, Annette Andre, Patricia Jessel, Inga Neilsen, Leon Greene, Myrna White, Pamela Brown, Roy Kinnear.

War Italian Style [*Due Marines e un Generale*] (1967). Released January 18, 1967. An American-International Pictures Production. Producer: Fulvio Lucisano. Director: Luigi Scattini. Script: Franco Castellano, Pipolo and Fulvio Lucisano. Photography: Fausto Zuccoli. Music: Piero Umiliani. Techniscope and Technicolor. Length: 84 minutes.

CAST: Buster Keaton (General Von Kassler), Franco Franchi, Ciccio Ingrassia, Fred Clark, Martha Hyer.

Final Shorts

Film (1965). Released in September 1965. An Evergreen Theatre Production. Producer: Barney Rosset. Director: Alan Schneider. Script: Samuel Beckett. Photography: Boris Kaufman. Editor: Sydney Meyers. Art Director: Burr Smidt. Camera Operator: Joe Coffey. Length: 22 minutes.

    CAST: Buster Keaton (Object/Eye), James Karen, Nell Harrison, Susan Reed.

The Railrodder (1965). Released in October 1965. A National Film Board of Canada Production. Producer: Julian Biggs. Director/Script: Gerald Potterton. Photography: Robert Humble. Music: Eldon Rathburn. Editors: Jo Kirkpatrick and Gerald Potterton. Sound Effects: Karl du Plessis. Sound Recording: George Croll and Ted Haley. Length: 21 minutes.

    CAST: Buster Keaton.

The Scribe (1966). Released in May 1966. (Filmed in October 1965, this was the last film in which Keaton performed.) A Film-Tele Production for the Construction Safety Association of Ontario. Producers: Ann and Kenneth Heely-Ray. Executive Producers: Raymond Walters and James Collier. Director: John Sebert. Script: Paul Sutherland and Clifford Braggins. Photography: Mike Lente. Editor: Kenneth Heely-Ray. Music: Quartet Productions, Ltd. Length: 30 minutes.

    CAST: Buster Keaton, Larry Reynolds (stunt double).

Bibliography

Abel, Richard, ed. *French Film Theory and Criticism: A History/Anthology, 1907–1939*. Vol. 1, 1907–1929. Princeton, NJ: Princeton University Press, 1988.

————. "Exploring the Discursive Field of the Surrealist Scenario Text." In *Dada and Surrealist Film*, edited by Rudolf E. Kuenzli, 58–71. 1987. Reprint, Cambridge, MA: MIT Press, 1996.

Agee, James. "Comedy's Greatest Era." In Agee, *Agee on Film*, 2–19. 1958. Reprint, New York: Grosset & Dunlap, 1969. First published in *Life*, 3 September 1949, 70–88.

Alexandre, Maxime, Louis Aragon, et al. "Hands Off Love." Translated by Paul Hammond. In *The Shadow and Its Shadow: Surrealist Writing on the Cinema*, edited by Paul Hammond, 183–92. 2nd ed. Edinburgh: Polygon, 1991. First published in *Transition* 6 (September 1927), and in *La Révolution surréaliste* 9–10 (October 1927).

Alexandrian, Sarane. *Surrealist Art*. Translated by Gordon Clough. 1970. Reprint, New York: Thames & Hudson, 1992. Originally published as *L'Art surréaliste*. Paris: Fernand Hazan, 1969.

Allen, Robert C. *Vaudeville and Film 1895–1912: A Study in Media Interaction*. New York: Arno, 1980.

Allen, Rupert C. "Commentary on Lorca's El Paseo de Buster Keaton." *Hispanofila* 48 (1973): 23–35.

Aragon, Louis. "L'Ombre de l'Inventeur." *La Révolution surréaliste* 1 (December 1924): 22–24.

Aranda, Francisco. *Luis Buñuel: A Critical Biography*. Edited and translated by David Robinson. New York: Da Capo, 1976.

Aron, Robert. "Films of Revolt." Translated by Richard Abel. In *French Film Theory and Criticism: A History/Anthology, 1907–1939*, Vol. 1, 1907–1929, edited by Richard Abel, 432–36. Princeton, NJ: Princeton University Press, 1988. Originally published as "Films de révolte," *La Revue du cinéma* 5 (15 November 1929): 41–45.

Artaud, Antonin. "Cinema and Reality." Translated by Helen Weaver. In *Antonin Artaud: Selected Writings*, edited by Susan Sontag, 150–52. New York: Farrar, Straus, and Giroux, 1976; Berkeley: University of California Press, 1986.

Baker, Stuart E.. *Georges Feydeau and the Aesthetics of Farce*. Theater and Dramatic Studies, Vol. 9. Ann Arbor, MI: UMI, 1981.

Balakian, Anna. *Surrealism: The Road to the Absolute*. New York: Noonday, 1959.

Barr, Richard L. Review of *Largely New York*, by Bill Irwin. *Theatre Journal* 42 (1990): 242–44.

Bazin, André. *What Is Cinema?* Translated by Hugh Gray. Berkeley: University of California Press, 1967.

Beckerman, Bernard. "Beckett and the Act of Listening." In *Beckett at 80/Beckett in Context*, edited by Enoch Brater, 149–67. New York: Oxford University Press, 1986.

Beckett, Samuel. *Film*. New York: Grove, 1969.

Bédouin, Jean-Louis, et al. "Data Towards the Enlargement of a Film: The Shanghai Gesture." Translated by Paul Hammond. In *The Shadow and Its Shadow: Surrealist Writing on the Cinema*, edited by Paul Hammond, 128–37. 2nd ed. Edinburgh: Polygon, 1991. Originally published as *L'Age du cinéma* 4–5 (August–November 1951): 53–58.

Benayoun, Robert. *The Look of Buster Keaton*. Translated and edited by Randall Conrad. New York: St. Martin's, 1983. Originally published as *Le Regard de Buster Keaton*. Paris: Editions Hersher, 1982.

Bentley, Eric. "Farce." In *The Life of the Drama*, 219–56. New York: Atheneum, 1964.

————. "The Psychology of Farce." In *Let's Get a Divorce! and Other Plays*, edited by Eric Bentley, vii–xx. New York: Hill and Wang, 1958.

Bermel, Albert. *Farce: A History from Aristophanes to Woody Allen*. New York: Simon and Schuster, 1982.

Bishop, Christopher. "The Great Stone Face." *Film Quarterly* 12, no. 1 (fall 1958): 10–15.

————. "An Interview with Buster Keaton." *Film Quarterly* 12, no. 1 (fall 1958): 15–22.

Blake, Lucas. "Acting Style in Silent Films." In *The Stars Appear*, edited by Richard Dyer MacCann, 33–47. Metuchen, NJ: Scarecrow, 1992.

Blesh, Rudi. *Keaton*. New York: Macmillan, 1966.

Bordwell, David, and Kristin Thompson. *Film Art: An Introduction*. 4th ed. New York: McGraw-Hill, 1993.

Bordwell, David, Janet Staiger, and Kristin Thompson. *The Classical Hollywood Cinema*. New York: Columbia University Press, 1985.

Brater, Enoch. Introduction to *Beckett at 80/Beckett in Context*. New York: Oxford University Press, 1986.

————. "Dada, Surrealism, and the Genesis of *Not I*." *Modern Drama* 18, no. 1 (1975): 49–59.

Breton, André. "As in a Wood." Translated by Paul Hammond. In *The Shadow and Its Shadow: Surrealist Writing on the Cinema*, edited by Paul Hammond, 80–85. 2nd ed. Edinburgh: Polygon, 1991. Originally published in *L'Age du cinéma* 4–5 (August–November 1951): 26–30.

————. *Manifestoes of Surrealism*. Translated by Richard Seaver and Helen R. Lane. Ann Arbor: University of Michigan Press, 1969.

————. *What Is Surrealism?* Translated by David Gascoyne. 1936. Reprint, London: Faber & Faber, 1978.

Brownlow, Kevin. *The Parade's Gone By.* New York: Knopf, 1968.

Brunius, Jacques B. "Experimental Film in France." Translated by Mary Kesteren. In *Experiment in the Film,* edited by Roger Manvell, 60–112. 1949. Reprint, New York: Arno, 1970.

Buñuel, Luis. "Buster Keaton's *College.*" Translated by David Robinson. In *The Shadow and Its Shadow: Surrealist Writing on the Cinema,* edited by Paul Hammond, 64–65. 2nd ed. Edinburgh: Polygon, 1991. Originally published in *Cahiers d'art* 10 (1927).

———— and Salvador Dalí. *Un Chien Andalou.* Translated by Phillip Drummond. London: Faber and Faber, 1994.

Buster Keaton Rides Again. Directed by John Spotton, with Buster Keaton, Eleanor Keaton, and Gerald Potterton. National Film Board of Canada, 1965.

Carroll, Noël. "Buster Keaton, The General, and Visible Intelligibility." In *Close Viewings: An Anthology of New Film Criticism,* edited by Peter Lehman, 125–40. Tallahassee: Florida State University Press, 1990.

————. "Entr'acte, Paris, and Dada." *Millenium Film Journal* 1, no. 1 (1977–78): 5–11.

Chaplin, Charlie. *My Life in Pictures.* London: Bodley Head, 1974.

Chesler, Judd. "Toward a Surrealist Film Aesthetic with an Investigation into the Elements of Surrealism in the Marx Brothers and Jean Vigo." Ph.D. diss., Northwestern University, 1976.

Chinoy, Helen Krich. "The Emergence of the Director." In *Directors on Directing: A Sourcebook of the Modern Theater,* edited by Toby Cole and Helen Krich Chinoy, 7–77. Rev. ed. New York: Macmillan, 1963.

Clair, René. *Cinema Yesterday and Today.* Translated by Stanley Appelbaum. New York: Dover, 1972.

Cook, David A. *A History of Narrative Film.* 2nd. ed. New York: W. W. Norton, 1981.

Cott, Jeremy. "The Limits of Silent Comedy." *Literature/Film Quarterly* 3, no. 2 (1975): 99–107.

Crafton, Donald. "Pie and Chase: Gag, Spectacle and Narrative in Slapstick Comedy." In *Classical Hollywood Comedy,* edited by Kristine Brunovska Karnick and Henry Jenkins, 106–19. New York: Routledge, 1995.

Dalí, Salvador. "An Abstract of a Critical History of the Cinema." Translated by Paul Hammond. In *The Shadow and Its Shadow: Surrealist Writing on the Cinema,* edited by Paul Hammond, 70–75. 2nd ed. Edinburgh: Polygon, 1991. Originally published in *Babaouo: Scénario inédit; précédé d'un Abrégé d'une histoire critique du cinéma; et suivi Guillaume Tell: ballet portugais.* Paris: Éditions des Cahiers Libres, 1932.

Dardis, Tom. *Keaton: The Man Who Wouldn't Lie Down.* London: André Deutsch, 1979; W. H. Allen, 1989.

Davis, Barbara N. "Lorca, Surrealism and the Teatro Breve." *Garcia Lorca Review* 6, no. 2 (1978): 95–110.

Deleuze, Gilles. *Cinema 1: The Movement-Image.* Minneapolis: University of Minnesota Press, 1986.

Desnos, Robert. *Cinéma.* Paris: Gallimard, 1966. Excerpts translated by Pamela Waxman for author.

DiMeglio, John D. *Vaudeville U.S.A.* Bowling Green, OH: Bowling Green University Press, 1973.

Drummond, Philip. Introduction to *Un Chien Andalou,* by Luis Buñuel and Salvador Dalí, v–xxiii. London: Faber and Faber, 1994.

Du Pasquier, Sylvain. "Buster Keaton's Gags." *Journal of Modern Literature* 3, no. 2 (1973): 269–91.

Earle, William. *A Surrealism of the Movies.* Chicago: Precedent, 1987.

Eberwein, Robert T. "The Filmic Dream and Point of View." *Literature/Film Quarterly* 8, no. 3 (1980): 197–203.

Edmonds, Andy. *Frame-Up!: The Untold Story of Fatty Arbuckle.* New York: William Morrow, 1991.

Edwards, Larry. *Buster Keaton: A Legend in Laughter.* Bradenton, FL: McGuinn & McGuire, 1994.

Eisenstein, Sergei. "Montage of Attractions." *The Drama Review* 18, no. 1 (1974): 77–84. Reprint of 1923 article.

Erebé, Judith. "Sur le film comique et singulièrement sur Buster Keaton." *Crapouillot* 59 (January 1963): 10–13. Reprint of 1927 article. Translated by Pamela Waxman for the author.

Esslin, Martin. *The Theatre of the Absurd.* Rev. ed. Garden City, NY: Anchor, 1969.

Everson, William K. *American Silent Film.* New York: Oxford University Press, 1978.

Feinstein, Herbert. "Buster Keaton: An Interview." *Massachusetts Review* 4, no. 2 (1963): 392–407.

Finkelstein, Haim. "Dalí and *Un Chien andalou.*" In *Dada and Surrealist Film,* edited by Rudolf E. Kuenzli, 128–42. Reprint, Cambridge, MA: MIT Press, 1996.

Friedman, A. B. "Buster Keaton: An Interview." *Film Quarterly* 19, no. 4 (1966): 2–5.

García Lorca, Federico. "Buster Keaton's Promenade." Translated by Tim Reynolds. *Accent* 17, no. 3 (1957): 131–33.

———. "Buster Keaton's Ride." Translated and adapted by Jack Spicer. In *After Lorca.* Toronto: Coach House, 1974.

———. "Buster Keaton's Spin." Translated by Alexander Hutchison. *Stand* 11 (1970): 4–6.

———. "Buster Keaton Takes a Walk." Translated by A. L. Lloyd. *Sight and Sound* 35, no. 1 (1965): 24–25. Reprinted in *Keaton: The Man Who Wouldn't Lie Down,* by Tom Dardis, 281–83. London: André Deutsch, 1979; W. H. Allen, 1989.

Gehring, Wes D. *Charlie Chaplin: A Bio-Bibliography.* Westport, CT: Greenwood, 1983.

Gentry, Clyde III. *Jackie Chan: Inside the Dragon*. Dallas: Taylor, 1997.

Giannetti, Louis. *Understanding Movies*. 6th ed. Englewood Cliffs, NJ: Prentice-Hall, 1993.

Gibson, Ian. *Federico García Lorca: A Life*. London: Faber & Faber, 1989.

Gilbert, Douglas. *American Vaudeville: Its Life and Times*. New York: Whittlesey, 1940.

Gillett, John, and James Blue. "Keaton at Venice." *Sight and Sound* 35, no. 1 (winter 1965–66): 26–30.

Gilliat, Penelope. "Buster Keaton." In *Unholy Fools*, 45–53. New York: Viking, 1973.

———. "An Interview with Buster Keaton." *London Observer Weekend Review*, 24 May 1964: 31.

Gold, Sylvanie. "He's a Clown with a Mission." *New York Times*, 8 August 1982: 4, 19.

Gontarski, S. E. *The Intent of Undoing in Samuel Beckett's Dramatic Texts*. Bloomington: Indiana University Press, 1985.

Goodwin, Michael. "Passing Through the Equal Sign: Fractal Mathematics in Sherlock Jr." 118–29. In *Buster Keaton's Sherlock Jr.*, edited by Andrew Horton. Cambridge: Cambridge University Press, 1997.

Green, Abel, and Joe Laurie, Jr. *Show Biz from Vaude to Video*. New York: Henry Holt, 1951.

Grindon, Leger. "The Role of Spectacle and Excess in the Critique of Illusion." *Post Script* 13, no. 2 (1994): 35–43.

Gunning, Tom. "The Cinema of Attraction: Early Film, Its Spectator and the Avant-Garde." *Wide Angle* 8, no. 3/4 (1986): 63–70.

———. *D. W. Griffith and the Origins of American Narrative Film*. Urbana: University of Illinois Press, 1991.

———. "Crazy Machines in the Garden of Forking Paths: Mischief Gags and the Origins of American Film Comedy." In *Classical Hollywood Comedy*, edited by Kristine Brunovska Karnick and Henry Jenkins, 87–105. New York: Routledge, 1995.

———. "Response to 'Pie and Chase.'" In *Classical Hollywood Comedy*, edited by Kristine Brunovska Karnick and Henry Jenkins, 120–22. New York: Routledge, 1995.

Gussow, Mel. "Profiles: Clown." *New Yorker*, 11 November 1985: 51–87.

Hale, Jane Allison. *The Broken Window: Beckett's Dramatic Perspective*. West Lafayette, IN: Purdue University Press, 1987.

Hammond, Paul, ed. *The Shadow and Its Shadow: Surrealist Writing on the Cinema*. 2nd ed. Edinburgh: Polygon, 1991.

Harrison, Mark. "New Vaudeville: Variety Artists in the Contemporary Theater." Ph.D. diss., New York University, 1989.

Havard, Robert G. "Lorca's Buster Keaton." *Bulletin of Hispanic Studies* 54 (1977): 13–20.

Higginbotham, Virginia. "The Experimental Farces." In "The Comic Spirit of Federico García Lorca," 100–104. Ph.D. diss., Tulane University, 1966.

Horton, Andrew, ed. *Buster Keaton's Sherlock Jr.* Cambridge: Cambridge University
Press, 1997.

———. *Comedy/Cinema/Theory.* Berkeley: University of California Press, 1991.

Houston, Penelope. "The Great Blank Page." *Sight and Sound* 37, no. 2 (spring
1968): 63–7.

Irwin, Bill. "Beauty in the Form, and Even in the Face." *New York Times*, 2 July 1995:
1, 10.

Jenkins, Henry. "This Fellow Keaton Seems to Be the Whole Show: Buster Keaton,
Interrupted Performance, and the Vaudeville Aesthetic." In *Buster Keaton's Sher-
lock Jr.*, edited by Andrew Horton, 29–66. Cambridge: Cambridge University
Press, 1997.

———. *What Made Pistachio Nuts?: Early Sound Comedy and the Vaudeville Aesthetic.*
New York: Columbia University Press, 1992.

Johnstone, Keith. *Impro: Improvisation and the Theatre.* London: Faber and Faber,
1979; New York: Theatre Arts Books, 1992.

Kamin, Dan. *Charlie Chaplin's One-Man Show.* Carbondale: Southern Illinois University Press, 1984.

Karnick, Kristine Brunovska, and Henry Jenkins, eds. *Classical Hollywood Comedy.*
New York: Routledge, 1995.

Kauffman, Stanley. "Melodrama and Farce: A Note on a Fusion in Film." In *Melodrama*, edited by Daniel Gerould, 169–72. New York: New York Literary Forum,
1980.

———. Review of Buster Keaton Festival. In *Living Images: Film Comment and Criticism*. 19–22. New York: Harper & Row, 1975. Originally published in *New Re-
public*, 24 October 1970.

Keaton, Buster. "Why I Never Smile." *Ladies' Home Journal*, June 1926: 173–74.

———. Interview. Edited by Joan and Bob Franklin. Oral History Project of Columbia University, New York, 1958.

——— with Charles Samuels. *My Wonderful World of Slapstick.* New York: Dou-
bleday, 1960.

Kerr, Walter. *The Silent Clowns.* New York: Knopf, 1975.

Kishpaugh, Dick. "The Real General." *The Keaton Chronicle* 2, no. 1 (1994): 1–2.

Kline, Jim. *The Complete Films of Buster Keaton.* New York: Citadel, 1993.

Koszarski, Richard. *An Evening's Entertainment: The Age of the Silent Feature Picture,
1915–1928.* Vol. 3, *History of the American Cinema.* New York: Charles Scribner's
Sons, 1990.

Kovács, Steven. *From Enchantment to Rage: The Story of Surrealist Cinema.* Cranbury,
NJ: Associated University Presses, 1980.

Král, Petr. "Larry Semon's Message." Translated by Paul Hammond. In *The Shadow
and Its Shadow: Surrealist Writing on the Cinema*, edited by Paul Hammond, 175–

82. 2nd ed. Edinburgh: Polygon, 1991. Originally published in *Positif* 106 (June 1969): 28–33.

Kramer, Peter. "Derailing the Honeymoon Express: Comicality and Narrative Closure in Buster Keaton's *The Blacksmith*." *Velvet Light Trap* 23 (spring 1989): 101–16.

———. "The Making of a Comic Star: Buster Keaton and *The Saphead*." In *Classical Hollywood Comedy*, edited by Kristine Brunovska Karnick and Henry Jenkins, 190–210. New York: Routledge, 1995.

———. "A Slapstick Comedian at the Crossroads: Buster Keaton, the Theater, and the Movies in 1916/17. *Theatre History Studies* 17 (June 1997): 133–46.

Krutnik, Frank. "The Clown-Prints of Comedy." *Screen* 25, nos. 4–5 (1984): 50–59.

———. "A Spanner in the Works?: Genre, Narrative and the Hollywood Comedian." In *Classical Hollywood Comedy*, edited by Kristine Brunovska Karnick and Henry Jenkins, 17–38. New York: Routledge, 1995.

Kuenzli, Rudolf E., ed. *Dada and Surrealist Film*. 1987. Reprint, Cambridge, MA: MIT Press, 1996.

Kyrou, Ado. "The Fantastic—The Marvellous." Translated by Paul Hammond. In *The Shadow and Its Shadow: Surrealist Writing on the Cinema*, edited by Paul Hammond, 167–69. 2nd ed. Edinburgh: Polygon, 1991. Originally published in *Le Surréalisme au cinéma*, 2nd ed. Paris: Le Terrain Vague, 1963.

Lebel, J. P. *Buster Keaton*. 1964. Translated by P. D. Stovin. London: A. Zwemmer; New York: A. S. Barnes, 1967.

Logan, Bey. *Hong Kong Action Cinema*. Woodstock, NY: Overlook, 1995.

MacCann, Richard Dyer, ed. *The Silent Comedians*. Metuchen, NJ: Scarecrow, 1993.

Madden, David. *Harlequin's Stick, Charlie's Cane*. Bowling Green: Bowling Green University Popular Press, 1975.

Maltin, Leonard. *The Great Movie Shorts*. New York: Crown, 1972.

Marzio, Peter C. *Rube Goldberg: His Life and Work*. New York: Harper & Row, 1973.

Mast, Gerald. *The Comic Mind: Comedy and the Movies*. 2nd ed. Chicago: University of Chicago Press, 1979.

Matthews, J. H. *An Introduction to Surrealism*. University Park, PA: Pennsylvania State University Press, 1965.

———. *Surrealism and Film*. Ann Arbor: University of Michigan Press, 1971.

———. *Surrealism and American Feature Films*. Boston: Twayne, 1979.

McCaffrey, Donald W. *Four Great Comedians: Chaplin, Lloyd, Keaton, Langdon*. London: A. Zwemmer; New York: A. S. Barnes, 1968.

———, ed. *Focus on Chaplin*. Englewood Cliffs, NJ: Prentice-Hall, 1971.

———. "The Mutual Approval of Keaton and Lloyd." *Cinema Journal* 6 (1966–67): 9–15.

McGerr, Celia. *René Clair*. Boston: Twayne, 1980.

McLean, Albert F., Jr. *American Vaudeville as Ritual*. Lexington: University Press of Kentucky, 1965.

McNamara, Brooks, ed. *American Popular Entertainments*. New York: Performing Arts Journal, 1983.

Meade, Marion. *Buster Keaton: Cut to the Chase*. New York: HarperCollins, 1995.

Megrue, Roi Cooper. *Seven Chances*. New York: Samuel French, 1916.

Milne, Tom. "Festivals '65: Venice." *Sight & Sound* 34, no. 4 (1965): 207.

Moews, Daniel. *Keaton: The Silent Feature Close Up*. Berkeley: University of California Press, 1977.

Musser, Charles. *Before the Nickelodeon: Edwin S. Porter and the Edison Manufacturing Company*. Berkeley: University of California Press, 1991.

———. *The Emergence of Cinema: The American Screen to 1907*. Vol. 1, *History of the American Cinema*. New York: Charles Scribner's Sons, 1990.

Neale, Steve, and Frank Krutnik. *Popular Film and Television Comedy*. London and New York: Routledge, 1990.

Oderman, Stuart. *Roscoe "Fatty" Arbuckle*. Jefferson, NC: McFarland, 1994.

Okkonen, Marc. *Buster Keaton and the Muskegon Connection: The Actors' Colony at Bluffton, 1908–1938*. Muskegon, MI: Dobb, 1995.

Oldham, Gabriella. *Keaton's Silent Shorts: Beyond the Laughter*. Carbondale and Edwardsville: Southern Illinois University Press, 1996.

Page, Brett. *Writing for Vaudeville*. Springfield, MA: Home Correspondence School, 1913.

Palmer, Jerry. *The Logic of the Absurd*. London: BFI, 1987.

Parshall, Peter F. "Buster Keaton and the Space of Farce: *Steamboat Bill, Jr.* versus *The Cameraman*." *Journal of Film and Video* 46, no. 3 (fall 1994): 29–46.

———. "Houdini's Protégé: Buster Keaton in *Sherlock Jr.*" In *Buster Keaton's Sherlock Jr.*, edited by Andrew Horton, 67–88. Cambridge: Cambridge University Press, 1997.

Patterson, Frances Taylor. *Cinema Craftsmanship*. New York: Harcourt, Brace & Howe, 1920.

Paul, William. "The Annals of Chaplin." In *Comedy/Cinema/Theory*, edited by Andrew Horton, 109–30. Berkeley: University of California Press, 1991.

Pearson, David B. "Playing Detective: Possible Solutions to the Production Mysteries of *Sherlock Jr.*" In *Buster Keaton's Sherlock Jr.*, edited by Andrew Horton, 140–57. Cambridge: Cambridge University Press, 1997.

Perez, Gilberto. "The Bewildered Equilibrist: An Essay on Buster Keaton's Comedy." *Hudson Review* 34, no. 3 (autumn 1981): 337–66.

Perlmutter, Ruth. "Beckett's Film and Beckett and Film." *Journal of Modern Literature* 6, no. 1 (1977): 83–94.

Rapf, Joanna E. "Moral and Amoral Visons: Chaplin, Keaton, and Comic Theory." *Western Humanities Review* 37, no. 4 (1983): 335–45.

——— and Gary L. Green. *Buster Keaton: A Bio-Bibliography*. Westport, CT: Greenwood, 1995.

Ray, Robert B. *The Avant-Garde Finds Andy Hardy*. Cambridge, MA: Harvard University Press, 1995.

Reid, Ashton. "Strictly for Laughs." *Collier's*, 10 June 1944: 66–67.

Rheuban, Joyce. *Harry Langdon: The Comedian as Metteur-en-Scène*. East Brunswick, NJ: Associated University Presses, 1983.

Robinson, David. *Buster Keaton*. Bloomington and London: Indiana University Press, 1969.

———. *The Great Funnies*. London: Studio Vista, 1969.

———. "Rediscovery—Buster." *Sight and Sound* 29, no. 1 (winter 1959–60): 41–43.

Rosemont, Franklin. *André Breton and the First Principles of Surrealism*. London: Pluto, 1978.

Rubin, William S. *Dada, Surrealism, and Their Heritage*. 5th ed. New York: Metropolitan Museum of Art, 1989.

Rubinstein, E. *Filmguide to 'The General.'* Bloomington: Indiana University Press, 1973.

———. "Observations on Keaton's "Steamboat Bill, Jr.'" *Sight & Sound* 44, no. 4 (1975): 244–47.

Sarris, Andrew. *The American Cinema: Directors and Directions, 1929–1968*. 1968. Reprint, New York: Da Capo, 1996.

———. "Buster Keaton." *The Primal Screen*. New York: Simon and Schuster, 1973.

———. "Buster Keaton and Samuel Beckett." *Columbia University Forum* 12, no. 4 (1969): 42–43

Saunders, Judith, and Daniel Lieberfeld. "Dreaming in Pictures: The Childhood Origins of Buster Keaton's Creativity." *Film Quarterly* 47, no. 4 (summer 1994): 14–28.

Schneider, Alan. "On Directing *Film*." In *Film*, by Samuel Beckett, 63–94. New York: Grove, 1969.

Scott, A. C. "The Performance of Classical Theater." In *Chinese Theater: From Its Origins to the Present Day*, edited by Colin Mackerras, 118–44. Honolulu: University of Hawaii Press, 1983.

Seidman, Steve. *Comedian Comedy: A Tradition in Hollywood Film*. Vol. 5, Studies in Photography and Cinematography. Ann Arbor, MI: UMI, 1981.

Slide, Anthony, ed. *The Encyclopedia of Vaudeville*. Westport, CT: Greenwood, 1994.

———. *Selected Vaudeville Criticism*. Metuchen, NJ, and London: Scarecrow, 1988.

Stein, Charles W., ed. *American Vaudeville as Seen by Its Contemporaries*. New York: Knopf, 1984.

Stewart, Garrett. "Keaton Through the Looking Glass." *Georgia Review* 33, no. 2 (1979): 348–67.

Sweeney, Kevin W. "The Dream of Disruption." *Wide Angle* 13, no. 1 (1991): 104–20.

Thompson, Kristin. *Breaking the Glass Armor: Neoformalist Film Analysis*. Princeton, NJ: Princeton University Press, 1988.

Tibbetts, John C. "Railroad Man: The Last Ride of Buster Keaton." *Films in Review* 46, no. 5/6 (July/August 1995): 2–11.

Tobias, Patty. "History of a Keaton Gag." *The Keaton Chronicle* 1, no. 2 (1993): 6–7.

Uraneff, Vadim. "Commedia Dell'Arte and American Vaudeville." *Theatre Arts* (October 1923): 321–28.

Usai, Paolo Cherchi. *Burning Passions: An Introduction to the Study of Silent Cinema.* London: BFI, 1994.

Vardac, A. Nicholas. *Stage to Screen: Theatrical Origins of Early Film.* 1949. Reprint, New York: Da Capo, 1968.

Wead, George. *Buster Keaton and the Dynamics of Visual Wit.* New York: Arno, 1976.

———. *The Film Career of Buster Keaton.* Boston: G. K. Hall, 1977.

Williams, Linda. *Figures of Desire.* Urbana: University of Illinois Press, 1981.

———. "The Critical Grasp: Buñuelian Cinema and Its Critics." In *Dada and Surrealist Film*, edited by Rudolf E. Kuenzli, 199–206. 1987. Reprint, Cambridge, MA: MIT Press, 1996.

Winn, Steve. "The Clown Who Can Fly—Almost." *Connoisseur*, September 1982.

Wolfe, Charles Clinton. "Spatial Disorientation and Dream in the Films of Buster Keaton." Ph.D. diss., Columbia University, 1978.

Yallop, David A. *The Day the Laughter Stopped.* New York: St. Martin's, 1976.

Index